POLICING AND WAR IN EUROPE

POLICING AND WAR IN EUROPE

Edited by
Louis A. Knafla

Criminal Justice History
Volume 16

GREENWOOD PRESS
Westport, Connecticut • London

ISBN: 0–313–31012–2
ISSN: 0194–0953

First published in 2002

Greenwood Press, 88 Post Road West, Westport, CT 06881
An imprint of Greenwood Publishing Group, Inc.
www.greenwood.com

Printed in the United States of America

The paper used in this book complies with the Permanent Paper Standard issued by the National Information Standards Organization (Z39.48–1984).

10 9 8 7 6 5 4 3 2 1

Contents

Preface

Volume 16 marks a new direction for *Criminal Justice History*. Each volume will center on a general theme or subject, which will include essays and reviews, and a title that reflects its contents. This volume highlights seven original articles on the history of policing in Europe from the eighteenth to the twentieth centuries, together with twelve reviews of books prominent in a field of war, crime, policing, and society that brings a multitopical focus to criminal justice studies. An introduction presents the articles and the themes that emerge from them, which will inform the history of crime and criminal justice. The book, as others in the series, concludes with a comprehensive index.

The following succeeding volumes have been contracted and completed for publication to date: Volume 17: *Gender, Class, and Sexuality in Criminal Prosecutions*; Volume 18: *Crime, Punishment, and Reform in Europe*; and Volume 19: *Violent Crime in North America*. Future volumes will be announced as they are prepared.

Introduction

Louis A. Knafla

The history of crime is usually conceived in terms of peacetime conditions. Personal crimes of violence such as murder, rape, and assault, property crimes such as arson, theft, and fraud, and regulatory offenses such as vagrancy, prostitution, and nuisances are often studied with primary reference to the role of victims, perpetrators, communities, and the state in a criminal justice system operating in peacetime conditions. External factors such as a major plague, dearth, or war are seldom considered unless they are examined specifically. However, some of the more prominent contributions to the historiography of crime and criminal justice in Europe have been on these factors. Europe, unlike North America, has been the battleground for most of this historiography. Possessed with class systems, conflicting versions of Christianity, and deep ethnic divisions, Europe also has been blessed with a passion for record keeping over the past millennia that has defied other civilizations east and west.

This volume in the *Criminal Justice History* series begins a sequence of books devoted to specific subjects. As an inaugural volume in the new series, it features the subject of policing and war in modern Europe. Military history has been one of the major growth areas of historical studies in the 1990s and one that has captured the interest of the reading public as well as students and academicians. Combined with the growth of the social history of crime, this has prompted research into the influence and effects of war on crime and criminality. It has also caused historians, sociologists, and political scientists to consider war as a factor, either directly or indirectly, in the role of states and communities in the criminal justice system.

An equally prominent area of growth in the historiography of crime and criminal justice has been the police, especially with regard to Germany, Italy, France, and England. Police history has focused on the police not only as law enforcement officials but also as specialist crime investigators and as men and women who have jobs, children, and families in the communities they serve. Like soldiers, they are not constantly in the heat of the chase, but they bear the conscience of the institution that has trained and nurtured them. The seven chapters that are contained in this volume, together with most of the books under review, provide some salient examples of modern research and critical thought on policing and war that will be useful to both current readers and future researchers.

Elaine A. Reynolds, in examining the Westminster night watch in the 1770s, compares and contrasts the police reforms of Sir John Fielding and Sir Charles Whitworth. She provides a detailed examination of the work of each kind of local official in law enforcement and assesses the impact of the Westminster Night Watch Act of 1774. The last major statutory landmark in local policing until the Metropolitan Police Act of 1829, the 1774 act emphasized the preventative function of the night watchman. It met the desire of parishes for greater local autonomy while establishing uniform duties and salaries. Reynolds concludes that it is difficult to interpret the importance of the act since it was legislated during a period of war when crime rates were unusually low. It was, however, a "significant forerunner to modern urban police organizations, and it developed out of a process of reform that involved both local and central government bodies."

War has always been linked to the crime problem. In early nineteenth-century France, imperialists interpreted criminality as a characteristic of a "backward, degenerate culture ripe for foreign control." Michael Broers' study of war and crime in Napoleonic Italy differentiates between criminality and crime or criminalized society and criminal activity. While the French were relatively successful in restoring civil order, they introduced efficient policing to win Italian support for French rule. This caused a reaction, however, which took the form of local political subversion that gave rise to organized banditry. Thus, the French process of state-building was confronted by victims who manipulated the state to their own ends and created a "legacy of fear" that was brought back to the minds of the Italian propertied classes from the uprisings of the 1790s. Conscription led to revolts, patronage to extortion and fraud. In the end, Italians seemed to prefer crime and corruption to a state culture founded upon war.

Richard W. Ireland's provocative study of "The Felon and the Angel Copier" explores the problem of criminal identity in the Victorian era in England and Wales. Rapid advances in transportation and communication led to demographic shifts in population that made it increasingly difficult to identify criminals in areas where most of the population were strangers. Failures to identify criminals in an era when transporting convicted felons out of the country was no longer possible led to fears of England itself becoming a penal settlement. Ireland addresses the problems of witness statements for police and prison officials in his study of Carmarthenshire. Governor Gardner, drawing from the use of photography in France and

Switzerland, introduced it to Bristol jails. This new method, supplementing written descriptions, enabled prison staff to create an inventory of criminal photographs that was used to assure the population that criminals and recidivists could be identified in the future.

Combining photography with the electric telegraph, Victorians now claimed that science could resolve social problems. Unfortunately, this development did not accord with reality. The Habitual Criminals Act of 1869 made only oblique reference to photography, and an examination of the photographs themselves reveals that they were crude likenesses unlikely to bring certain identification. Criminals were held down to have photographs taken, and often they were unnamed. Given no system with which to file them, a yearly "Register of Distinctive Marks" was issued in the 1880s. The use of photographs then changed to one of confirming identity. This became part of the new world of criminal stereotyping that became a feature of their criminology and public discourse and now of ours today.

Little has been written on private policing in the nineteenth century, let alone in the twentieth. Barry Godfrey examines the emergence of the new police in Yorkshire in the middle decades of the nineteenth century and analyzes their relationship with the private police of the worsted factory inspectorate. His examination of petty and quarter session records in the West Riding, 1844–76, reveals that over 3,000 cases of fraud and embezzlement were reported by factory inspectors and their agents. Workers were searched at the gates, and their houses and sheds were searched on warrants signed by justices of the peace (JPs). Employers used the advice of their inspectors as to whether charges should be preferred, and JPs had nearly 80 percent of those charged arrested without the inspectors present.

Worsted Committees, supported financially by taxes, private corporations, the sale of seized goods, and fines, arranged settlements with the accused that included compensation to the factory owners. Their services were advertised in newspapers, as were the outcomes of their settlements. Since the police did not have the right of access to factories and warehouses without their owners' permission, the committees kept their distance from both the local police and local prosecution societies. The inspectors were reduced in number drastically by William Gladstone's budget of 1859 but restored in 1870 with lower salaries and men of lower qualities. This resulted in a much less effective enforcement system. Godfrey argues that the employers' private police were the most dynamic element of policing in modern England's history. They reveal the extent to which public police and private enterprise have theoretical inconsistencies and how a private system could be cheaper, more efficient, and easier to control than a body subject to publicly elected officials.

"Street, Beat, and Respectability" marks the symbolism of Mark Clapson and Clive Emsley's study of the culture of the late Victorian and Edwardian urban policeman. Using heretofore unused sources such as the *Police Re-*

view and house-to-house police surveys, the authors are able to depict policing on the streets with graphic detail. Streets are colored in pencil according to their class and character. Thus, streets colored black were "vicious, semicriminal poor, and the very poorest," streets colored pink were respectable working class, and those colored orange were "wealthier middle class and landed wealthy." The police themselves lived "in the pink." Since the governments of the day refused to recognize police unions, the police educated their own recruits and defended their professional status "no matter what." With a fixed wage, a pension, and long-term commitment to the job, police were nonetheless depicted as "sex-absorbed," with an overdeveloped interest in unclothed women. They were men who could, observing a malcontent, give him "a clip around the ear 'ole" on a cold winter's night.

Policing, as we have seen above, could be affected decisively by war. One of the most graphic descriptions of what police could do to their society is provided by Simon Kitson's case study of the destruction of the old district of Marseille after the Allied invasion of North Africa on 12 November 1942. Marseille was considered the "Chicago" of Europe in the 1930s, a city noted for its riots against governments and its black markets, where police sided with demonstrators and were part of the illicit trade. The German Gestapo recommended destroying the "old district," leaving 40,000 people homeless; the French police argued to remove the "criminal element." Included among these people were Jews, both French and foreign. The French capitulated.

Five thousand German troops and police embarked on the destruction of the old town, assisted by some 7,000 to 9,000 French police. The French warned some people to evacuate, comforted others, and then participated in the looting that occurred afterward. The orders came from the Vichy regime, and many local officials participated willingly, as if the orders had come from the Republic. Internal evidence suggests that the French police believed that saving a few people was worth their participation. In the end, the French participated, and Kitson queries the outcome had they decided to defend their city. Without the assistance of the French, "the roundups would have been extremely limited as the Germans had neither the manpower nor the local knowledge to perform them on a similar scale."

German police were quite different from their English counterparts. The major differences are contained in David Smith's study of the British reorganization and reform of the German police in the British Zone of Germany following the close of World War II. The Inspector General of the Public Safety Branch (PSB), Gerald Halland, had as his goal a Germany "demilitarized, denazified, and disarmed." He wanted the Germans to police communities by earning the respect of their citizens, not by instilling fear. The goal, however, was not achieved. Police morale suffered from inadequate food rations, poor accommodations, and few arms. The British desire to have them under local, democratic control was frustrated by the Ministry of the Interior, which tried to enforce control by the central state. Thus, police federations were instituted, and their trade unions secured by the Police Act of 1949.

By that date, Foreign Office officials wondered in private if it had been a mistake to enforce British ideals in a Germany "contrary to their whole tradition." The Newsome Commission had reported publicly that German compliance with the PSB was simply "lip service." Nonetheless, Smith does not lay blame for this failure because the British model was alien to the German people. It failed because the PSB "was forced to follow contradictory policies." By the mid–twentieth century, few police forces in the industrial West were nonunion, unarmed, and unprejudiced. The esprit de corps that was the hallmark of a good army was also the hallmark of a good police force.

Several themes emerge from these studies. First, while factors ranging from geography to ideology have played a major role in bringing diversity to modern European history, elements in these studies suggest that policing in Europe—from Germany to Italy, France, and England—has certain common characteristics that can be called "European." Second, we have learned, especially in this century, that war often compromises the values of society. One can see examples here of how war influences the ways in which police institutions conceive of and conduct their work. In some of these situations, this has been revealed as dangerous to the physical and mental health of the citizen. Third, the evidence suggests that police, like soldiers, must use discretion in their work. The rigid institutions of policing and warring, which were created out of necessity, appear to depend on decision-making at the bottom in order to be ultimately successful regardless of what has been planned at the top. In this respect, the modern state may lack in reality that cohesive homogeneity that historians, political scientists, and commentators have come to expect since the age of the industrial and technological revolutions.

War on the streets might be different from war between states, just as police are different from soldiers. In each of these forms of warfare, there are willing and unwilling participants. Some of the perpetrators, called culprits or invaders, may claim a higher purpose and fight on to what they regard as a higher ground. But each situation has its own rules, and the terms for contesting it are not altogether indifferent. The nation-state today may have a monopoly on violence. Its communities, however, will never lack for ingenuity in gaining control of what happens on its streets. Neither will the citizen lose initiative, whether as the victim of a crime committed within the community or as a member of a group threatened with its extinction by outside forces.

In conclusion, the history of policing and policemen, and of military history and warfare, are two major growth fields of modern history. Bringing these two areas together to bear on problems of civil society and the nation-state in times of war reveals that local problems of law enforcement cannot be understood properly without reference to the larger issues of the state. As we have seen in the brief discussion above, once one examines the interaction of these institutions it becomes apparent that the internal and external policies of the state have a direct impact upon the nature and success of policing in its communities.

POLICING AND WAR IN EUROPE

Sir John Fielding, Sir Charles Whitworth, and the Westminster Night Watch Act, 1770–1775

Elaine A. Reynolds

For many the real story of policing in London began in 1829 with the establishment of the Metropolitan Police, headquartered at Scotland Yard.[1] Thus, much of the historiography of policing has been concerned with the origins of Scotland Yard, held up as the very model of a "modern" police force, that is, a centralized, standardized, professional police force. Many historians of varying persuasions, from Sir Leon Radzinowicz to Douglas Hay, have argued that the eighteenth-century ruling classes were stubbornly resistant to innovations in policing.[2] The English apparently preferred the risks of robbery to the dangers of a centralized "French" police, that is, one more bureaucratic and less flexible than the old, locally controlled system. Only when frightened by the specter of the French Revolution and domestic radicalism did England's ruling classes finally come to their senses and provide London with a centralized, uniformed, professional police force.

More recently, I and others have challenged this rather Whiggish view of the origins of modern policing.[3] What I and others have found is that although there was considerable resistance to *centralized* policing, Parliament and local leaders did not reject all reforms. There is a long history of police reform that stretches back into the first half of the eighteenth century. Studies have been made of the reform efforts of the Fieldings, who, while successful at establishing the force of detectives that became the basis for the Bow Street Runners and Patrols, were less successful at broader-based reform.[4] What has not been studied, however, is the issue of how the work of the Fieldings compares to other contemporary efforts at police reform.[5] By comparing and contrasting the efforts of Sir John Fielding to reform the Westminster night watch in 1770 with those of Sir Charles Whitworth in 1774, I will show that police reform happened when local and central government worked together and when reforms were grounded in the structures and experience of local bodies.[6] As John Styles expresses it, parish vestries and magistrates were "willing to respond with enthusiasm, flexibility and some expenditure to proposals . . . [for reform] if they were based on the existing law enforcement apparatus" and when such reforms aimed at "policing appropriate to local circumstances."[7] In addition to shedding light on the process of reform, this chapter will also address the issue of what motivated reformers. Because the fears generated by post–French Revolution radicalism were not a factor in the early 1770s, we must look for other reasons why innovations in policing were sought and implemented. It is my contention that, for local authorities in particular, the great fear was not riots and radicals but more common or garden varieties of theft and robbery.

The primary focus of reform efforts in the 1770s was Westminster. Officially named the City and Liberty of Westminster, it included nine parishes, four extraparochial areas, and the Liberty of the Rolls.[8] The population grew slowly in the eighteenth century, from approximately 130,000 in 1700 to 165,000 by the first census in 1801. Areas that had been fashionable for the rich and famous in the seventeenth century, such as Covent Garden, became more crowded and less salubrious in the eighteenth century. Covent Garden was known for its theaters, gaming houses, night cellars, and prostitutes. The wealthy and powerful migrated west and north, into the parishes surrounding the palaces of Whitehall and Westminster, where Parliament and the royal court resided.[9]

The parishes bordering Westminster to the east and north were a mixture of respectable, middle-class neighborhoods, such as St. George, Bloomsbury, being developed by the Duke of Bedford, and outright slums such as St. Giles-in-the-Fields (hereafter cited as St. Giles) and Saffron Hill.[10] It is significant that these notorious areas were places where the intersection of boundaries between the City of London, Westminster, and several parishes and small liberties made for jurisdictional confusion.

The parish was the basic unit of local government in England. The parish vestry supervised the operation of the poor law, the paving of streets, garbage collection, and the services and property of the local church. Vestries were either "open," which meant any householder who paid the local rates was considered a member, or "select," when the board was self-elected, vacancies being filled by nomination and election of the remaining vestrymen. Most of the powerful and wealthy parishes in Westminster had select vestries, such as St. James, Piccadilly, and St. George, Hanover Square. But many of the crowded, older parishes kept the open system. This was the case, for example, in St. Anne, Soho.[11]

A key officer in eighteenth-century law enforcement was the constable. Constables were the unpaid keepers of the king's peace. Nominated by vestries and sworn into office by magistrates, constables were householders who served for one year and then passed the office on to the next man in the rotation. By the eighteenth century, the use of hired substitutes was common, often subject to the approval of vestries but not always. Constables were pivotal figures, however, because it was their authority, as sworn officers of the law, to arrest and detain suspected criminals and malefactors that empowered watchmen to do the same. Thus, the supervisory role of the constable was legally very important.

Beadles were paid parish servants who performed a variety of functions, including assisting the overseers of the poor, keeping order in church on Sundays, and supervising the night watch. It was the watchmen, augmented by patrols in some parishes, who stood as guardians of the night streets, walking specified beats at regular intervals of the night. They carried lanterns to light their way and called the hours. The legislative authority to tax local residents for the beadles and night watch for most of Westminster dated to legislation passed in the 1730s and 1740s.[12]

The work of all local authorities and officers was overseen by justices of the peace. There were two benches of justices that mattered for the areas under consideration in the 1770s: Middlesex and Westminster. By the 1760s, the Westminster bench had lost much of its power and prestige, most people preferring to take their complaints and business to the Middlesex sessions.[13] However, the Westminster sessions were chaired by London's sole professional magistrate, Sir John Fielding.

Sir John Fielding had succeeded his more famous brother, Henry Fielding, as the government's only paid magistrate after Henry's early death in 1754. Headquartered at Bow Street, Henry and John Fielding were recognized nationally for their work as magistrates. Henry founded a force of plain-clothes detectives that became known eventually as the Bow Street Runners, whom historians have seen as the direct ancestors of Robert Peel's bobbies. Although blind, John Fielding held the post of chief magistrate at Bow Street for twenty-five years, earning in the end £400 a year and a knighthood.[14] Thus it was only natural that when Parliament turned its attention to the topic of crime in 1770, it consulted Sir John Fielding.

SIR JOHN FIELDING AND THE 1770 COMMITTEE ON BURGLARIES AND ROBBERIES

The initial charge to the 1770 committee was to enquire "into the several Burglaries and Robberies that of late have been committed in and about the Cities of *London* and *Westminster*, and to consider of more effectual Methods to prevent the same for the future."[15] The main focus of the committee's report, given to the House of Commons on 10 April 1770, concerned the night watch. The witnesses, however, were not from parochial watch committees or vestries. There were only three: Sir John Fielding, Bow Street magistrate; James Sayer, deputy high steward of Westminster; and Mr. S. Rainsforth, high constable of Westminster.[16]

Fielding presented statistics to show the extent and growth of property crime in recent years, commented on the causes of such increases, and noted some of the difficulties magistrates faced in carrying out their functions.[17] He also pointed out that ballad singers should be prevented from singing in the streets, as this allowed crowds to gather and provided opportunities for pickpockets.[18]

Most of Fielding's remarks and all of those from Sayer and Rainsforth, however, concerned the night watch of Westminster. They were critical of the number, age, character, and wages of watchmen and constables and of the lack of interparish cooperation. Their recommendations for how to improve the situation were, for the most part, straightforward: Watch committees should appoint younger men of character, hire more of them, and pay them better. The witnesses also suggested other changes in the organization and discipline of the night watch.[19] The most drastic of Fielding's recommendations concerned who would direct the actual operation of the night watch. Fielding stated:

> If the new Provisions for the Watch can be established by the Commissioners remaining where they are, it will save Trouble, . . . so that the Appointment, Distribution, Direction, Wages, Number, and Punishment of the Watch, may be in the Magistrates, by a new Commission, and the Paying and Clothing be in the present Commissioners.[20]

What Sir John was proposing was that parish watch committees or vestries could continue to collect the watch rate and act as paymasters but that all the decisions on how and where that money would be spent would be made by a committee of magistrates, taken from the Westminster bench of justices, of which he was chairman.

The parliamentary committee endorsed virtually all of the recommendations made by Fielding, Sayer, and Rainsforth. In the debate in the House of Commons, however, the resolutions on the night watch attracted virtually no attention. Cobbett's *Parliamentary History* does report: "The Resolution, that ballad singers were a great cause of the increase of robbers . . . was so ridiculous, that the Clerk could not read it for laughing; indeed the whole House joined him, and after some droll defence of them, as itinerant Muses, etc. the Resolution was postponed."[21] Only one resolution became law in a bill that allowed receivers of stolen property to be convicted as the principal offenders and sentenced to fourteen years transportation.[22]

Nothing more was heard from Parliament on the subject of night watch reform, however, for two years. Why is not exactly clear. The failure of Parliament and local governments to respond with enthusiasm to Fielding's ideas for reform did not mean, however, that they were opposed to all reform. This became clear when Parliament took up the issue of the Westminster night watch again in 1772.

THE WESTMINSTER NIGHT WATCH ACT

When the subject of the Westminster night watch resurfaced in 1772, the approach to reform was distinctly different. Heading the committee "to enquire into the state of the Nightly Watch, within the City and Liberty of *Westminster*" in 1772 was Sir Charles Whitworth, Member of Parliament (MP) for Minehead.[23] Whitworth was, with rare exceptions, a consistent government supporter. He was chairman of the Ways and Means Committee of the House of Commons from 1768 until his death in 1778.[24] Sir John Fielding was not asked to testify for Whitworth's committee. Instead, information and cooperation was sought from the parishes. The legislation that finally emerged from this enquiry in 1774 reflected a desire for a greater degree of uniformity but it was combined with continued local autonomy; it was "based on the existing law enforcement apparatus."[25] The act was also a conduit for the spread of local reform. Reforms and practices developed in some parishes were applied to all.

Although the bill that emerged from the committee's recommendations did not make it out of committee before Parliament rose for the summer,[26] the committee report and its resolutions were ordered printed. The report reveals important information about both how the parochial watch system of Westminster was structured and how other areas compared. The parishes under scrutiny included all those in Westminster and, additionally, St. Andrew, Holborn; St. George-the-Martyr; St. George, Bloomsbury; St. Giles-in-the-Fields; and the Liberty of Saffron Hill. The report also provided statistics on how much money was spent annually on the night watch, how many watchmen were employed, and at what rates of pay for all the parishes concerned in the bill.[27]

In terms of total expenditure, St. James, Piccadilly, topped the list at £1,497 per year. In decreasing order of magnitude, the others were St. George, Hanover Square (for midsummer 1770 to midsummer 1771)—£1,431; St. Margaret and St. John—£1,250; St. Martin—£894; St. Andrew and St. George-the-Martyr—£856; St. Anne—£809; St. Clement Danes—£670; St. Paul—£646; Saffron Hill—£280; St. Mary-le-Strand—£89; the Savoy—£17. Watch rates ranged from four to six pence in the pound. The committee, like Sir John Fielding in 1770, commented that the maximum rate limits set by prior acts of Parliament had proved to be too low for several parishes by 1772 and they were having difficulty raising sufficient funds.[28]

The numbers of watchmen varied greatly, depending on the size of the parish. St. Mary-le-Strand employed only three men, while St. George, Hanover Square, had sixty-one watchmen and four patrols and St. Martin-in-the-Fields had eighty-five watchmen. The committee apparently was not interested in the numbers of beadles or constables. There is no information regarding these officers in the report.

There was also a range of salaries for the night watchmen of Westminster, but this did not vary as widely as the numbers of men employed. Winter rates of pay ranged from a low of 10d. per night in St. Anne, Soho, to a high of 1s.2d. paid in the united parishes of St. Margaret and St. John and in St. Clement Danes and St. Paul, Covent Garden. Summer salaries varied from 8d. in St. Anne to 10d. in the same three parishes as paid the higher winter rate. St. Paul and St. James, Piccadilly, also paid their men an intermediate rate in the spring and autumn months. In St. George, Hanover Square, the watchmen and patrols apparently were paid one shilling a week all year round. St. Mary-le-Strand and St. Martin paid an average of just over a shilling a week year-round.[29]

Outside Westminster, the united parishes of St. Andrew, Holborn, and St. George-the-Martyr had the best paid watch. The vestry employed thirty regular watchmen and six armed patrols. The watchmen were paid 1s.3d. per week in winter and 1s. in summer. Patrols received 1s.6d. in winter and 1s.3d. in summer. Saffron Hill hired thirteen watchmen year-round, assisted by an additional two patrols in the four winter months. The watchmen's weekly salaries ranged from 1s. to 1s.2d. per night, depending on the season; winter patrols were paid 10s.6d. a week. In the tiny Liberty of the Savoy, a single watchman stood guard there and for his trouble received 1s.2d. a night in winter and 10d. in summer.[30] These wages were comparable to or below those paid to unskilled laborers. However, a watchman's work was steady, year-round, unlike the seasonal nature of both skilled and unskilled jobs.[31]

The longest entry in the committee report dealt with the united parishes of St. Giles and St. George, Bloomsbury. No figures were given for numbers of watchmen or funds collected. Instead, there was this explanation:

> Your Committee received from these Parishes Two Returns, One of which gave the Account of the United Parishes, and the other of *St. George, Bloomsbury* only; from whence it appears, that they are under no particular Act of Parliament, but exercise their Authority under the Statute of *Winchester*—that the Constables collect the Money from the Inhabitants, who pay what they please; and that the Constables never account for the same: That the above Statute relates only to Inhabitants keeping Watch and Ward; above 200 Inhabitants do not pay any Thing; and most of them are so dissatisfied with this Mode of Watching, that they have entered into voluntary Subscriptions to pay other Watchmen than those provided by the Constables . . . there are Two Divisions and Two Constables, whose Jurisdiction extends equally over the whole Parishes.[32]

In essence, St. Giles and St. George in 1772 were at the stage of development where the parishes of Westminster had been in 1735–36. Funds were being collected to pay watchmen, and not necessarily collected with any great success, under the rather dubious legal covering of the medieval Statute of Winchester, and there was no legal power that could be brought to bear on either the residents to make them pay or on the constables to make them account for what funds were collected.

After offering this information about the state of the watch, the committee made four resolutions. The first was: "That it is the Opinion of this Committee, That the present Mode of Watching, and Pay of the Watchmen, within the City and Liberty of *Westminster*, is very irregular and various, and ought to be put under proper Regulations." The second resolution followed on from the first, that "it would tend to the Safety of the Inhabitants" if a regular and uniform night watch, with the addition of patrols, "was established under proper Regulations." Next, the committee decided that it would be necessary to levy a rate in order to pay for the proposed improved watch. The final resolution addressed the question of who should have authority over constables. The resolution stated:

> that it is the Opinion of this Committee that Constables of the Night should be appointed, who as well as the Beadles, Watchmen, and Patrole Men, should be under the Directions of proper Persons *in each Parish*, to be called Directors of the Watch [Emphasis added].[33]

Since most of the parishes already had the authority to levy rates and professional night watches, these resolutions were not proposing any great shift in the parochial system. The committee was proposing, however, that while there would be a degree of structural conformity from parish to parish, each locality would still be free to administer the system within its boundaries as it saw fit. The last resolution, however, proposed a more fundamental change. If implemented as read, it would have meant that the parish watch committees would have more direct authority over the constables. The authority of the bench of justices, thus would be diminished. This was distinctly different from then current practice and from what Sir John Fielding had proposed in 1770.

On 15 February 1773, the committee's resolutions were adopted, but the bill that was brought in did not get out of committee. For the next session, that of 1773–74, Whitworth changed his tactics.[34] In November 1773, Sir Charles published the draft of the bill as a pamphlet, with an introductory letter addressed "To the Inhabitants of Westminster." He pointed out that an improved night watch was necessary because nighttime was when thieves and robbers "put in Practise their Schemes of Villainy." He asserted that "The Welfare of Society depends upon securing the Honest and Industrious from the Violence" of thieves and robbers.[35]

Sir Charles also made a point of saying, in his introduction, that the bill had "undergone the Examination of most of the VESTRY-CLERKS these last two years" (capitals his). Gaining the support of the vestry clerks undoubtedly helped Whitworth gain the support of the parish vestries of Westminster. As the chief administrative officer for the vestry, a vestry clerk, who was often a lawyer as well, was in an advantageous position to lobby effectively among the vestrymen.[36]

From the vestry records it seems that the clerks for St. James, Piccadilly, were especially active. Mr. Thomas Thomas and Mr. Luke Ideson testified before the House of Commons committee in February 1772. They also met with the clerks from the other parishes and agreed to work together to improve the watch.[37] In the spring of 1774, the vestry ordered the clerks, Mr. Ideson and Mr. James Dyson, to follow the progress of the new version of Whitworth's bill.[38]

The body of Whitworth's pamphlet summarized the current state of the night watch and of his proposed plan. This plan called for the establishment of minimum standards—each parish or liberty was to have no less than a stipulated number of watchmen and patrols. Thus, in 1772, there was a total of 348 watchmen and 8 patrols employed in Westminster and the adjacent parishes. The proposed plan called for at least 323 watchmen and 55 patrols, a total increase of 22 men. The patrols would be mandatory only during the winter months, but "the Number as well as Duty may be augmented at the Discretion of each respective Parish." Beadles would be required to patrol their parishes, to check on the watchmen and patrols, keeping a book in which they were to record any lapses of discipline, as was done in St. George, Hanover Square. This was the bare bones of Whitworth's plan. He also stated, "The above Plan has been already experienced with good Effect in the Parishes of St. Andrews Holborn [*sic*], and St. George-the-Martyr; and the Bill is formed upon the 10th of George II for Saffron Hill, etc."[39]

The bill proposed minimum wage rates for watchmen and patrols and lifted the rate ceiling. Section five of the bill stipulated that every patrol was not to be paid less than 1s.3d. a night and watchmen not less than 10d. a night from Lady Day to Michaelmas or less than 1s.2d. in the winter half of the year, from September to March. The watch rate that would provide the funds to pay wages was not to be more than 6d. in the pound per year, "according to the Yearly Rent or Value of the Houses, [etc.]."[40]

Hours of duty were spelled out precisely. In the summer, from May to August, watchmen were to be at their stands from 10:00 P.M. until 5:00 A.M. Winter hours, in effect from November to February, were ten to seven, and during the fall and spring, watchmen were on duty from ten to six. Winter patrols were to be on the streets from 11:00 P.M. until 6:00 in the morning. If a parish chose to use patrols in other seasons, the minimum hours of duty would be from eleven to five.[41]

Whitworth's bill also explicitly emphasized the preventive function of the night watch. It stated "That every Watchman [other than patrols] shall every Night Half-hourly during his Whole Time of watching, go round his Walk or Beat, and loudly, and as audibly as he can, call or proclaim the Time of the Night or Morning." Watchmen and patrols were instructed to try doors and windows, to see if they were secure and to notify the occupants if they were not. These men were "authorized and impowered to arrest and apprehend all Night Walkers, Malefactors, Rogues, Vagabonds, and other loose idle and disorderly Persons, whom he [or they] shall find . . . disturbing the public Peace, or that he shall have Cause to suspect of any evil Designs. . . ." Any suspects apprehended were then to be turned over to the constable of the night for formal charging.[42]

The bill also gave statutory sanction to certain practices developed over the years in Westminster since the 1730s through trial and error. For example, the vestries of St. George, Hanover Square, and St. James, Piccadilly, had agreed to instruct their watchmen to come to each other's assistance, regardless of parish boundaries. This came about, however, solely because of a tradition of administrative cooperation between these two particular parishes. Whitworth's bill made such cooperation mandatory between all parishes:

> that in Case any One or more of the said Watchmen shall want any Assistance to enable him or them to perform any Part of the Duty herein and hereby required to be by him or them done, then and in every Case any other of the Watchmen of the same or any adjoining Parish, Liberty, Precinct or Place have knowledge or Notice thereof by the Rattle, or other Signal Outcry, or otherwise to repair to and assist such Watchman or Watchmen wanting Assistance, by the best Ways [and] Means in his or their power. . . .[43]

This bill included other changes that had developed out of the experiences of the previous forty years. One was the keeping of written records of violations of the rules and regulations by watchmen, which facilitated disciplinary procedures. Another practice included using a scale of disciplinary actions, starting with reprimands, moving through fines of varying amounts, leading ultimately to dismissal. The employment of rate collectors who were paid on a percentage basis was another procedure developed in the earlier decades that had now become common. In this bill, the rate collectors were to be allowed, "for his or their Trouble . . . as they [the vestries] shall think fit, not exceeding *Six Pence* in the Pound of the clear Monies collected."[44]

The creation of the rank and function of patrol watchmen was another change that originated in one parish and was to be extended by Whitworth's bill to all. It appears that this practice was developed in either St. Andrew, Holborn, or Saffron Hill. St. Marylebone, a parish that bordered St. George, Hanover Square, to the north, was using patrols to supplement stationary watchmen by 1772.[45] St. George, Hanover Square, considered "an Augmentation of the Watch by a Patrol" in 1772 but postponed any final decision when Lord Litchfield suggested the vestry wait until Parliament considered Whitworth's bill, which was due to come up in the next session.[46] As it turned out, it was just as well that the vestry waited. The bill, as has been noted, did require each parish (with the exception of the Savoy) to employ patrols in the winter. Patrols, unlike watchmen, were constantly on the move and did not call the hours. Since this was a more physically strenuous job, patrols were paid more.

The bill also allowed, but did not require, vestries to create a watch committee that would meet monthly to handle complaints and discipline of the night watch. It also stipulated that all decisions and actions of the committees "shall be subject to the Controul [*sic*], Alteration or Revocation, of the said Vestries, Trustees, directors or Governors of the Watch, and Governors and directors of the Poor. . . ."[47] This provision followed the example of St. George, Hanover Square, which had established such a committee in 1736.

Section 18 of the proposed bill began: "And for the more effectually preventing the Appointment of improper Persons to be Deputy Constables. . . ." As has been previously discussed, the use of deputy or substitute constables was not a new practice in the eighteenth century. The 1756 act that increased the number of constables for Westminster had set a fine of £8 for anyone who chose to use a substitute and set down which occupations were or were not acceptable trades for constables. James Sayer had complained in 1770 that the rich escaped serving and had recommended increasing the fine levied on those who chose not to take up the office from £8 to £20.[48] Whitworth's bill was thus another effort to regulate the use of deputy constables.

As Sayer had also pointed out in 1770, the problem was how to ensure that the men hired as deputy constables were honest, sober, and conscientious. The bill stated that "no Person whatever shall be appointed a Deputy Constable in and for the said City of Westminster, or Liberty thereof, who shall not at the Time of such Appointment be an Householder, and Resident in the Parish . . . for which he shall be appointed. . . ." They were also required to produce a certificate signed by a churchwarden (or chapelwarden for nonconformists), "signifying that he hath been approved at some Vestry, or other Public Meeting of the Inhabitants. . . ."[49] The idea that a resident in a particular locality was best suited to know and provide policing for his community was part of the tradition that saw the constable as a community representative as well as the keeper of the king's peace.[50] It also made good tactical sense because someone familiar with the neighborhood would be more likely to recognize strangers or those known to be criminals. This clause, then, attempted to maintain the connection between community and law enforcement but also gave vestries some control over the quality of men allowed to be deputy constables.

Whitworth's bill also proposed changes in the penalties for any constable who did "not watch and abide in the Watch House during all the Hours and Times hereby directed and appointed for keeping Watch." Anyone guilty of neglect of duty still had to be brought before a magistrate and convicted. However, the fines now would range from five shillings, if absent for one to three hours, or ten shillings for more than three and less than five hours, to the maximum of twenty shillings, if the constable of the night defaulted for more than five hours. Any fines collected went into the watch fund for the parish in which the offense occurred. If unable to pay, the offender could be jailed and sentenced to hard labor for up to three months.[51]

Thus, what Whitworth planned to do was to take the provisions of previous acts of Parliament relating to the night watch, incorporate in a statutory form what some parishes had developed in practice, and add some innovations. This combination of reforms would then be extended to all the parishes of Westminster and some of its neighbors. In this way, there would be at least minimal uniformity for the whole of the district and yet also the flexibility for each parish to adapt that system to its needs.

Sir Charles took steps to gain the support of the parish vestries by careful attention to the concerns and interests of parish authorities. In addition to vestry clerks, Whitworth lobbied the members of vestries, especially the powerful select vestries of the West End. For example, in late January 1774, Lord Trevor told the vestry of St. George, Hanover Square, that he had received a copy of the Westminster night watch bill from Sir Charles Whitworth, "which contained some Clauses by which this Parish would be materially affected. . . ." The vestry took the bill into consideration at their next weekly meeting.[52] The suggestions offered by the vestry of Hanover Square illustrate how sensitive local authorities were to any possible attempts to usurp their power.

The alterations in the bill proposed by the vestry of St. George, Hanover Square, were a minimum wage of £18 5s per year for watchmen, "the same to be regulated, and paid as to the different parts of the year, at the Discretion of the Vestries of each Parish"; that the watch rate should be determined "according to a Pound Rate upon all Occupiers of Houses," not assessed on the yearly rent or value of houses; that the meetings of the watch committees could be limited to the first week of the month "but that the particular day be left to the Discretion of the Board." Finally, the vestry was "willing to admit additional Watchmen, under the Name of Patrols; but as to their particular Duty, they desire it may be left to the Judgement of each Vestry."[53] From these, it is also clear that this vestry was very jealous of its authority to regulate its night watch.

An additional suggestion from the vestry of St. George, Hanover Square, indicates the status of watchmen was changing. The vestrymen stated, "They are of [the] Opinion that a Clause should be added for the Protection of Watchmen, etc. when on their Duty; and to make it highly Penal, to assault, or resist them."[54] They were asking that watchmen be afforded a legal status similar to that of constables. To assault an officer of the law in the course of his duty was a more serious offense than assaulting a private person.[55]

In addition to seeking their suggestions for improving the bill, Whitworth sought the support of the Hanover Square vestry on behalf of the bill after it was introduced in the new session of Parliament in February. In April, Sir Charles Whitworth wrote to the vestry, "purporting that the Committee on his Watch Bill would meet after the Holidays and that he would send Notice of the day." The vestry ordered a fresh copy of their suggestions sent to Whitworth and to those vestrymen who were members of the House of Commons. The vestry also instructed their clerk to inform those members of "when the said Committee meets and desires their Attendance there." Whitworth had thus convinced the vestry to lobby its own members on behalf of the bill.[56]

In May, Mr. Parry, the vestry clerk for Hanover Square, reported he had attended the parliamentary committee meeting on the night watch bill. He informed the vestry that the committee had adopted the recommendation that the minimum wage for watchmen be expressed in a yearly figure instead of a per-day sum.[57] While assaulting a watchman was not made a felony, a paragraph was inserted in the final version to stipulate that if "any Person or Persons assault or resist any Watchman whilst in the Execution of his Office, or shall promote or encourage the same; every such Person shall, for every such Offense, forfeit and pay any Sum not exceeding Five Pounds."[58]

Other than these changes and some additional clauses dealing with the interaction of St. Clement Danes, St. Mary-le-Strand, and the Savoy, the final version of the Westminster Night Watch Bill was the same as Whitworth's published draft. On 27 May 1774, the bill as amended was read for a third time and finally passed by the House of Commons. A week later, the House of Lords also passed it and on 14 June it received the royal assent.[59] One final indication of the extent to which this bill was a cooperative effort between local and central government is in an entry in the vestry minutes for St. James, Piccadilly, for 18 June 1774. Mr. Ideson, one of the vestry clerks, reported that one of the clerks of the House of Commons had been particularly helpful in regard to the night watch bill. Ideson told the board "that it was thought reasonable by the Vestry Clerks of the several Parishes . . . that some pecuniary allowence by way of a Gratuity ought to be made. . . ." The vestry agreed and left it to the discretion of the vestry clerks to decide the amount.[60] Thus it is clear that this bill passed in large part because of the support it received from parish leaders and officials as well as from parliamentary leaders. And this was the key difference between this reform effort and that advocated by Sir John Fielding four years earlier.

The final version of the Westminster Night Watch Bill was the same as Whitworth's published draft with the addition of some minor amendments made at the suggestion of a few parishes. The act "for the Better Regulation of the Nightly Watch and Beadles within the City and Liberty of *Westminster*, and Parts adjacent" (14 Geo. III c.90) was the last major statutory landmark in the development of the night watch system in Westminster until the Metropolitan Police Act of 1829. The organizations and practices established by the 1774 act provided preventive policing. The emphasis, whether in the preambles to acts of Parliament or in the rules and regulations issued by parish vestries and watch committees, was on the preventive function of the night watch. This function was a limited one. Watchmen were not expected to be detectives, investigating crimes once they had occurred in the expectation of discovering the guilty party or parties, nor were they expected to act as riot police. Although the tumults associated with the career of John Wilkes were undoubtedly fairly fresh in the minds of many, not once did the issue of riots and crowd control arise in either parliamentary or parochial discussions. Very few political riots or demonstrations occurred in the hours when the night watch was on duty.

It was not riots and tumults, though the 1760s and 1770s were punctuated with them, that caused the authorities of Westminster to reexamine their system of preventive policing. Whitworth's prime concern was the villainy of thieves and robbers who worked under cover of night. Concern about the rising level of street crime and property crime of all types spurred renewed interest in local police reform. Additionally, the direction of watch reform was not from the top down but was more circular and even lateral. This act passed with the carefully solicited support of powerful vestries, such as St. George, Hanover Square, and St. James, Piccadilly. The parliamentary legislation applied reforms successful in one parish to many; parishes adopted innovations made by their neighbors; Whitworth made use of suggestions from local leaders; vestry clerks coordinated parochial support of the bill. The overlap in personnel between central and local government made this kind of exchange even more likely in Westminster, where MPs were also likely to be vestrymen. The result in 1774 was a significant degree of cooperation and uniformity in parochial law enforcement, particularly in the West End.

CONCLUSION

Sir Charles Whitworth's Night Watch Act was implemented in the autumn of 1774. The additional watchmen and patrols required by the act were duly hired; deputy constables were appointed; wages were increased.[61]

of Westminster Abbey. The tasks of the Court of Burgesses were similar to that of vestries, including paving and lighting the streets. The burgesses were also responsible for appointing annually the unpaid, amateur constables who were to keep the king's peace in Westminster. By midcentury, however, the vestries, dominated largely by wealthy and powerful aristocrats, had superseded much of the work of the burgesses. The power and authority of the burgesses, who were mostly small tradesmen, were no match for the more powerful and well-connected select vestries. For example, in the 1730s, the parish vestries had succeeded in obtaining parliamentary legislation that allowed them to rate local inhabitants for a professional night watch where the Court of Burgesses had failed. In the 1770s, the burgesses still appointed constables, however. For more on the Court of Burgesses, see Sydney Webb and Beatrice Webb, *The Manor and the Borough*, vol. 1 (1906; reprint 1963), 214. For the decline of the Court of Burgesses, especially in the area of law enforcement, see my forthcoming work on the development of the night watch in the eighteenth century, chap. 2. See also Robert Shoemaker, *Prosecution and Punishment: Petty Crime and the Law in London and Rural Middlesex, c. 1660–1725* (Cambridge, 1991), 265–70.

12. For a fuller discussion of the authority of constables, beadles, and night watchmen, see Reynolds, "The Night Watch and Police Reform in Metropolitan London, 1720–1830," 22–27; for the 1730s legislation, see chap. 2 of Susan Reynolds, *The Night Watch and Police Reform in Metropolitan London, 1720–1830* (Basingstoke, UK, 1998).

13. Ruth Paley, " 'An Imperfect, Inadequate and Wretched System'?: Policing London before Peel," *Criminal Justice History* 10 (1989): 101.

14. Critchley, *A History of Police*, 32–33.

15. *House of Commons Journals* (1770), 32, 784, 798. Hereafter cited as *CJ*.

16. High constables were officers appointed for each hundred in a county. They acted as intermediaries between Quarter Sessions and petty or parish constables, communicating decisions and instructions from magistrates to constables. Like other local officials, high constables also had a wide range of administrative duties that became wider as the eighteenth century went on. They collected county rates, inspected roads and bridges, and monitored the weights and measures used in markets. See Sydney Webb and Beatrice Webb, *The Parish and the County* (1906; reprint 1963), 489–502; and Styles, "Sir John Fielding and the Problem of Criminal Investigation," 143–49.

17. *CJ* 32, 878–79.

18. Ibid., 879, 880–81.

19. *CJ* 33, 879–80.

20. Ibid., 879.

21. The testimony and resolutions printed in the *House of Commons Journals* also appear in William Cobbett and T. C. Hansard, eds., *The Parliamentary History of England from the Earliest Times to the Year 1803* 16, cols. 929–42. The subsequent debate is reported in cols. 942–43. V.A.C. Gatrell has recently offered an intriguing analysis of ballads about hangings. He notes that at this time (1770s) the audience for such ballads was not limited to the lower social classes and that gentlemen as well as the laboring poor understood the cant and bawdy language of street ballads. But as the gap between upper and lower classes widened in the later 18th century, Gatrell points out that these songs were another aspect of street

culture that were increasingly repressed after 1790. It would seem that lawmakers of later generations were not as amused by such songs and their singers as these men were in 1770. See V.A.C. Gatrell, *The Hanging Tree: Execution and the English People, 1779–1868* (Oxford, 1994), 109–55.

22. *CJ* 32, 883, 908, 982. For the provisions of the bill, see Radzinowicz, *A History of the English Criminal Law*, 3: 71–73.

23. *CJ* 33, 416.

24. Sir Lewis Namier and John Brooke, eds., *The House of Commons 1754–1790* (London, 1964), 3: 632–34. See also the entry for Sir Charles Whitworth in *Dictionary of National Biography* 21, 162–63.

25. Styles, "Sir John Fielding and the Problem of Criminal Investigation," 149.

26. *CJ* 33, 447, 759–60, 788, 791, 953.

27. *Report of the Committee who were appointed to enquire into the State of the Nightly Watch of the City and Liberty of Westminster* (London, 1772), 4–6. Hereafter cited as *1772 Westminster Committee Report.*

28. *1772 Westminster Committee Report*, 4–6.

29. Ibid.

30. Ibid.

31. For wages, see Peter Mathias, *The First Industrial Nation: An Economic History of Britain 1700–1914* (New York, 1969), 4–6; for seasonality of work and cost of living, see L. D. Schwarz, *London in the Age of Industrialisation: Entrepreneurs, Labour Force and Living Conditions, 1700–1850* (Cambridge, 1992), 103–23, 161–78.

32. *1772 Westminster Committee Report*, 4.

33. *1772 Westminster Committee Report*, 6–7.

34. *CJ* 34, 130, 141, 171.

35. Sir Charles Whitworth, *The Draught of an Intended Act, for the better Regulation of the Nightly Watch and Beadles within the City and Liberty of Westminster, and Parts adjacent* (London, 1773), iii–iv. There is a copy of this pamphlet in the Guildhall Library, while the Westminster City Archives has a copy of the act. Hereafter cited as *Draught of an Intended Act.*

36. Whitworth, *Draught of an Intended Act*, iv. On the roles and status of vestry clerks, see Webb and Webb, *Parish and County*, 35, 124–29.

37. Westminster City Archives, St. James, Piccadilly, Vestry Minutes, 13 and 19 Feb. 1772.

38. Mr. Thomas resigned in February 1774 and was replaced by Dyson. Westminster City Archives, St. James, Piccadilly, Vestry Minutes, 10 and 19 February and 9 March 1774.

39. Whitworth, *Draught of an Intended Act*, v–vi.

40. Ibid., 18. Rate ceilings were a common feature of earlier parochial night watch acts.

41. Ibid., 19–22.

42. Ibid., 24–25.

43. Ibid., 25–26.

44. Ibid., 26–33, 40–44.

45. See, for example, Marylebone Public Library, St. Marylebone, Vestry Minutes, 7 January 1773, when two patrols were disciplined. St. Marylebone maintained one of the better watches in metropolitan London. See my "St. Marylebone:

Local Police Reform in London, 1755–1829," *The Historian* 51 (May 1989): 446–66.

46. Victoria Public Library, Westminster City Archives, St. George, Hanover Square, Vestry Minutes, 20 April 1772, 1 May 1772.

47. Whitworth, *Draught of an Intended Act*, 52–55.

48. *CJ* 33, 880.

49. Whitworth, *Draught of an Intended Act*, 37.

50. In discussing seventeenth century village constables, J. A. Sharpe notes: "Central government control over the localities was ultimately dependent upon the parish constable, who would often find the laws he was expected to enforce and the administrative instruction he had received from quarter sessions at odds with local ideas and the best interests of his fellow villagers . . . much of the criticism that has been made of the constable and other parish officers has arisen from a failure to appreciate that contemporary assumptions about the role of such officers were very different from modern ideas on 'police.' " See J. A. Sharpe, *Crime in Early Modern England, 1550–1750* (London, 1984), 77. See also Keith Wrightson, "Two Concepts of Order: Justices, Constables, and Jurymen in Seventeenth-Century England," in John Brewer and John Styles, eds., *An Ungovernable People: The English and their Law in the Seventeenth and Eighteenth Centuries* (London, 1978), 24; and Joan Kent, *The English Village Constable 1580–1642* (Oxford, 1986), 282–311.

51. Whitworth, *Draught of an Intended Act*, 31–34.

52. Westminster City Archives, St. George, Hanover Square, Vestry Minutes, 26 January 1774.

53. Westminster City Archives, St. George, Hanover Square, Vestry Minutes, 26 January, 3 February 1774.

54. Westminster City Archives, St. George, Hanover Square, Vestry Minutes, 3 February 1774.

55. H. B. Simpson, "The Office of Constable," *English Historical Review* 10 (1895): 636.

56. *CJ* 31, 432, 543; Westminster City Archives, St. George, Hanover Square, Vestry Minutes, 4 April 1774.

57. Westminster City Archives, St. George, Hanover Square, Vestry Minutes, 2 May 1774.

58. 14 Geo. III c.90, s. 1927.

59. *CJ* 34, 540, 766, 788, 801, 814.

60. Westminster City Archives, St. James, Piccadilly, Vestry Minutes, 18 June 1774.

61. See, for example, Westminster City Archives, St. James, Piccadilly, 6 October, 7 November, 7 December, 10 December 1774, and St. Clement Danes, Minutes of the Governors of the Nightly Watch, 19 September, 10 October, 7 November 1774. We get a glimpse of a few of the newly appointed deputy constables from parish records. St. Clement Danes chose to appoint Samuel Baldwin, who already worked for the parish as a watchman. St. James chose to appoint householders, mostly petty tradesmen of the kind one would expect to find in a well-to-do parish like Piccadilly. They included a carver, a chandler, a jeweller, a cheesemonger, a carpenter, a baker, a painter, a coach joiner, a cabinet maker, a shoemaker, and three wigmakers.

62. J. M. Beattie, *Crime and the Courts in England 1660–1800* (Princeton, N.J., 1986), chap. 5; and Douglas Hay, "War, Dearth and Theft in the Eighteenth Century: The Record of the English Courts," *Past and Present* 95 (1982): 117–60. Beattie notes that the court records do not permit a comparison of arrest records for officers of the night watch over time, and for most parishes that is also the case. Very few parish charge books survive. I know of only one, in the John Harvard Library, Southwark, for the Clink Paving Commission, which supervised the night watch for the Clink Liberty in Southwark.

63. Radzinowicz, *History* 3: 85.

War and Crime in Napoleonic Italy, 1800–1814: Regeneration, Imperialism, and Resistance

Michael Broers

This chapter is a contribution to a wider attempt to reevaluate the nature of the Napoleonic Empire, at least in its Italian context.[1] New studies of the phenomenon of cultural imperialism in the context of the developing world have enhanced and expanded the range of enquiry surrounding the nature of imperial rule and its ideological bases.[2] The fundamental goal of this study is to integrate the experience of Napoleonic rule in Italy into the framework of cultural imperialism simply because a thorough investigation of the archival sources have yielded results that make such a connection seem remarkably applicable to the primary sources. Hence, a basic assumption of this study is the existence of a cultural, moral mission on the part of Napoleonic imperialists toward the subject people of the Italian peninsula.[3]

The choice of the relationship of war and crime to the process of French imperialism also seems a natural one. Crime and disorder were the hallmarks of Italian society at the end of the eighteenth century[4] as war was at the heart of the Napoleonic state.[5] The relationship between the two produced a series of flashpoints between rulers and the people they ruled in Napoleonic Italy that preoccupied contemporaries to a considerable degree. War and crime were central to contemporary experience; they belong among the primary concerns of any historicist approach to the period.

The paramount place of crime in the history of Italy in this period requires careful handling, however. Two specific concepts have influenced its introduction into the analysis of cultural imperialism in this particular context. The first derives from concepts developed in the study of "classic imperialism" in the Third World. Important work has centered on the perception of the ruled native population by imperialist officialdom. This turns on the need to justify an imperial presence through the cultivation of an official image of the native as lazy, backward, and also as criminalized.[6]

These assumptions appear present in the attitudes of the French administrators of Napoleonic Italy just as much as in the ranks of the rulers of the overseas empires of the later nineteenth century. Each component of this image is almost always present in every colonial experience, but in degrees that vary in accordance with local conditions.

In Napoleonic Italy, the criminalized element in the official view of the native assumes a particular importance. This is because the French inherited a society that perceived itself as gripped by something akin to a "crime wave." There is certainly a considerable amount of empirical evidence to suggest that these indigenous concerns about the prevalence of crime during the late *ancien régime* were not without foundation. Working as they did within the intellectual framework of cultural imperialism, the French interpreted the prevalence of crime as the manifestation of a deeply criminalized society, whose structures and social relationships were conditioned and even controlled by crime.[7] There are particular cases when this assessment may be correct, and they will be explored in some depth. However, what also emerge are very different views of the problem of law and order taken by the French imperialists and the native Italian elites. While the former interpreted crime in the imperialist context of a backward, degenerate culture ripe for foreign control, the latter looked to their imperial masters simply for practical protection from a practical problem that they regarded as normal in its nature, if not in the proportions it seemed to be assuming at the turn of the eighteenth and nineteenth centuries. That is, the study of crime in this particular historical context has as much to do with contemporary perceptions as factual realities.

The second conceptual element is already implicit and in need of clarification before proceeding further. It is quite simply the need to distinguish criminality from crime, and a society that is regarded as criminalized from one faced by a high degree of criminal activity.[8] The imperial experience of Napoleonic Italy provides a useful example of these two concepts pulling at each other. The French imperialists interpreted what they saw as a criminalized society; the native population did not. This fundamental, if often fine, distinction emerges most clearly where the interests of rulers and ruled people managed to find some common ground. Policing had a very different context for each of them, even though it was a central concern to native elites and imperial administrators alike.

The historical reality of Napoleonic Europe is dominated by warfare. Thus, it was inevitable that the phenomena of crime and cultural imperialism would be worked out in the context of war. They became part of the process of the militarization of European society that occurred in these years. The Napoleonic Empire emerged as a direct result of wars of conquest and its conquests were quickly harnessed to that same war effort. The issue of crime was interpreted from the outset in the context of cultural imperialism, but both, in turn, were absorbed into the military ethos of the Napoleonic regime.

THE *ANCIEN RÉGIME*: POLITICAL PEACE AND SOCIAL CHAOS

The Italian peninsula had known a remarkable degree of peace in the second half of the eighteenth century until the campaigns of the late 1790s. Although the plain of the Po Valley and the mountain passes of Piedmont, Lombardy, and the Veneto were among the traditional battlefields of European military history, they had been used little in the wars of the eighteenth century until Napoleon opened his "second front" against the Austrians in 1796. The second Italian campaign of 1800–1801 concluded the military process begun in 1796, and in this way, the peninsula reverted quickly to its former circumstances as one of those parts of Europe comprehensively removed from the immediate theaters of war throughout the period 1801–14. There are two regions that are vital exceptions to this—Calabria and the uplands of the Veneto—and the examples they provide of the impact of war on the pattern of crime stand out in the history of the period.[9] However, as regards the greater part of the Italian peninsula, any discussion of the relationship between war and crime must be set in the context of the indirect, rather than the immediate, effects of war. It is a question of influence rather than impact. The Italian peninsula was ruled by a state at war and was made to play a full part in its massive war effort, but only on its extreme southern and eastern margins did its involvement in the Napoleonic wars become direct. Thus, the discussion of war, crime, and criminality must center on the aftermath of the campaigning of the late 1790s on the one hand and the effects of participation in the Napoleonic war effort on the other. In the long term, the first and second Italian campaigns are, perhaps, best seen as short interludes, punctuating only briefly a trend that had removed Italy from the forefront of European warfare from the end of the War of the Spanish Succession until the First World War.

The general picture is one of peace at the military level, but this should in no way be taken as a sign that Italian society was at peace with itself on the eve of the Napoleonic campaigns or that it returned to tranquillity after their conclusion; far from it. The states and regions of *ancien régime* Italy are marked by their variety. The peninsula contained a multitude of different topographies, economic and social units, and political cultures, but they almost all shared the problem of serious disorder throughout this period, its persistence fed by the intrinsic weakness of the states into which Italy was divided.[10] Whatever problems the French may have created in the course of the first and second Italian campaigns, they overlay other older, deeply rooted patterns of disorder, which the states of the *ancien régime* had been either unable or unwilling to confront.

Organized banditry existed in all the Italian states. Even the supposedly well-governed absolutist Kingdom of Piedmont-Savoy was not exempt from this phenomenon, especially along its southern border with Liguria, while in the Kingdom of Naples, the Papal States, and the Republic of Venice, the problem reached very serious proportions in the last decades of the eighteenth century. Organized banditry had several different *raisons d'être*. Along the borders of the northern states, it was an offshoot of smuggling—itself engendered by the mercantilist policies of the Habsburg and Savoyard governments that the introduction of the Napoleonic Continental System did much to perpetuate in the period 1800–*14*. Over much of the Mezzogiorno (the southern region of Italy) it was an extension of baronial power, part of a running war with the pretentions of reforming monarchs to control the countryside and with the rising rural bourgeoisie. Everywhere, it was connected with the wider problem of neglect by the feudal nobility of any aspect of their juridical privileges that did not bring them direct financial gain.

Deeper sources of social and economic dislocation engendered more incoherent, erratic explosions of popular disorder. Demographic pressures, coupled with rackrenting and attempts to introduce new agricultural practices combined to produce a mass of localized peasant *jacqueries* (revolts) throughout the peninsula in the last years of the eighteenth century. They centered on the upland valleys of the Apennines and the Alps but probably found their apogée in the Viva Maria risings of the 1780s and 1790s in the valleys of Tuscany.[11]

Italy also possessed some of the largest and most crime-ridden urban centers in eighteenth-century Europe. In contrast to the impotence they displayed in the countryside, most *ancien régime* states had lavished attention on urban crime and urban policing, if to little real avail. They had also been more ready to draw direct links between the problems of crime and poverty in an urban context than in a rural one, an interesting comment on their ignorance of rural conditions more than on their sensitivity to urban ones, perhaps. Social control in the cities revolved less around the small civic police forces than around the support offered by charitable institutions, which often owed more to the largesse of the Church and local *notabili* (nobles) than to the state, per se. The concerted efforts of the Savoyard monarchs in this sphere are an important exception to the general rule.[12] Although such trends are notoriously difficult to know with any real precision, it is fairly clear, in general outline, that urban crime was intensifying in the late eighteenth century as demographic and economic pressures created spasmodic but frequent influxes of rural poor into the cities. This was certainly how the authorities interpreted events, as seen in the tighter controls they sought to impose, not only in the administration of public charity but also on the movements of the poor in an urban context. The summation of their policy was one of exclusion, of keeping rural crime as "unlinked" to urban centers as possible, both by controls on entry to cities and by a more restrictive distribution of charity.

The archives of the *ancien régime* states abound in criminal legislation, much of it ferocious in tone and meticulous in content, but when set in its social and institutional context, it becomes clear that much of this represents a retreat from government rather than an attempt to extend the parameters of the state. Literally in many cases, the governments of the *ancien régime* simply tried to shut the gates on the rising tide of rural disorder. Concurrently, the feudal baronage was also withdrawing from the exercise of any form of social control or policing that did not serve its immediate financial ends. A multitude of local and regional variations qualify this, but its uniting themes are, on the one hand, the serious structural dislocation of large sectors of Italian society in the late eighteenth century and, on the other, the intrinsic institutional weakness of the states of the *ancien régime*. This troubled heritage must be set beside the more transient, if traumatic, dislocations created by the fighting of the late 1790s. In any assessment of Napoleonic rule in Italy it must always be remembered that the new rulers inherited a society more crime-ridden than war-torn.

THE PROCESS OF PACIFICATION: FROM THE AFTERMATH OF WAR TO THE PROCESS OF STATE-BUILDING

The Aftermath of the 1790s: Pacification and Vendetta

It must always be borne in mind that the relationship between Italian criminality and the Napoleonic wars is not identical with French policies concerned with the repression of disorder or other aspects of social control. Nevertheless, the point where the aftermath of war most influenced the wider aims of French policing policies was in their concern with "political subversion" and, above all, its links to organized banditry. It should be noted, however, that this formed only one aspect of a much broader policy of trying to win support for French rule through a more efficient, effective approach to the problem of violent crime in general, and organized banditry in particular. When viewed in this wider perspective, it also becomes clear that although politicized, counterrevolutionary banditry was a very real problem in many parts of Italy, it was hardly the major source of banditry in itself.

In confronting political brigandage, the French can be seen most clearly in the role of "cleaning up their own mess." This aspect of disorder was a direct consequence of the military conquest of Italy and, in particular, of the massive counterrevolutionary risings of 1799.[13] When French rule was reestablished in Italy after 1800, a very careful watch was kept not only on areas that had been the major centers of the revolt but also on those people at the local level who were regarded as its leaders. This process was not an easy one, because only in a few places—most notably in the Tuscan valleys near Arezzo, Piedmont, and parts of Calabria—had the revolts achieved any high levels of organization. Elsewhere—in most places, in fact—the revolts had been small-scale affairs, truly popular in character. This made them particularly worrisome for the new regime in its attempts to secure a grip on the country.

As long as French interest in Italy remained confined to a purely military occupation, the potential for renewed local revolts on the pattern of 1799 was of little consequence; they could be picked off individually. However, when it became a matter of establishing a permanent administrative presence at every level of society, the protection of their local officials—and of all those who collaborated with them—depended on rooting out counterrevolutionary elements. Even here, the French were always careful not to take this policy too far. The suppression of counterrevolutionary brigandage was essential to the establishment of their rule, but their main goal was always to try to disassociate the disorders of the war period from common crime.

Above all, they sought reconciliation with many counterrevolutionary leaders, symbolized by the general amnesty decreed by Napoleon in 1802 as soon as French hegemony had been reestablished over most of northern Italy. In this respect, the attitude of the French to political brigandage in Italy—or, more precisely, the potential for it—was subsumed into the general policy of *ralliement* (rallying). *Ralliement* was the essence of the Napoleonic regime.[14] Rooting out the former leaders of political brigandage always took second place to the appeasement of former opponents. Surprisingly little action was taken in these kinds of cases, as a careful analysis of those reported to the authorities reveals. It was only when former rebels actually took up arms and reverted to banditry that the French reacted and, when they did so, tended to portray the rebels less as subversives than as ordinary criminals.

This attitude was made easier to sustain because such incidents tended to occur in areas with a well-established tradition of apolitical banditry. There is strong evidence that bands led by activists of 1799 continued to operate along the border between the Papal States—which became part of the French Empire in 1809—and the Kingdom of Naples, and there is similar evidence for other parts of the Mezzogiorno. Even in some of these cases, however, it is probable that the bands' continued existence owed at least as much to the subsequent character of French rule as to the residues of the war years. This would certainly seem to be so where members of the regular clergy "turned outlaw," usually with considerable success, following the introduction of the French Concordat, which deprived them of their vocations. It is also very important to note that almost all cases of serious brigandage of a politicized nature were confined to central and southern Italy. What banditry remained in the north, following concerted French efforts to eradicate it, was not tinged by the politics of the 1790s.

When the focus shifts from the specific problem of organized banditry to more fluid manifestations of violence and disorder, the heritage of the 1790s becomes much more important, if also markedly more complex. The dislocation created in the wake of the rapid political changes of the period 1796–1801 both spawned and sharpened a host of individual personal vendettas that persisted into the following decade, and probably beyond. The series of administrative purges that followed each military conquest and reconquest created a vast number of persecuted, frightened, and embittered men at every level of society. Revolutionaries and counterrevolutionaries alike had seen their careers ruined, their lives endangered, and their property confiscated—or what was left of it after it had been looted by their rivals. It was in this way, and at this level, that the legacy of the war years made its deepest impact on Italian society, long after the more spectacular but more transient products of wartime dislocation, notably waves of petty crime, had subsided. The administrative chaos of the war years had opened the floodgates to anarchy at almost every level of a social structure that was already riddled with vendettas and personal rivalries and where law and order were fragile, to say the least.

In the face of this, the French were remarkably successful in the restoration of civil order in most of the peninsula between 1801 and 1814. They were less successful where the personal vendettas of the *ancien régime* had become entangled with the political rivalries of the 1790s and then with acts of violence in the postwar period. Here, the ravages of war became enmeshed with the social anarchy never far from the surface of *ancien régime* life.

Even where the newer divisions created by the war overshadowed older ones, they expressed themselves in the old ways: verbal and physical abuse together with the destruction of property. An instructive example of this centers on Belmondo, a royalist landowner in the mountain village of Pietraporzio, in the Piedmontese Alps. Before the revolutionarly wars, Belmondo had been a militia commander and a municipal councilor, and he owned extensive properties, employing over a dozen shepherds. However, he lost his official posts during the first period of French rule, 1798–99. Not surprisingly, he led his men for the king during the counterrevolution of 1799, and his first victim was the man who had replaced him as militia captain under the French.[15] In 1799 Belmondo was alleged to have sacked his rival's house and to have raped his rival's wife.[16] Here, personal vendetta merges with political rivalry. Belmondo's hatred of his pro-French rival went back to 1794, at least, and it was said to center on this woman. Until the war, their hatred had remained on a purely personal, if bitter, basis, and although Belmondo's loss of office may be presumed to have raised their rivalry to "a higher plane," as it were, it is still the case that the circumstances created by the war gave him ample scope for revenge. Between 1796 and 1799, this pillar of the local community soon acquired a taste for banditry, if he did not have one already. Nor was this the end of the story. Belmondo withdrew from public life under the French, wealthy enough to live off his rents and properties, but not from the public eye. Throughout the fourteen years of French rule that followed, his local rivals continually tried to bring him before the courts on a variety of offenses, all of which carried jail sentences.[17] The French did not doubt that Belmondo was a source of trouble, but the chief of police in Turin was equally clear in his own mind that many of the charges against him were "dictated in great part by animosity and the spirit of faction" and that "he is rather too much the object of hatred for the local authorities."[18]

A list of similar cases would be endless, but another aspect of the relationship between traditional vendetta and the aftermath of war is illustrated by a case that surfaced on the border of Umbria and Tuscany in 1810–11. It also reveals another way that vendetta could be conducted. Whereas the case of Belmondo emphasizes passion, these incidents rest on careful calculations made within a complex network of village relationships. In the autumn of 1810, rumors reached the French police in Florence that a revolt was being planned in the Val di Pierla, a mountainous area described by a police official as "places where, in the past, the inhabitants have shown themselves to be of a bloodthirsty and turbulent character, and to be brigands."[19] The main conspirators were found to be three substantial local landowners, one a priest, all of whom had been prominent in the fighting of 1799 and whose subsequent political behavior had been far from tranquil. Their village, their church, and their houses were ransacked by the police; guns and seditious literature—"relics of 1799"—were found, along with letters from fellow conspirators in Umbria.[20] However, a close investigation of the source of the denunciation showed it to come from another village notable who was in debt to one of the conspirators and who had been the defendant in a murder trial in which another conspirator had been a witness for the prosecution. From this point on in the investigation, the police recognized the possibility that the letters might have been "planted" and began to consider the arms cache—all hunting rifles, after all—in a new light. A few weeks later, the man who had denounced the plot fled the village and joined a brigand band led by his brother, his evidence further undermined by the growing realization that the conspirators had too many longstanding quarrels among them for them to have acted together. The denunciation had been carefully constructed to draw the attention of the authorities to the events of 1799, as well as to the possibility of their repetition, in the likelihood of touching an official nerve.[21] In this case, and a host of others like it, calculation of the official response to certain allegations was the key tactic, and one of the surest ways of getting a response was thought to be to resurrect the specter of the war years.

The official goal of French policy was to forge an amalgam of former revolutionaries and counterrevolutionaries, under the umbrella of Napoleonic rule. The reality was an amalgam of old quarrels with more recent ones, and the clearest manifestation of that reality is a passion for mutual denunciation to the authorities by rival factions in thousands of towns and villages, an amalgam of a very different sort from that intended by the French state but one that still pervades the public life of both France and Italy. It was the denunciation that linked the individual to the state most closely. It became the most useful service they could render each other and almost the only effective bond between them. It was by and through the well-prepared denunciation that this society sought to make use of the new state that had been imposed upon it by conquest; it was through this medium that the notables of provincial Italy sought to enmesh the French in their own quarrels. The denunciations are the firmest, most numerous form of archival evidence that this society was, indeed, looking toward the new state and seeking its help, but only for its own ends and to help it to settle its own kind of problems.

The aftermath of the war played a pivotal role in this process. On a tactical level, as has been seen, the authors of denunciations played on fears of the past, and indeed they were often motivated by vendettas with at least part of their origins in the 1790s. Finally, their investigation by the authorities illustrates how difficult it was for the French to fight their way through the complexities of local hatreds and maintain their objectivity. The overwhelming trend of the evidence, as suggested in the examples cited above, indicates that the French sacrificed tight security in the interests of *ralliement* and that the majority of denunciations, especially those harking back to political divisions, fell on stony ground, if only after thorough investigation.

The study of the art of denunciation reveals the heart of a process whereby the legacy of the wars of the 1790s was absorbed into a crime-ridden society, rather than altering the character of that crime. The residues of the war years simply became a part, albeit a major part, of much older conflicts. Arguably, this is indicative of the more general character of the relationship between the state and its citizens that was being shaped in Italy during the period of Napoleonic rule. The denunciation was the strongest bond between them. Put another way, their relationship was criminalized at its very core. It depended on the usefulness of state repression in settling personal scores. As will be seen below, there was little else to the relationship beyond this, while the state itself sought to avoid involvement in the very aspect of its work that most interested its subjects.

At this point, the very real gulf in perception emerges between the rulers and those among the ruled they sought to appease and enlist. The French regarded the very collaboration they were offered as criminalized: the denunciation. This was why they strove not to become involved in it. To the ruled it was a traditional weapon in the defense of society as well as of personal interest. In practice, the indigenous interpretation proved the stronger. It was one of the few avenues of approach the French could find into the heart of Italian society, and they took it, if always with reluctance and extreme caution.

In the final analysis, what emerges is the tenacity of the *società bloccata* (blocked society). Its world of personal vendettas and intense rivalries—small in scale but never "petty"—proved stronger than the tidal wave of war and revolution, shaking off the dislocation of the former and absorbing the politicized divisions of the latter into itself. The "earth shattering events" of the great age of European revolutions were sucked into this world; they did not transform it. Another layer of hatreds was added to the existing ones. The political culture created by the French Revolution was criminalized, at least by its own lights. Rather than leaving criminality in its wake, the aftermath of war, like the ideology of revolution, was criminalized in its turn.

The Restoration of Order: The Legacy of Fear and the "Dangerous Classes"

The "culture of denunciation" represents the uses to which the criminal legacy of war could be put; it shows how the victims of war and revolution attempted to manipulate the repressive machinery of the state to their own ends. In contrast to this calculated manipulation of war—a deliberate attempt to criminalize war—was the legacy of fear that the popular risings of the 1790s had implanted in the minds of the Italian propertied classes. Whereas the denunciation was an attempt by the propertied classes to condition the thoughts of the police, the revolts of the late 1790s imposed themselves on the collective psyche of the Italian bourgeoisie. The revolts were a nightmare come to life. Popular collective violence on this scale had been unknown for most of the eighteenth century until the tide of war and revolution unleashed them between 1796 and 1801. It would far exceed the limits of this communication to explore their nature in depth, but it is revealing enough simply to recall how much the counterrevolutionary risings of 1799 frightened even those who led them. Cardinal Ruffo was not the least among them, despite being the most successful *capo* (chief) of all.[22]

In this context, what matters most is the general climate of fear these revolts left behind them. They consolidated a bourgeois vision of the popular classes as the "dangerous classes," well before the process of modernization became perceptible in most of the Italian peninsula. This fear, in turn, enabled first the French and then successive regimes, well into the twentieth century, to use the issue of law and order as a central facet of the role of the state and as a way of achieving consensus in a society otherwise so riven with divisions.

The popular fury unleashed by the general collapse of authority can be reasonably attributed to the war. As with the more atomized phenomena of vendetta and denunciation, it was less the fighting itself than the latent social forces it released that left enduring traces. The mass risings of 1799 were almost exclusively counterrevolutionary, and thus their targets were the *giacobini* (Jacobins), the pro-French reformers. Ultimately, this section of the propertied, educated classes came to interpret these events as an assault on the Enlightenment itself by a barbarous populace, urban and rural alike. This evolved into a vision of "the intelligentsia beseiged," which was still vivid a century later and dominates liberal interpretations of these events written for the centenary of 1799.

The Puglian historian, Serrafino La Sorsa, incapsulates this outlook, in his account of the rising of 1799 in the coastal town of Molfetta:

> The memory of what took place . . . during 1799 has remained alive among our people of the south, as terrible events in which the lower orders (*la plebea*) [common people] showed what they were capable of, and with what insolence they knew how to impose themselves on other classes, 1799 is still spoken of as a dismal and savage event which has left an indelible mark on the popular memory.[23]

The step to seeing the rebels as criminals and savages was not a big one. It was taken most emphatically by Brigidi, in 1882, in his classic study of the Viva Maria rising of 1799 in Tuscany. He described the rebels who entered Siena thus:

> vile and ruthless men, come out of the last dregs of *la plebea*, part of that thriving, violent rabble that is to be found, always and everywhere, in every period of acute social confusion. . . . These brutal men, with their horrendous faces, their frightening physionomy, their arms bared, their heads uncovered, disheveled, with cutlasses in hand . . . *la canaille* [the rabble] . . . [24]

It is equally important to remember that this violent spectacle frightened many reactionaries as well, but its victims were the pro-French, reform-minded *giacobini*, and it is not surprising that the memory of 1799 did much to bind them to the French—and to the policy of efficient policing—in the years ahead. After 1814, it would bind almost all of them to any government that could keep order, and these considerations would play a key role in the process of unification, 1859–61. As John Davis has said with great incisiveness, "The perception is much more tangible than the empirical reality . . . crime in particular and disorder in general came to hold an often central place in the politics and culture of the new state [post-Unification]."[25] 1799 had a central place in the folk memory of the progressive intelligentsia, and the most vivid part of that particular nightmare was the criminal savagery of *la plebea*, unleashed by war.

In the short term, in the context of the period of Napoleonic rule, this outlook persuaded the French to place the restoration of order at the center of the wider policy of *ralliement*. It was to be their main tactical weapon in the cause of reconciliation, and there is much evidence to suggest that it worked. The fear engendered during the war years led most sections of the Italian elites to accept, and often to welcome, the heavy hand of the Napoleonic police state.[26] Although unpopular for its desire to protect them from each other—as witnessed by the mass of denunciations they produced against each other—the new state won considerable support for its efforts to protect the propertied classes from *la plebea*. In the sphere of law and order, at least, the perceptions of the Italian elites met the political priorities of the Napoleonic state, and law and order assumed a very great importance for all concerned in this period.

It was against this background that the French were able to pursue the restoration of order—the suppression of organized banditry in particular—all over Italy throughout the period. If they had a "trump card," this was it, given the psychological climate engendered by the war and its attendant anarchy.

The Case of Calabria: "The Exception that Proves the Rule"

The Calabrian peninsula was the one part of Italy that remained firmly "in the front line" of the Napoleonic Empire throughout the period of French rule. The island of Sicily was only a few miles away, still held by the exiled Bourbon court and protected by the British navy, and together they waged a perpetual, if limited, war of harassment against the region from 1805 onward. In Calabria, the French had to approach the restoration of order, and the fight against brigandage in particular, in a very different context from elsewhere in Italy. These circumstances provide a useful foil to events in the rest of Italy and help to place the more general experience of French rule in a wider perspective.

The French failed conspicuously to break banditry in Calabria. In contrast to the rest of the peninsula, the *gendarmerie* in Calabria was never able to operate as a normal, sedentary police force, but only as an auxiliary to the regular troops, fighting as *colonnes mobiles* (flying columns) with no permanent territorial assignations. The French won most of their direct confrontations with the bandits; they captured scores of them in a series of ruthless campaigns that reached their height in those led by General Manhes between 1810 and 1811. Particularly in the first years of their rule, there were signs that they were getting support in their efforts from a wide spectrum of the population, but fail they did. Unlike in the north, new bands always appeared in place of the old ones.[27]

It is very tempting to blame the failure of French counterinsurgency policy in Calabria on the Anglo-Bourbon policy of destabilization, and there is a school of thought, led by Angela Valente, that adheres to this view. That such a policy existed, there is no doubt. The occasional raid by the Royal Navy kept the coastal areas in a continual state of unease, but far more important was the supply of English gold coming from Palermo. This provided an alternative source of patronage for the bandit chiefs at the very point when some of their "normal" patrons, the feudal barons, seemed to be turning against them and toward cooperation with the French. This change of allegiance had been preceded by clear, enthusiastic signs of cooperation from many peasant communities, the frequent excesses of the French themselves notwithstanding.[28]

All this follows a contemporary pattern very typical of much of the rest of Italy, the argument being that it was undermined not for internal reasons but because Calabria was still a war zone. As such, it might be viewed as an almost unique case, and an examination of the development of British policy toward Calabria shows the very thin line that stood between the success of French pacification and the region becoming another Spain. The British and the Bourbons, certainly, were held back from large-scale intervention only through lack of resources. The British opted to concentrate their efforts on Portugal and Spain, where a foothold on the European mainland already had been established. Even the activities to which they restricted themselves were enough to create considerable continuities with the upheavals of the 1790s. In practical human terms, this was a region unique in not having a real period of peace, however brief, under Napoleonic rule. The disruption and disorder fostered by Anglo-Bourbon policy undoubtably had repercussions far beyond the limits of its direct intervention. Calabria thus represents a striking example of an area deeply disrupted by war, as a deliberate result of British grand strategy.

Nevertheless, such analysis does not address the question of the exceptionally disturbed, crime-ridden society that existed in Calabria prior to the revolutionary wars. Calabria represents a case where the concept of criminality might acceptably be applied to the social structure of the region. Banditry had become institutionalized in a very real sense: Bandits were not so much tolerated as retained by the feudal baronage and the bourgeois-dominated municipal councils, the *università*, who sought to rival them. In contrast to the smuggler-bandit-merchant networks of the Piacentino or the Piedmontese-Ligurian border, the bandits of the Mezzogiorno fulfilled no economic role in their society. They existed, and their existence was fostered, for ends that were generally admitted to be criminal by definition. There was no pretense that this was otherwise, even within their own communities.

This, in turn, raises the further question of whether the French would have been able to create stability under any circumstances. The region had known disorder, poverty, and structural crime, involving all levels of society, on a scale terrifying even by the standards of the rest of the Mezzogiorno. It is arguable that the devastating earthquake of 1781 did more to push Calabria over the threshold of anarchy than the revolt of 1799.[29] The Bourbon state had always been a shadowy, almost marginal presence there, and it is questionable if the French could have advanced its scope as rapidly there as elsewhere, even in more favorable circumstances.

What is certain is that the Napoleonic state itself did not have the resources to police the area professionally. With its manpower overstretched in terrain that is still among the most difficult to govern in Europe, the French had little alternative but to employ tactics that were more military than police-like in character and that provided order more transient than secure.

Here, the proper comparison would seem to be with Spain rather than with most of the rest of Italy, but with the vital difference that the Bourbons in Palermo, unlike the Cortes of Cadiz, made no attempt to discipline or organize the bandits who fought for them. Nor was there a direct British presence to instill the prospect of victory. Calabria was a region adrift.

ITALY AND THE NAPOLEONIC WAR EFFORT: THE PROCESS OF STATE-BUILDING

From "Counter"revolution to "Anti"revolution

There is a very important distinction be to made between the influences of the wars of conquest of 1796–1800 and the impact of French rule itself on the structure of crime in Italy and, arguably, on the criminalization of Italian society.

The phenomena of organized banditry and politicized private vendetta are residues of the anarchy of the revolutionary period. They originated as direct responses to the French invasion and adapted themselves to the new conditions of imperial rule. In the case of vendettas, this meant the deliberate attempt to manipulate the new state through denunciation. In that of banditry, where it still existed on an appreciable scale, it was either as a direct continuation of resistance, as in Calabria, or as a rallying point for new sources of discontent, most notably conscription and the new lease of life given to traditional smuggling by the Continental Blockade. This was how the effects of the wars of conquest blended into the new problems created by Italy's incorporation into the Napoleonic Empire and the demands it imposed on its people. The main new source of disorder was undoubtedly conscription, something virtually unknown in the small, weak states of the *ancien régime*.

Put another way, the distinction between the disorder engendered by the direct military conquest—with its attendant anarchy—and the new problems created by the subsequent French occupation might best be approached in the context of the concept formulated by Roger Dupuy and Colin Lucas.[30] This draws a clear, if often interrelated, distinction between "counterrevolution" and "antirevolution." The former belongs to the more or less politicized resistance that emerged as a direct ideological response to the emergence of the revolutionary state and its ideology. In an Italian context, this can be related quite readily to the revolts of 1799 and their complex aftermath. The culture of the vendetta/denunciation obviously is not rooted in these events, but it was influenced heavily by them, while the example of Calabria—although almost unique—still illustrates the continuity of armed resistance to French rule from 1799 into the later period.

Elsewhere, there are fewer traces of continuity, and this is where the concept of antirevolution comes to the fore. Resistance to conscription and taxation was less an attempt to preserve the old order than a rejection of the most oppressive acts of the new one. It was a defiance of the new state, its ways, and its demands. In this, it represents a new wave of disorder. In an Italian context, where these two types of resistance find common ground is less in their relationship to the consequences of war—or even in their shared anti-French motivation—than in the fact that they operated within the same social, economic, cultural, and geographic circumstances that had, in their turn, made law and order so central an issue for Italian society.

Conscription: The Advance of the State and Popular Resistance

The French themselves came to judge the effectiveness of their rule, as distinct from its popularity, by their ability to enforce conscription. They saw it as the "acid test" of their capacity to rule. They were probably right to use this as their yardstick. It is not without significance that conscription was not introduced into the Napoleonic Kingdom of Naples until 1809, and only then after protests from Murat, and that it was never actually applied in Calabria, the most unruly part of the French empire in Italy. Conversely, the Kingdom of Italy—centered on Lombardy—and the Piedmontese departments became among the most reliable recruiting grounds in the whole empire.[31]

These extreme examples should also serve as a warning about equating the issue of conscription too closely, or too widely, with the problem of disorder. Calabria never achieved the same degree of law and order as most of the rest of Italy, despite the fact that conscription was unknown there for most of the period. Conversely, the Piedmontese departments witnessed their most tranquil period between 1810 and 1813, exactly that point when the demands of conscription were at their highest.

Where the older, deeply rooted sources of disorder had already been broken, conscription did not readily lend itself to the growth of crime;

where organized banditry had ceased to exist, there was no "hard core" with which deserters or refractaries could coalesce. In these circumstances, resistance degenerated into passive resentment. At the other end of the scale, in areas so prone to disorder that normal administration could not function, the new regime did not attempt to enforce an institution everyone admitted was loathed popularly. Seen in this light, the relationship between conscription and disorder, although very real, is not as straightforward as it might at first appear.

This is not to say that the enforcement of conscription did not create serious problems for law and order. Far from it. Attempts to enforce conscription were crucial causes, but not the sole ones, of two of the most serious, widespread revolts in the history of Napoleonic Europe: that of the Piacentino—in the Apennine valleys between Genoa and Piacenza—and that in 1809, over a wide area centered on Bologna that reached right across central Italy, south of the river Po. If the revolts of 1799 epitomize counterrevolution in its Italian context, those of 1805–6 and 1809 are among the clearest on record of antirevolution.

The revolt of 1805–6 in the Piacentino was triggered by the new forms of taxation imposed by the French and, above all, by their attempts to raise a militia for service in the Kingdom of Italy following their annexation of the area, which had been part of the Duchy of Parma-Piacenza-Guastalla. They met with little real resistance in the lowland parts of the Duchies, but the mountain communities opposed these new demands with marked ferocity. The French were able to crush the rising, but only with great difficulty, and they kept a close eye on these valleys thereafter. The revolt of 1805 is a clear example of tenacious resistance rooted in the same collective, communal structures that also nurtured the highly organized smuggling bands of the area. The incursions of the French state—driven, initially, by the demands of its war effort—hardened these structures against them and transformed them from networks created to sustain smuggling into sources of armed revolt. The revolt seems to have been led by the smuggling bands and innkeepers with whom the smuggler-merchants were closely linked as well as by more "conventional" local *notabili* such as the clergy.

When set in a fuller regional context, the role of crime and, possibly, of criminality in the revolt becomes very central. Crime was built into the social fabric and economic life of the region. Smuggling was central to the economy, and those who controlled it stood at the center of local life. Care must be taken to equate this with the concept of criminality, of course. However, there were other features of the culture of the Piacentino that might be said to mark it as a criminalized society. Leaving the question of banditry based on smuggling aside, the French still found much to their eyes to equate with a society criminalized to the core as reflected in the patterns of daily social behavior and in the mores governing male sociability.

The inhabitants of the valleys of the Piacentino were renowned for their violent behavior as well as their criminal activities. The area had its share of blood feuds, but its outstanding characteristics were the profusion of spontaneous acts of violence and the penchant of its youth for carrying arms. None of this marked the behavior of the people of the lowlands of the plain around Parma, and French officials often contrasted their sullen obedience with the rebelliousness of the highlands.[32] These communities not only had a vested interest in resisting the new state—in remaining unpoliced in the fullest sense of the term—they also had the collective structures to mount formidable resistance to such attempts. Organized crime played a large part in those structures, and the demands of the Napoleonic war effort transformed them into the mainsprings of a wider popular rebellion.

There are obviously strong parallels to be made with risings such as the Vendee, Spain, the Tyrol, and those of 1799 in Italy itself, especially those in Calabria, Liguria, and Piedmont, where bandit/smugglers played an important part in the organization of resistance. However, what sets the Piacentino in a different category is the thoroughly antirevolutionary character of its resistance. There was nothing overtly ideological about the rising. The rebels' demands, as embodied by the placards they posted and the declarations they had read from the local pulpits, were devoid of appeals to religion or the old order.[33] They fought to thwart the progress of the new state, rather than to restore the *ancien régime*. That they were able to do so, however briefly, depended in no small measure on the highly criminalized character of their communities.[34]

The revolts of 1809 in central Italy have much in common with that of 1805 in the Piacentino, in that they were thoroughly antirevolutionary in their character and origins.[35] The risings began in several hill communes in the Apennines west of Bologna, initially over new taxes related to milling and flour production. As in the Piacentino, the revolts originated among tightly knit communities with a history of banditry and smuggling, and they seem to have been equally devoid of ideological motives. Where they differed from that of 1805 was in the course they took once the rebels spread beyond their own area and into the plains around Bologna and Ravenna. Here, their ranks were swelled by deserters from the French army—usually Italians or non-French conscripts—whose presence seems to have changed the character of the revolt. When the original rebels dispersed, probably returning home, the deserters remained to form the hard core of new, smaller bands that continued to ravage wide areas of the countryside for several months. It is probable that the deserters were able to contribute some degree of military experience to the revolt. It is certain that many among them simply could not return home or melt into the local community. This gave the risings a particularly desperate character in their final phase.

These revolts were also a chilling reminder to the Napoleonic authorities of the potential for disorder that could be generated by the close liaison between conscription and crime. Even the nature of the demise of the risings was a cause for concern. The revolt of the Piacentino had a discernible center and, thus, it could be crushed. Those of 1809 were diffuse; they were a target in perpetual motion with no center by their final phase, and as a result, they were not crushed, as such. Rather, they dissipated themselves as the bands of deserters were gradually isolated and hunted down, seemingly unable to integrate themselves into the indigenous criminal structures. In the revolts of 1809, an even older pattern can be seen reasserting itself, that of the rampant soldiery. It serves as a reminder that the modern, Napoleonic military machine operated in a world that was still an early modern one in many respects. The horrors of the Thirty Years War could repeat themselves all too easily when and where the system of conscription, and the armies it produced, were not properly policed and were then able to tap local sources of discontent. These revolts show the explosive potential of a war effort applied to a deeply unstable society. It is arguable that the experience contained the potential to criminalize it.

These two massive revolts represent incidences of what happened when the policing of conscription broke down. As with the example in Calabria, in the context of the relationship of criminality to counterrevolution, they are the exceptions that prove the rule. In the main, the French imposed conscription on most of the people of Italy with ruthless efficiency, and in so doing, they created the most effective system of policing the peninsula had ever known. The mechanics of conscription brought the whole apparatus of the state closer to the heart of Italian society than any other single facet of its activities. At the moment of every *levée* (levy), the prefects toured their departments, canton by canton, meeting with the *maire* (mayor) of each commune in the process. That is, the highest official of local government was brought into direct contact with his lowest subordinates every time this process occurred. As the demands of the Empire grew for more men, *levées* (levies) took place at least four times a year, and sometimes five or six.

The *gendarmerie* (constabularies) and units of regular troops accompanied the prefect on these tours, thus bringing a strong police presence to rural areas on a very frequent, regular basis. These *battues* (rounds) became occasions for the prefects to learn a great deal more about their departments and their *administrés* (those under their governance). They were also used for dealing with disorder in a much wider sense than those aspects of it related directly to conscription. While on these rounds, prefects not only learned about local sources of crime at first hand; they also had the capacity at hand to deal with them. In this way local troublemakers of long standing were often brought to justice, usually at the promptings of the communities involved. This kind of direct, decisive action was unknown under the *ancien régime*. It was also the surest way of penetrating the reality of local vendettas.

When Napoleonic officials moved into this territory—this local, immediate level of policing—they were soon led to challenge those clandestine but formalized social relationships that had either filled the gap left by the weakness of the *ancien régime* state or had exploited its weaknesses. The most spectacular examples of this are the campaigns against the baronial-backed bandits of the Mezzogiorno. More generally, and more importantly, it was represented by the challenge mounted by the state to the matrix of patronage in Italian society.

The exigencies of the war effort made it impossible for the French to tolerate this world of favors and obligations, just as much as their concept of the state made it anathema to them, ideologically. As the demands of war mounted, it became increasingly impossible to grant dispensations, to adhere to the codes of protection and reciprocity demanded by an order based on patronage. This is illustrated very clearly in the deep resentment, and astonishment, felt within the Italian propertied classes at the creation of the Gardes d'Honneur in the last, desperate years of Napoleonic rule. The Gardes were meant to be an elitist—as distinctly opposed to elite—force, drawn from the sons of the wealthiest landowners of each department. In reality, it was seen by the government as a means of conscripting men whose families had been wealthy enough to buy them out. This amounted to an assault on patronage and influence, even if coated in the sugar of blatant snobbery. The institution met with repugnance throughout Italy, and the reports of the prefects reveal how at odds with indigenous attitudes it was. The initial reaction of most families concerned was shock, that collaboration had not brought them the tangible benefit of privileged exemption. This was followed by reversions to well-established patterns of bribery and appeals for protection to better-established patrons in the Church or the aristocracy. Most prefects took a determined stand against this. As a result, not only did they alienate large sections of the elites they had so carefully cultivated until now, but they also extended the bounds of "criminality" to embrace the concept of patronage itself.

The antagonism between the modern state and this aspect of the old order was a wound that had festered since 1789. Although the Napoleonic regime had done much to heal it, the demands of war now tore it open again. By the last years of the Empire, much of the process of *ralliement* verged on being undone, not just because the institution of conscription had been extended to the propertied classes, but because this act destroyed their hopes that the new state could be absorbed into the pattern of patronage that was natural to them. Instead, they became "criminalized" in the eyes of the administrators.

Where French rule brought new standards of legality, the collision of different cultures becomes less dramatic but potentially more serious for the future evolution of the modern state in Italian culture. In this respect, too, the institution of conscription had a considerable part to play in a wider, more profound process. It was the catalyst that brought a deep abyss into view. Whereas the popular classes opposed conscription with armed force, the propertied elites sought to do so by manipulating the only real "loophole" in the system, those provisions that allowed replacements to be bought.[36] The system was a complex one, hedged in with restrictions, mainly because it was a concession the state disliked. It was tolerated only as a necessary expedient. When it became an unaffordable luxury, all pretense within the Italian elites that the new order might be compatible with the essence of the old evaporated. In this way, the issue of the Gardes d'Honneur has a much wider significance than might at first appear to be the case.

Beyond the circle of great landowners, the buying of replacements found a niche for itself in Italian criminal life. It opened up a whole new vista for extortion and fraud that was rapidly exploited by local officials, who readily issued false birth certificates for a fee, by doctors and surgeons who issued medical exemptions, and by "conmen" who procured replacements who never turned up. At this level, the adaptability of Italian criminality to a wholly new institution was remarkable. There is abundant evidence to show how seriously the French regarded this problem and how difficult they found it to eradicate. This genre of offense is an instance of the introduction of conscription expanding the horizons of crime, and it should be set alongside those instances of brigandage where the nucleus organized bands, as in Piedmont and Calabria, or created new ones, as in the revolts of 1809. It must also be said, however, that these phenomena were tied to conscription and the war effort so directly that they disappeared with its abolition in 1814. Any assessment of their impact on longer-term evolution of Italian crime must be set in this context.

The general resentment created by the demands of war—the genuine fear felt in many families and communities at the prospect of being sucked into the vortex of the Napoleonic war machine—was probably more decisive in shaping attitudes to state authority than the immediate crime generated by the circumstances of the wars. It was in this way, and at this time, that people at all levels of society learned not only to hate the French, for this had been accomplished between 1796 and 1800, but to hate the state itself. This whole process brought the state into the heart of society and, in so doing, brought into sharper focus the huge gap between official definitions of criminality and those concepts of patronage, privilege, and obligation intrinsic to Italian culture.

This took place on two different levels, one confrontational but episodic and regionalized, the other subtler but more diffuse and profound. Smuggling, and its attendant banditry, had always been illegal, but this usually had been something most states had been powerless to control. As a result, there were parts of Italy where it had become not only a way of life for those directly involved, but the cornerstone of the local economy, as in the Piacentino, the uplands of the Veneto, or the border between Piedmont and Liguria. Under French rule all this came under a more powerful, determined assault than the *ancien régime* had been capable of mounting, but it did not really amount to a redefinition of the bounds of legality.

The challenge to patronage and, implicitly, a political world that centered on local, personalized sources of authority, redefined criminality. In its relentless drive to harness Italian manpower for the war effort, the Napoleonic state pushed deference and reciprocity aside, just as in its desire to restore order and professionalize the administration of justice it often ignored the denunciations through which local factions sought not only to destroy their rivals but also to enlist the help of the state. Seen from the vantage point of the ruled, this was how allegiances were created.

The French Path to Redemption: From Criminal to Warrior

If there is one unifying theme in the impact of the Napoleonic wars on Italian criminal life and possibly the development of true criminality, it would seem to be the fundamental gap it exposed between rulers and the ruled over the nature of civil society.

War had played no part in the lives of those who lived under the small states of eighteenth-century Italy. In stark contrast, the Napoleonic Empire had been born of war and knew no other condition throughout its life. This vast difference affected the relationship between rulers and the ruled in this period, and their cultural estrangement emerges at its most striking in their respective attitudes to war itself. A useful conclusion emerges particularly because, in the course of their experience in ruling Italy, many French officials developed a specific opinion about the nature of the relationship of criminality to war, which turned exactly on the vast cultural gap they perceived between the Italians and themselves.

Military service was a traditional way of dealing with many offenders. The weak states of the *ancien régime* saw this as an expedient means of coping with normal offenders, nothing more. It was a useful way of removing them from the communities or even the families they terrorized. Frightened rural councilors and frustrated bourgeois families found great relief in its application to their unruly members, be it an "unsocial" bandit or a profligate son. Indeed, there is a mass of evidence, particularly in Tuscany and Umbria, of desperate appeals by well-to-do parents for the enrolment of delinquent sons in the French army. Some such petitions refer to youths already in jail and the genuine panic felt within their families at the prospect of their imminent release. It need not even have involved violence; a wealthy widow of the Roman bourgeoisie—the former mistress of a prominent counterrevolutionary—was more than ready to send her son to the forefront of the hottest battle in 1812, when there were several to choose from, in order to avoid an unsuitable marriage. Her counterrevolutionary past did not prevent her appealing to this end to the prefect of Rome, a young French noble, who shared her view that it was the only way to save an honest family.[37] In this milieu, conscription became a much needed, and far more effective, substitute for the *lettre de cachet* (arbitrary warrant of imprisonment), a method of policing that may have been dying out in France by the Revolution[38] but that was certainly alive, well, and in demand, in Tuscany in the 1780s and 1790s, where the practice was to exile bourgeois delinquents to the wastes of the Maremma.[39] Now they could be sent to Spain, the Baltic, or the Balkans, and they often were.

Similarly, particularly as the demands of the last campaigns steadily drained their manpower, there are increasing instances, again to be found mainly in Tuscany and the former Papal States, of the French making treaties of sorts with brigands, enrolling their bands en masse as irregular units, usually for service in Spain, in return for a full pardon.[40] On one level, this policy represents a serious retreat by the French from their determination thoroughly to uproot banditry. This was a real break with their own standards of policing, forced upon them by the demands of war. It is also one of the rarer examples of where an identity of interest could be found between some segments of Italian society and the state concerning the institution of conscription.

However, when the French ideological justification for these policies is understood, the artificiality of even these limited grounds for consensus is first exposed and then cut away. For the French, conscription was far more important than simply coping with disorder or even rendering the war effort its most essential service. Conscription became a means of cleansing the Italian social fabric of criminality; it became a tool of social regeneration. Whereas the indigenous elites regarded their society and even their own families as prone to individual, if frequent, outbreaks of criminal activity, the French saw Italian society and culture as criminalized to the core. What the indigenous elites saw as a pressing practical problem in need of drastic action was interpreted by the French as a clear sign of degeneracy and cultural inferiority. The other side of this coin was their own sense of cultural superiority: the basis for the evolution of a policy of genuine cultural imperialism.

The French officials who governed much of Napoleonic Italy were often young men, *auditeurs du Conseil d'État* (auditors of the Council of State), especially by the last years of the Empire.[41] Whatever their family backgrounds, royalist or revolutionary, they had been brought up in the martial spirit of both the Revolution and the Empire, and they shared with their contemporaries in the officer corps a strong belief in the intrinsic worth of military service and the martial values instilled by war.

That such attitudes and instincts were lacking in most of the Italian peoples—with the notable exception of the Piedmontese—was seen as a source of regret but also as a fault easily remedied by the successful application of conscription. For the young administrators of the Napoleonic Empire, war had a creative, positive role to play in the reform of society and the eradication of criminality in particular. In their eyes, the long period of peace enjoyed by the peninsula before their arrival had not been a blessing for its youth, patrician and plebe alike. In the mountains of the Roman departments, the problem was seen in terms of channeling the natural aggression of rustic youth to patriotic ends, but a peaceful disposition was regarded as equally regrettable.[42]

The director-general of police in Florence stressed the need to educate the propertied classes of Tuscany in their ancient history.[43] His colleague in Rome saw more potential in the Roman aristocracy, but there was still a great deal to do.[44] He saw even more potential in the Umbrian aristocracy.[45] As has been seen, these hopes were illusory; the same young nobles portrayed here as ready to embrace the martial values of the new order were one and the same with those who refused to join the Gardes d'Honneur only a few months later.[46] This "epidemic" had been triggered by the attempts of the leading noble family of the area, whose head was a senator of the Empire, to have their son exempted from the Gardes. The final irony came when several young Umbrian nobles took to the hills in plebian fashion, joining brigands led by a relative of one of their number, to avoid service in the Gardes d'Honneur.

Incidents of this kind were relatively rare within the elite, but by the last years of French rule they had become increasingly common among more plebian conscripts. The panic-stricken letter of the *maire* of San Stefano to his *sous-préfet* (subprefect) in Arezzo in southern Tuscany paints a typical portrait of the circumstances that rapidly engulfed much of central Italy, as French rule, and with it the policing of conscription, fell apart.[47] Conscription was sighted by all local officials as the main spark of revolt against the Empire in its death throes, and it was aggravated by the ferocious reprisals the French took against the families of deserters. Clearly the nobility and moral worth with which the French invested war was lost on Italians of all classes. The experiences of those at the front, when they reached those at home, did much to counteract the martial values the French strove to promote and the arrival of letters home was dreaded by the authorities.[48] For the French this spelled the end of an illusion.

Regeneration and "L'homme Nouveau à l'Italienne"[49]

From much of the evidence cited, it is clear that the French placed their hopes in the youth of Italy, patrician and plebian alike, for their dream of regeneration, literally, through the inculcation of martial virtues. The implications for the future of the modern state in Italy have already been explored. This is the vantage point of the ruled. As is also clear, the rulers had their own set of values and priorities, which stretched far beyond the immediate needs of the war effort. So central was military service to the French for the pursuit of moral rebirth that they pursued it at the risk of all else, not only out of necessity, but from principles rooted in their vision of the Enlightenment.[50]

This intellectual baggage led the French to link martial virtues, criminality, and the Italian environment, both cultural and physical, in a very coherent vision of a people in desperate need of salvation from itself. Its starting point was a robust cultural self-confidence based on the firm belief that the Revolution and the Napoleonic conquests it produced had "regenerated" the French themselves. They saw themselves as having combined intellectual sophistication with martial valor, an unprecedented degree of military success with the highest level of civilization ever known in the West. The best elements of the Revolution, the Enlightenment, and the *grand siècle* (majestic age) of Louis XIV had come together under Napoleon. It was an imperial vision, and it was their duty to raise up the other peoples of their empire in the same way.

There is no real doubt that the French found a genuinely serious problem of law and order in Italy. However, they perceived this as criminality. This was because they interpreted these impressions primarily through the prism of Enlightened concepts of social development and Revolutionary *civisme* (good citizenship) that criminalized all before them.

The role of the physical environment, and of climate in particular, was central to the thought of the Enlightenment about the human condition. The influence of the Mediterranean climate on human behavior held a very special place in the Enlightenment view of the world. It was seen as conducive to irrationality, and generally to be shunned. In this intellectual construct, the Mediterranean heat became one of the prime sources of criminal behavior, and references abound to it in the official correspondence of the period. French administrators felt no need to hide their belief that the Italian climate blunted the finer sensibilities and enflamed the grosser passions; in their eyes, it produced violent behavior almost as a matter of course. For the director-general of police in Florence, only a change of scene, neatly provided by conscription, could cure Tuscan criminals.[51] When the French applied Enlightened theory to what they thought they saw in Italy, it seemed to them that crime was carried on the very breeze, and it led them to hope quite seriously that the Mediterranean conscripts of the *Grande Armée* would return better men from the Russian snows. There was no doubt in the official, imperial mind that the Italian climate was morally debilitating in itself.

Faced with the generally accepted need to regenerate their meridional *administrés*, the French were led to pose themselves one of the central dilemmas of all Enlightened thinking on the human condition: the relative influence of geography, and of climate in particular, on the formation of society, as opposed to the intrinsic power of human reason to overcome the physical environment. This dilemma was posed at its most direct by David Hume in his essay "*Of National Character*," a work that took as given a series of national and racial characteristics and then set about divining their origins in relation to the relative influence of environment and intellect.[52] The empire builders of Napoleonic Italy, like Hume, came to see reason as the more powerful of the two, while never dismissing the importance of the environment. Even their ultimate faith in Humian optimism left them faced with an enormous task: "There is much to do . . . but it must not be denied that it is impossible to obtain results in a country in need of complete regeneration, and where all its received ideas must be changed."[53]

Italy was rife with decadence in the eyes of its new rulers. A devastating combination of a morally debilitating climate, weak government, and perhaps above all else, the culture of the baroque Church had created an atmosphere of general decay that tainted even those not directly involved in criminal activities. It warped the natural intelligence of all classes of men, engendering a devious, criminalized mentality in their approach to human relations. In 1812, the prefect of the Apennines spoke thus of his *valligiani* (valley dwellers): "We have to cope with the kind of men who are as used to calculating the danger as much as the reward and who act only in proportion to the interest or the risk that must be run."[54] The prefect of Perugia detected a similar outlook on life among the Umbrian nobility. Weak government had allowed their very real intelligence to degenerate into a taste for intrigue; all they understood was "a firm hand." The innate genius of their subjects was turned only to ignoble ends.[55]

The French held the Church more responsible for all this than anything else. The predominant place it held in Italian life had destroyed the moral fiber of its faithful. Its long domination of Italian culture had left the French little upon which to build. This contrasted greatly with their view of their own cultural heritage, where the decadence of the late *ancien régime* and the excesses of the Terror had shaken, but not destroyed, the heritage of the *grand siècle* and the eighteenth-century Enlightenment. These foundations had allowed the French to redeem themselves through the Revolution. Their perceptions of Italy led them to believe that a similar, indigenous regeneration was impossible there and that the Church was to blame. It fostered ignorance and superstition, the breeding grounds of crime, at every level of society, just as the ready alms it was thought to provide were seen as encouraging sloth, a trait always latent in hot climates and the first step to petty crime. These aspects of clerical influence were only symptoms of a much deeper malaise diagnosed by the French.

The new administrators were very explicit in their belief that the culture of baroque Catholicism had sapped Italians of their manhood. While weak government and the climate had brutalized them, "Jesuitical values" had made them devious and effeminate. A French official in Parma saw the links between clerical culture, crime and moral depravity in terms resonant with the influence of Diderot.[56] The ultimate remedy was in education, but education of a very particular kind. Conscription and militarized workhouses—discipline and regular work—were their recipe for the youth of the lower classes, but the youth of the elite was targeted for an equally intense experience of French militarism. The former Jesuit boarding school of Santa Caterina had attracted the sons of noblemen from all over Italy since the seventeenth century. Although closed initially by the French, they were quick to reopen it in 1806, but with a very different ethos. Parents withdrew their sons by the score, just as they protected their elder brothers from the Gardes d'Honneur.[57] From the French point of view, what is most striking is the utter contempt for clerical education and the unequivocal belief in martial virtues as a cure for them.

The French imperial administrators inherited the concept of regeneration from the Revolution, and they clung to it all the more fiercely in the face of what they beheld in Italy. Regeneration and that transparency of moral conduct that went with it were perceived as light years removed from the world of intrigue they found, which they equated with criminality. They had also inherited the warlike *machismo* of 1792 and injected it with their own resurgent, more conventional militarism. These were powerful elements of their ideology, and they were the complete antithesis of the baroque culture of *ancien régime* Italy. There could be no place for crime in a regenerated world, and there could be no regeneration without martial values. In the French official mind, militarism and morality were inseparable, all the more so because they were diametrically opposed to the system of values perceived as the root cause of decadence and, therefore, of crime. To militarize Italy was to redeem her, nothing more, nothing less. *L'homme nouveau* (new man) was a warrior, almost from the outset.

It would be an understatement to say that this ideology fell on stony ground among Italians of all classes, everywhere. Yet the French imperialist vision of regeneration through martial virtue was seized upon by Mazzini and incarnated in the person and deeds of Garibaldi. In both *Risorgimento* and regeneration, warrior virtues were at the heart of morality and patriotism, without which criminality would never be defeated. Such theories have remained close to the official heart and, therefore, the property of an intellectual elite, a narrow minority. The majority of Italians of all classes continued to prefer the anarchy of a crime-ridden, even criminalized, society to redemption through war. Patronage, and with it a high degree of corruption and, therefore, of crime, remained a more preferable form of social cement than a state culture founded on war.

NOTES

1. The author wishes to thank both the Carnegie Trust and the Universities of Scotland for their support of the doctoral thesis upon which several portions of this chapter are based. The bulk of the archival research was carried out thanks to the generosity of the British Academy Small Grants in Aid of Personal Research. In Paris, the author wishes to extend very special thanks to M. Michel Fleury and Mme. F. Auffrey of the Institut de la Francophonie. Thanks are also due to the participants of the International Association for the History of Crime and Criminal Justice (IAHCCJ) seminar of June 1993 held at the Maison des Sciences de l'Homme in Paris, at which an earlier version of this chapter was read. Particular thanks are offered to Louis Knafla, Clive Emsley, and Pieter Spierenburg.

2. Among the huge and growing corpus of work in this field perhaps the most influential voice has been that of Edward W. Said in two seminal works of synthesis and interpretation: *Orientalism, Western Conceptions of the Orient* (London, 1978) and *Culture & Imperialism* (London, 1993).

3. Similar concerns to those of this study, if set in a slightly different set of preoccupations, emerge in S. J. Woolf, "French Civilization and Ethnicity in the Napoleonic Empire," *Past & Present* 124 (1989): 96–120.

4. A theme brought to the fore in the opening chapters of J. A. Davis, *Conflict and Control, Law and Order in Nineteenth Century Italy* (London, 1988).

5. Amid the vast literature on Napoleonic warfare, its social and cultural aspects are discussed in their military context in J. A. Lynn, "Toward an Army of Honour: The Moral Evaluation of the French Army, 1789–1815," *French Historical Studies* 16 (1989): 31–52; H. Lachouque, *Napoléon et la garde impériale* (Paris, 1957); and *The Anatomy of Glory, Napoleon and His Guard*, ed. A.S.K. Brown et al. (New York, 1962). On the wider impact of conscription and the war on the civilian population, A. Forrest, *Déserteurs et Insoumis sous la Révolution et l'Empire* (Paris, 1988); I. Woloch, "Napoleonic Conscription: State Power and Civil Society," *Past & Present* 111 (1986): 101–29.

6. An important contribution to this in a Malayan context but with very wide conceptual implications for the study of cultural imperialism is S. H. Atalas, *The Myth of the Lazy Native* (London, 1977). This work emphasizes the need for the British to develop a view of the Malays as idle because of the essentially economic nature of British exploitation of that particular colonial society. In the immediate context of Napoleonic Europe, Woolf ("French Civilization and Ethnicity") points to the emphasis on social and economic backwardness made by French officials in the Illyrian provinces.

7. This definition of criminality is in large part derived from the work of Michel Foucault, especially *Surveiller et Punir* (Paris, 1975).

8. See Foucault, *Surveiller*, 209–16, for a penetrating analysis of the emergence of the concept of criminality in France in the late *ancien régime*.

9. On Calabria, see U. Caldora, *Calabria Napoleonica* (Naples, 1960); G. Cingari, *Giacobini e sanfedisti in Calabria nel 1799* (Messina-Florence, 1957); idem, *Brigantaggio, proprietari e contadini nel sud* (Bari, 1976). On the Veneto, see C. Bullo, "Dei movimenti insurrezionali del Veneto sotto il dominio francese, e specialmente del brigantaggio del 1809," *Nuovo Archivio Veneto* 15 (1898): 353–69, 441–67, 607–23, 721–45.

10. Davis, *Conflict and Control*, 17–119.

11. G. Turi, *"Viva Maria": le reazione alle riforme leopoldini, 1790–99* (Florence, 1969).

12. On the policing of Turin, see D. Balani, *Il Vicario tra Città e Stato, l'ordine pubblico e l'Annona nella Torino del Settecento* (Turin, 1987). On Savoyard charity, see R. Davico, "Pauperismo urbano e contadino in Piemonte sotto Vittorio Amadeo II" (Ph.D. diss., Università degli Studi, Turin, 1963). On Bologna, see A. De Benedictis, *Patrizi e comunità: il governo del contado bolognese nel 1700* (Bologna, 1984). See especially *Città e Controllo Sociale in Italia tra XVIII e XIX Secoli*, ed. E. Sori (Milan, 1982). In a wider context, see S. J. Woolf, *The Poor in Western Europe* (London, 1986).

13. The classic general account is G. Lumbroso, *I moti popolari contro i francesi, 1796–1800* (Florence, 1932). For a more recent attempt at a general assessment, M. G. Broers, "The Parochial Revolution: 1799 and the Counter-revolution in Italy," *Renaissance & Modern Studies* 33 (1989): 159–74.

14. F. Bluche, *Le Bonapartisme: aux origines de la droite autoritaire* (Paris, 1980), 13–94.

15. Archivio di Stato, Cuneo [hereafter ASC], Mazzo 228, Polizia, Belmondo to Prefect, dept. Stura (22 August 1812).

16. ASC Mazzo 229, Polizia, Maire of Pietraporzio to Prefect, dept. Stura (1 September 1812).

17. Archives Nationales, Paris [hereafter ANP] F/7 8923 Police Générale (dept. de la Sture), Director-General of Police, Turin to Minister, 3 arrond. of Police (15 October 1812).

18. Ibid.

19. ANP F/7 8802 Police-Générale (dept. de l'Arno), Director-General of Police, Florence to Minister, 3 arrond. of Police (10 October 1810).

20. ANP F/7 8802 Police-Générale (dept. de l'Arno), Director-General of Police, Florence to Minister, 3 arrond. of Police (6 November 1810).

21. ANP F/7 8802 Police-Générale (dept. de l'Arno), Director-General of Police, Florence to Minister, 3 arrond. of Police (22 December 1810).

22. There is an ample literature on 1799 in the Kingdom of Naples. See especially Cingari, *Giacobini*. For a recent assessment, see J. A. Davis, "1799: The *Santafede* and the Crisis of the *Ancien Régime* in Southern Italy," *Society & Politics in the Age of the Risorgimento*, eds. J. A. Davis & P. Ginsborg (Cambridge, 1991), 1–25.

23. S. La Sorsa, *I moti rivoluzionari a Molfetta nei primi mesi del 1799* (Trani, 1903), v.

24. E. A. Brigidi, *Giacobini e realisti, o Viva Maria: Storia del 1799 in Toscana* (Siena, 1882), 11.

25. Davis, *Conflict and Control*, 2.

26. In a Piedmontese context, see M. G. Broers, "Revolution as Vendetta: Na-

poleonic Piedmont, 1794–1821," *Historical Journal* 33 (1990): 573–97, 787–809. In a Tuscan context, see J. P. Filippini, "Difesa dell'Impero o difesa della società? Le misure di Haute Police nella Toscana Napoleonica," *Rivista Italiana di Studi Napoleonici* 17 (1980): 9–66.

27. Caldora, *Calabria Napoleonica*; P. Villani, *Mezzogirono tra riforme e rivoluzione* (Rome-Bari, 1973). A. Valente, *Giacomo Murat e l'Italia Meridionale* (Turin, 1965).

28. Valente, *Murat*.

29. Cingari, *Giacobini*, 33–38.

30. C. M. Lucas, "Résistances populaires à la Révolution dans le Sud-Est," *Mouvements populaires et Conscience sociale (XVI–XIX siècles)*, ed. C. Langlois (Paris, 1985), 117–35; R. Dupuy, *De la Révolution à la Chouannerie* (Paris, 1988).

31. On Piedmont, see M. G. Broers, "The Restoration of Order in Napoleonic Piedmont, 1794–1814," (Ph.D. diss., Oxford, 1986). On the Kingdom of Italy, see L. Antonielli, *I Prefetti dell'Italia Napoleonica* (Bologna, 1983).

32. The major archival sources are ANP F/1e 85, 86, 87, Pays annexés et réunis, Administration-Générale États de Parme, Plaisance et Guastalle and ANP F/7 8926, Police-Générale, (dept. du Taro) in a dossier misleadingly entitled "Délits de conscription 1805–06."

33. Several original examples exist in ANP F/7 8926, Police-Générale (dept. du Taro).

34. On the long history of smuggling, banditry, and their place in these communities, see O. Raggio, "Social Relations and Control of Resources in an Area of Transit: Eastern Liguria, Sixteenth to Seventeenth Centuries," *Domestic Strategies: Work and Family in France and Italy, 1600–1800*, ed. S. J. Woolf (Cambridge and Paris, 1991), 20–34.

35. The most informative secondary source is L. Valente, "La Corte Speciale per i dellitti di Stato del Dipartimento del Reno, (1809–1811), Inventario Analitico" (Ph.D. diss., Università degli Studi, Bologna, 1973). See also G. Manzoni, *I briganti di Romagna, 1800–1815* (Imola, 1973).

36. On the buying of replacements, see Woloch, "Napoleonic Conscription."

37. ANP F/7 8899, Police-Générale (dept. Rome) Prefect, dept. Rome to Minister, 3 arrond. of Police (22 August 1812).

38. M. Foucault and A. Farge, *Le Désordre des Familles, Lettres de Cachet des Archives de la Bastille* (Paris, 1982); C. Quetel, *Par le Roy—Essai sur les lettres de cachet* (Toulouse-Privat, 1981); F.-X. Emmanuelli, "Ordres du Roi et lettres de cachet en Provence à la fin de l'ancien régime," *Révue Historique* 373 (1974): 357–92.

39. A mass of petitions of this nature survives in Archivio di Stato, Florence, Serie Buon Governo Filze 461, 463, 464, 465, 468, 469, and 470, which cover the period 1808–9, the first years of French rule. Soundings taken for the years 1785, 1793, and 1802 in this series show such petitions to have been equally common during the *ancien régime* although this evidence is at present very impressionistic.

40. A spectacular example of this occurred in Tuscany in 1813. The most important band operating around Arezzo—the center of the 1799 revolt—led by one Bonaccia was granted a full pardon by the French. Originally assigned to a labor battalion in Corsica, the bandits were allowed to keep their arms and were sent instead to Spain as a counterinsurgency unit. In fact, although the bulk of the band

did exactly this, Bonaccia managed to evade service altogether and formed a new band from the deserters of the *levées* of 1813 and 1814: ANP F/7 8809, Police-Generale (dept. de l'Arno) Rapport au Ministre de la Police-Générale (2 September 1813).

41. On the *auditeurs*, see C. Durand, *Les auditeurs du Conseil d'État de 1803 à 1814* (Aix-en-Provence, 1958).

42. ANP F/7 8899, Police-Générale (dept. Rome) Director-General of Police, Rome to Minister, 3 arrond. of Police (20 September 1812): "the absence of almost any signs . . . of civilization illustrates the savage morals of these areas. . . . No one understands anything in this truly barbarous country where youth turns to banditry whereas for ages in France it has turned instead to soldiering."

43. ANP F/7 6523(A), Police-Générale (Toscane, Rapports du Directeur) Minister, 3 arrond. of Police to Director-General of Police, Florence (August 1810):

> Nothing is better proof of the vices of the old administration and institutions of these little states than the alienation of their inhabitants from the profession of arms who have inherited none of the instincts of their earliest ancestors or of the warlike peoples who have successively invaded this beautiful part of the Empire.

44. ANP F/7 8888, Police-Générale (dept. Rome) Director-General of Police, Rome to Minister, 3 arrond. of Police (14 September 1810):

> Although the martial spirit is not entirely foreign to the tastes of the local inhabitants, we will never see them turn into warriors unless we convince them that (military) service is the quickest path to glory and honor. . . . This taste for military life is even more noticeable among the Romans because it was never part of the policy of the previous government, who never promoted it through influence or public education.

45. ANP F/7 6531, Police-Générale (Italie, Plaque II) Director-General of Police, Rome to Minister, 3 arrond. of Police (10 October 1812): "The Emperor will find officers easily among the aristocratic youth of this department and the rich families of the second rank who seek to draw themselves closer to the nobility."

46. ANP, Archives Privées [hereafter AP] Fonds Roederer 29-AP-15, P. L. Roederer to L. Roederer (24 July 1813): "an epidemic which is going to entail many families protesting against the enrolment of their children, in terms that will hardly be helpful."

47. ANP F/7 8809, Police-Générale (dept. de l'Arno) Maire of San Stefano to S. Prefect, arrond. Arezzo (July 1813):

> We are on the point of being massacred; the government will probably avenge us. But we will be no more. . . . Apart from the conscripts who have been called up already, all the communes have joined Bonaccia (the bandit chief), so that a hundred of them charge about our area with impunity and their number grows every day . . . the seeds of rebellion have been sown. . . . I envisage that in the moment of crisis, the malcontents of town and country will be able to unite with the brigands. All the families of the conscripts who have been run off their farms (by the French) because of their refusal of their children (to obey the call-up) are among the malcontents.

48. ANP F/7 8807, Police-Générale (dept. de l'Arno) Bulletin aux prefets des departements de la Toscane (28 April 1813): "These letters written by young soldiers to their relatives . . . passing from hand to hand among families and communities . . . gain more credibility than all the utterances of the government: they

could obliterate any sort of public enthusiasm until the first imperial victories revive it."

49. "Baroque piety" may almost be taken as a given term. M. Vovelle, *Piété Baroque et déchristianisation en Provence au XVIII siecle* (Paris, 1978), and M. Agulhon, *La vie sociale en Provence intérieure au lendemain de la Révolution française*, 2 vols. (Paris, 1971), find a working definition in the "good practices" set out by the Council of Trent. For two standard analyses that emphasize the elements of popular piety, see S. Burgalassi, *Il compotramento religoso degli italiani* (Florence, 1968); V. L. Tapie, *Baroque et classicisme* (Paris, 1957).

50. The concept of regeneration as a potent force in the ideology of the revolution has been analyzed brilliantly in M. Ozouf, *L'homme régénéré* (Paris, 1989); idem, "Regeneration," *A Critical Dictionary of the French Revolution*, eds. F. Furet and M. Ozouf (Cambridge, Mass. and London, 1990): 806–17; idem, "La révolution française et l'idée de l'homme nouveau," *The French Revolution and the Creation of Modern Political Culture*, vol. 2, *The Political Culture of the French Revolution*, ed. C. M. Lucas (Oxford, 1988): 213–32. For this concept in the wider context of the Enlightenment, see B. Baczko, *Lumières de l'Utopie* (Paris, 1978).

51. ANP F/7 8805, Police-Générale (dept. de l'Arno) Director-General of Police, Florence to Minister, 3 arrond. of Police (16 July 1813):

> It seems proven to me that of all the policing policies (available) enlistment is that one most essential for Tuscany and the one which will do the most good, because I regard it as the only way to rid the Grand Duchy of a horde of individuals who . . . do not want to do anything with themselves thanks to the attraction of idleness in hot countries, which inevitably turns them to crime to make a living.

52. After distinguishing between "moral" and "physical" causes, Hume decides, "That the character of a nation will depend on moral causes, must be evident to the most superficial observer; since a nation is nothing but a collection of individuals, and the manners of individuals are frequently determined by these causes." However, he also added that "the basest passions"—lust and drunkenness—could be exaggerated by climactic conditions, that is, exactly those passions which played a major part in much criminal behavior. David Hume, "Of National Character," *Essays Moral, Political and Literary*, 2 vols. (London, 1898), 244–58.

53. ANP F/7 8888, Police-Générale (dept. Rome) Minister, 3 arrond. of Police to Director-General of Police, Rome (19 April 1811).

54. ANP F/7 8795, Police-Générale (dept. Apennines) Prefect, dept. Apennines to Director-General of Police, Turin (12 October 1812).

55. ANP AP Fonds Roederer 29-AP-15, P. L. Roederer to L. Roederer (3 December 1811):

> Here we are in a country where the best class of person is very shrewd. They grasp even the slightest hint. If the man in charge lets himself be perceived as hesitant, he will be pounced upon as such immediately and will lose his freedom to act; thus he will remain forever, and forever, and also forever if (he acts with) firmness and justice he will be the absolute master of the country.

56. ANP F/1e 87/88, Pays annexés et réunis (Administration-Générale, États de Parme, Plaisance et Guastalle, Rapport sur la situation de l'Administration de

Parme) Subdelegate, arrond. Parma to the Administrative Prefect, Parma (15 June 1806):

A morality which is inseparable from a holy and firm piety is rather rare, and the (presence of) vice is the direct result of this absence of a break to moderate them. . . . You would probably be surprised if I told you how numerous the victims of seduction and debauchery are; how little domestic virtues are valued! How familiar among the youth of all classes are these venemous sarcasms that strike people down with ridicule! Your soul would probably be revolted if I told you that young things between eight and ten years old are delivered into prostitution . . . the state must attack this penchant for liscence at its very roots. . . . It must reduce the number of priests.

57. ANP F/1e 85, Pays annexés et réunis (Administration-Générale, États de Parme, Plaisance et Guastalle) Director of the Lycée, Parma to Minister of the Interior (25 August 1806).

I can gather together 150 young people from the leading noble families of Italy, and I made these little counts, marquises and princes enact "The Dragon of Thionville" and "The Battle of Austerlitz". . . . Your thoughts will quickly grasp all the political and moral advantages (involved). There are complaints that I give these children too military an education; that is to say that it is not exclusively monastic. . . . I manage to break, a little, the grip of home and of family. This is a fitting nursery for subjects based on the love, the laws and the practices of my homeland.

The Felon and the Angel Copier: Criminal Identity and the Promise of Photography in Victorian England and Wales

Richard W. Ireland

THE PROBLEM

On 22 March 1865 a prisoner was admitted to Carmarthen Gaol in southwest Wales on remand, accused of being "concealed in a house with intent to commit felony." The governor of the jail, George Stephens, recorded the details of prisoner number 1076 in the Felon's Register. He noted that the prisoner was five feet four inches in height (about average for a male prisoner in this jail at that time) and had a very dark complexion. He was a laborer from Queenstown in Ireland who had been residing most recently in Merthyr Tydfil, and his name was John Phillips.

Or was it? "John Phillips" had already served prison sentences in Swansea and Gloucester and, indeed, in Carmarthen itself, where he was held pending a sentence of seven years transportation for housebreaking in 1853. On that occasion as prisoner number 463, he had given his name as George Flynn and his occupation as "sailor." After his discharge from his second spell in custody at Carmarthen (after serving two months with hard labor on conviction by the Llanelli magistrates), "John Phillips" apparently continued in his criminal activities. In 1870 he was imprisoned at Merioneth as "John Stanmore," in 1872 in Montgomery as "John Hanley."[1]

In November of the same year, two prisoners were committed to the same jail to face trial for burglary and stealing money, for which offenses both subsequently received terms of fifteen years penal servitude and were removed from Carmarthen to Millbank. The first, "Charles Williams," a "bell hanger," also had a record of custody and, indeed, of escape from custody at Ruthin in North Wales and also at Cardigan. He, too, had been in Carmarthen Gaol before, in 1852 as "Owen Pritchard," a "farm servant," and two years previously he had served a sentence in Stafford as "William Davies." Governor Stephens, in recording his details in 1865,

Figure 1: "John Phillips" alias "George Flynn" alias "John Stanmore" alias "John Hanley"

allowed himself some skepticism in relation to the information with which "Williams" provided him. Under his register's heading "Place of Birth," Stephens has written "near Wrexham, says Swansea," and for "Last Residence," he records "Says Swansea."[2] His accomplice, another "bell hanger" called William Davies, had also been imprisoned twice at Ruthin, on at least one occasion using the name "Daniel Ryan." Again Stephens is cautious as to the prisoner's place of birth and last residence, recording "Says Swansea" for both.[3]

Which, if any, of the names given by "Phillips," "Williams," and "Davies" were their "real" ones I do not know,[4] but these men may be seen not simply as recidivist burglars with a talent for inventing plausible aliases. Rather, they may be taken as personifications of a problem that haunted and threatened the major reconstruction of the criminal justice system that occurred in the nineteenth century. The small photographs that George Stephens glued next to the names of "Phillips" (Figure 1), "Williams," and "Davies" are also significant in that they represent a belief that the problem might be solved and that its solution lay in scientific advancement. It is with these issues, the difficulties of establishing the identity of persons accused of crime and the steps suggested and undertaken to combat those difficulties, that this chapter is concerned.

I deliberately have started my discussion with practical examples from a local jail, and we will return to the experience within that jail many times, not simply for the reason that in George Stephens we find, as we shall see, one of the unacknowledged pioneers of custodial photography. In a work that has as one of its principal concerns the limitations of central bureaucratic control, the practical obstacles that threatened the realization of the Victorian dreams of a uniform, predictable penal system, it would, I think, be wrong to start with the dreamers—the bureaucrats and legislators—rather than with the position of those to whose lot the implementation of policy fell. And while there is no doubting the importance of those much-observed (both by contemporaries and historians) metropolitan institutions such as Millbank or Pentonville, it should not be forgotten that the identification of prisoners who might be sent to them often depended to a large extent on actions taken in more far-flung and less renowned jails.[5] The cases that we have mentioned earlier were problems in Carmarthenshire, but not simply for Carmarthenshire, and we will have cause to examine the practice of other penal institutions and the activities of central government in the course of the discussion. Moreover, I hope to establish that the engagement with the issue of criminal identity and the promise of photography in the nineteenth century should be seen not merely as a search for a practical solution to a practical problem but also as the locus of discussions that may give wider insights into views (sometimes shifting, often competing) of the nature of criminality, the purpose(s) of the penal system, and the role of science in societal direction.

To an individual in the late twentieth century, an "identity crisis" signifies an internal, private difficulty. While the criminal justice system may occasionally experience doubts on the issue of *identification* ("is X the person who was seen by the witness?"), it seldom entertains them on the issue of *identity* ("who is X?"). "I.D." is routinely carried in the pocket, asked for, and provided in various "official" forms (passports, library cards, and the like), or converted into numerical form (the PIN). "Identity" can be discovered, in the final resort, on the tips of our fingers, in the extent of our dental work, and even within our genetic structure. Contemporary concern focuses not on how little we know of our fellow citizens but on how much, or perhaps more accurately, on how much they might know about us. It is probably because of the relatively unproblematic nature of identity in our own day that historians have failed largely to appreciate the immense difficulties that a penal system with no such confidence might face. The issue of identity was a very real and pressing problem in the Victorian jail.

THE DEMOGRAPHIC AND PENOLOGICAL CONTEXTS

The problem was, of course, by no means a new one in the nineteenth century. In medieval times, the offender whose identity was established by personal claim alone, rather than being socially underwritten, one who was not in a tithing and had no lord to warrant him, was subject to formal legal prejudice.[6] Moreover, the associated fear of the anonymity of the mob, in particular the fear of the urban crowd, was by no means a novelty in Victoria's reign but had a considerable history, and indeed the very difficulty of the recognition and detection of itinerant criminals had been addressed by Sir John Fielding in his General Preventative Plan of 1772, in which a scheme for national distribution of descriptions of suspicious persons and fugitives was advanced and, indeed, was followed by the circulation of a newspaper "The Hue and Cry" in 1773.[7] Within the nineteenth century, however, both legal and more general social developments were to ensure that the issue of criminal identity came to be recognized as a question of acute official concern.

It is tempting to begin discussion with a rehearsal of this official concern, voiced, for example, before the Carnarvon Committee in 1863, or perhaps with the climate of fear of the habitual offender that found articulate expression in the late 1850s and early 1860s. Yet to do so would be to ignore the wider and more fundamental changes that I suggest underlay that concern or that climate and that constitute an important part of the background to the particular events that led to such discussions. Clearly, however, there are major difficulties in offering sweeping generalizations about demographic or penological changes and their effects in the longer term, in ignoring the contingent and particular, and in presenting "trends" or "preoccupations" as universal and unilinear. In setting the scene for the midcentury engagement with the problem of criminal identity, I offer in the next few paragraphs a number of very general observations on factors that I believe to have been of some significance in the etiology of that engagement. Thereafter, by considering in more detail the experience of the town of Carmarthen and its surrounding shire, and in particular the evidence of its jail records from the 1840s to the 1870s, the significance of these factors in the day-to-day administration of the penal system may be revealed in sharper focus.

It is difficult in the context of this chapter to do more than rehearse clichés in assessing the demographic changes that industrial and technological advances produced in the nineteenth century. Whether or not the attendant greater urbanization did, in truth, contribute to the growth of a "society of strangers" is perhaps less significant than the way in which the growth of the city could be perceived.[8] Victorian journalists and philanthropists might enter the slums like explorers and missionaries, but to many of the opinion formers or legislators the slums remained areas that held masses rather than collections of individuals. Although most noticeable in the great cities, the factory and the lodging house, with their concentrations of humanity and their at least apparent relative anonymity, were also to be found, of course, in smaller towns. It was not only their own growth that reduced the distance between towns, however. Improved communications, such as the railways, as well as importing a sizeable often "alien" workforce into an area during their construction and operation, also served to shrink the country both physically and psychologically. The capacity of people to move, quicker than rumor, away from the traditional ties that had added a communal dimension to "character" became both literally and figuratively part of the landscape. Mobility, its architecture, engineering, and promises, pressed for public attention. It would be surprising indeed if such factors—the potential for anonymity that inhered in both urban concentration and easy transit—had no impact at all when the context of the question of disputed identity is considered.

Certainly, I suggest changes in the penal system played their part in pushing the question of criminal identity up the agenda in the nineteenth century. The now familiar label used to describe the transition from the penal world of the eighteenth century to that of the nineteenth is contained in the antithesis of the "punishment of the body" (by hanging, whipping, the pillory, and the like) and the "punishment of the mind" (in the prison, in particular the penitentiary).[9] The formula is, as representative of the totality of the penal experience of either the "old" or "new" regimes, capable of working grave mischief. It ignores elemental continuities within penal practice. Capital punishment, though it might be controversial and only rarely (and after 1868, privately) applied, remained of potent symbolic significance, albeit a disputed one, throughout the nineteenth century. More significantly, the purported antithesis neglects the extent and flexibility of nonphysical sanctions, including imprisonment, in the preceding period. We may also observe that the formula courts the familiar, though seductive, danger of fixing our attention upon the superior courts' responses to the most serious forms of wrongdoing at the expense of ignoring the numerous bindings over and other penalties that were imposed for minor infractions in both periods. Unglamorous as it might sound, it might be suggested, with only a slight element of mischief, that penality within the nineteenth century as a whole and particularly the latter part should be characterized by the imposition of the fine or the withdrawal of a license rather than by the construction of Pentonville. Bearing these points in mind, however, we may recognize that the shorthand description of the transition of penality from the assault directly on the body to its constraint in the prison contains a germ of truth. Incarceration certainly attained a new significance. It is clear also that those punishments that acted directly upon the body raised the issue of identity, if at all, only in an indirect way—*this* body is whipped, *this* body placed in the pillory, *this* body is hanged. While the giving of a "character" might act as a dispensation from punishment and might arise over questions of eligibility (a pardon from the death penalty, for example), ideas of identity are, as I will argue shortly, less central in respect of these punishments than it would be for the Victorian prison system.

Of crucial importance was the demise of one particular penal measure, transportation. The story of transportation and its decline is well documented and needs no rehearsal here.[10] I would observe only that although the origins of this sentence have been found by authors in the Transportation Act of 1717 or in a statute of 1597,[11] its genesis and character are to be discovered by looking considerably farther back. The expedient of "moving on" the troublesome offender is an ancient and familiar one in English law and one that had been regulated by statute as early as the twelfth century.[12] The procedures and destinations may have changed, but the sentence of transportation rested ultimately on the old and simple philosophy "out of sight, out of mind." It was this philosophy, as much as the actual penalty, that fell to be reassessed in the nineteenth century. In the eighteenth and early nineteenth centuries transportation had been an important method of dealing with criminals, the gravity of whose offenses or the regularity of whose offending qualified them for the penal colonies. As such, their identity could be material as a qualification for the measure, but was not crucial to its essence as a penalty, for this simply involved, as it always had, the removal of the convict outside the jurisdiction. The last convict ship sailed as late as 1867, but by that time transportation had long been in decline, subject to criticism at home and objection from abroad, and the pronouncement of the sentence had increasingly resulted in journeys no farther than to the hulks at Portsmouth or Woolwich. The demise of transportation is better viewed as a process than an event.

It was, however, an important process. "As long as transportation provided the means of flushing large numbers of England's criminals to the antipodes, there was no need to consider how to control or incapacitate them at home,"[13] observe Radzinowicz and Hood, and there is no doubt as to the significance of the rundown of the export of criminality. Certainly, the end of transportation did not create the problem of domestic recidivism, as becomes apparent when the whole range of penal experience, rather than simply the position of the more serious offender, is considered, but it did provide the backdrop against which the concern with "ticket-of-leave men," which grew in the 1850s and 1860s and exploded in such moral panics as the 1862 garotting scare, is to be understood.[14] That there was concern in the popular press and in government circles as to the problem of "habituals" is well known. It was a concern that, fuelled by increasing intelligence from the country-wide police force after 1856 and from the consequences of the reformation of the criminal statistics in the following year, grew into a major preoccupation. Estimates of the number of such individuals varied, but the estimates were invariably alarming. But the debate that surrounded the fear "lest England herself became a penal settlement"[15] recognized that dealing with such recidivists was only half of the problem; finding them was the other half.

Let me attempt to bring together those factors which I believe lay behind the increasing concern with criminal identity, not a new problem in itself, in the Victorian period. The end of transportation meant that those who beforehand might be eliminated from the concerns of the penal system now formed an important domestic presence and challenge to the penal structure. Moreover, the challenge was heightened when the hardened criminal could disappear into urban anonymity or by geographical migration. In a curious apparent ambivalence, Victorian social commentators could point to both the dangers of established urban areas of vice and criminality, parts of London or (in a Welsh context) of Cardiff or Merthyr Tydfil,[16] and also express alarm at the problem of transient criminals roaming the country. Not only did settled criminal districts apparently exist in the heart of population centers, but criminals, paradoxically, could not be expected to stay in them! So, on the latter point, Mayhew, dividing the population into the "wandering" and the "civilized tribes," warned of the preponderance of criminals in the former group.[17] Back in 1839, Sir Edwin Chadwick had warned of the migrations of the "marauding hordes."[18] Whether in the anonymity of the crowd in the urban "rookery" or the alias of the wandering felon, the problem of criminal identity was apparent. Moreover, the changes in the penal system had seen not only the demise of transportation but also the decline in direct corporeal penal measures in which issues of "character" were less immediately important. The prison was to take center stage and, as it did so, the distinction between the neophyte and the hardened offender became important as integral to the nature of the custodial experience. The midcentury prison enterprise was more ambitious than the simple confinement of a collection of bodies; it was underwritten by models, controversial and disputed as they were, of reform of character, of intervention in the lives of moral individuals. Even those who came to believe as the century wore on that there was a class of humanity for whom no such reform was a realistic hope nonetheless had to ground that belief in a supposed capacity to recognize who the personalities who comprised that class were. Ideas of "character," "moral individuals," and "personalities" made the task of identification significant in a way that the whip, the noose, and the voyage to Van Dieman's land had not.[19]

There was also another point at issue. A failure to identify criminals jeopardized the very drive toward consistency, predictability, and uniformity of punishment that marked so much of the nineteenth-century discourse of penality. The arbitrariness of the earlier "system," with its elements of discretion and its face-to-face negotiation, was to be replaced by consistency. It had been this arbitrariness in prison conditions, as well as their squalor, that had been revealed by Howard's survey, and the drive to uniformity would reach its culmination a century thereafter in the reduction of local prisons to national control. In the interim period of flow of statutes, inspectors' reports and Select Committee recommendations demonstrate the movement toward consistency: Cell sizes might be standardized, minimum dietaries laid down, forms of labor prescribed, and so on. Sir Walter Crofton, as late as 1870, had no doubts about the pernicious effects of deviation from regularity, and his words, I suggest, represent a concern evident in many earlier measures: "There is want of uniformity in our treatment of prisoners which is fatal to the repression of crime."[20] Crofton well knew, as one vigorously involved in debates about the problem of the habitual criminal,[21] that uncertainty in the recognition of the old hand undercut any plans for a graded but uniform punishment across classes of prisoners. It was possible to legislate for a national police force, or even for a national prison system, but if John Phillips could be George Flynn in Carmarthen, John Stanmore in Merioneth, and John Hanley in Montgomery, the whole penal enterprise was threatened by a crucial handicap. In brief, there could be no satisfactory national penal system without a "national prisoner."

The climate of concern regarding habitual criminals in the late 1850s and early 1860s brought the issue of criminal identity sharply into focus, and the rehearsal of the problems before the Carnarvon Committee on Prison Discipline in 1863 allowed suggestions to be considered for their amelioration. I suggest, however, that it is proper to see the anxiety in the context of more general and protracted changes in the criminal justice system and the society it overlay. And, as we shall see, the problems were not amenable to immediate solution. A prisoner taken for an offense would have every incentive to conceal his real name, his previous record, and any information that could give clues as to these, such as place of birth or last residence. The prevalence of dissimulation was well appreciated by the prisoners themselves, by prison officials, and even by the writers of popular amusements. The governor of Coldbath Fields, T. H. Colvill, told the Carnarvon Committee that "an old prisoner, upon a new conviction, always changes his name, and so makes it more difficult to trace his history."[22] Michael Davitt, reflecting on his own prison experiences and obviously eager to demonstrate his mastery of argot, affirmed, "The great majority of convicts hide their real under assumed names, many of them having a fresh 'moniker' (name) each conviction, to be dropped for obvious reasons, upon release."[23] In *The Ticket-of-Leave Man*, a melodrama written in 1863 with an eye firmly on contemporary concerns, it is the issue of identification that is central. At one point in the drama the detective Hawkshaw, addressing one Theophilus Wake, observes of the villain Dalton, alias "Downey" alias "The Tiger," "He has many outsides as he does aliases. You may identify him for a felon today and pull your hat off for a parson tomorrow." As the audience knew but Hawkshaw did not, Wake is in fact none other than Dalton.[24] Examples of the recognition of the extent of the problem could be multiplied, but it is hard to better the laconic comment of the warder of Coldbath Fields, vouchsafed to Henry Mayhew: "All *Smiths* are doubtful."[25]

CARMARTHENSHIRE SOCIETY AND CRIME

The immense practical importance of the problem becomes easier to appreciate when we shift focus from the general to the particular and consider the demographic and criminological patterns within a specific area. The county of Carmarthenshire, and in particular the county town, at midcentury provided homes, albeit often temporary and in less than reputable boarding houses, for many who had been born outside its boundaries. As well as soldiers, sailors, and passing drovers, there were other identifiable groupings. Cornish miners had been attracted to the area and formed a distinct element of the population, as did the Irish for whom West Wales was an obvious destination on emigration. "Rows" involving members of these groups are recorded not infrequently in the notebooks of the Carmarthen police,[26] even when no prosecutions followed. While the social diversity of the county as a whole, which still supported a large agrarian economy with considerable traditional stability, should not be overstated, in bustling centers such as the county town, it should not be underestimated either. Clearly, opportunities for mobility were expanding.[27]

The improved roads, the importance of which for the criminal history of Carmarthenshire in the context of the "Rebecca" disturbances is well known,[28] significantly assisted communications in the county. So, too, did the railway links to Carmarthen that were opened and consolidated in the 1850s.[29] The railway played a considerable role in providing the locus of opportunity for crime—its crowded stations favored by pickpockets,[30] its sidings a source of iron and coal for thieves,[31] its carriages the haunt of fare dodgers.[32] Railway servants of many descriptions, from the examples of two stationmasters[33] and a "carriage fitter up"[34] to the more frequent examples of railway laborers,[35] were to trickle fairly steadily into Carmarthen jail in the 1850s and 1860s, and the majority gave a place of birth outside the county. How many criminals, apart from its own servants, the railway bought into the county is a matter upon which it is impossible to speculate. There is evidence of individual criminals using railway travel to facilitate their careers elsewhere in Wales,[36] and one assumes that it happened in Carmarthenshire. In particular perhaps one might speculate that a crime with potentially high returns that was suited to "hit and run" tactics, such as the introduction of counterfeit money, might be facilitated by rapid transport. Birmingham counterfeiters had used Wales as a market for "flash money" in the past and a gang operating at Carmarthen fair in 1860 had been noted as outsiders, as having "spoke English," although how they arrived in the town I do not know.[37] Indeed, my suspicion is the majority of individuals who committed offenses in Carmarthenshire who had made their way there from outside continued to do so by traditional methods such as "tramping" or begging rides on carts. Nonetheless, as argued earlier, increased ease of communication may be seen as having a symbolic as well as an actual role in raising questions of identity as the railway station was erected as a temple to transience.

Those who administered law and order in the country were aware of the benefits of the railway, for they used it frequently themselves. They also used the steamship. In March 1858,[38] PC David Williams conveyed Bridget Connolly and her two children out of the county to Waterford in Ireland in a journey that took only eight and a half hours in the Meleakoff Steam Ship.[39] In 1850, Governor Stephens could leave the jail on 11 September to convey the transport of Thomas Hughes to Millbank by steam packet and be back at work on 15 September,[40] where a predecessor of his, Governor Waugh, had taken seven days to perform a similar duty by coach in 1823.[41] Those involved in the processes of law enforcement at midcentury, even in Carmarthenshire, knew well that it was getting easier for people to move around the country.

When the official records of criminality are examined, we find some apparent basis for a fear of itinerant criminals in Carmarthenshire. The records of course must be used with considerable caution—in an argument concerning the unreliability of information provided by prisoners, it would be unwise to rely uncritically upon that information in the construction of that argument. It is, moreover, no part of my thesis that the records indicate in any sense a "correct" distribution of the amount of criminality between "locals" and "outsiders." The polarity between the two may be acknowledged to be overstated (a regular visitor from a neighboring county might be well known in Carmarthenshire, for example), but more importantly there is reason to suggest that "outsiders" were more likely to fall within the criminal justice system than others who had acted in similar ways, suspicion focusing official attention and the issue being less likely to be ignored or unofficially settled than if the malefactor were a "local." Thereafter it is possible that in an example of "deviancy amplification" the processing of such individuals may be seen to confirm a suspicion that in its turn thereby is promoted, and increased action follows against members of the group defined as problematic. While the figures do not in themselves establish such a pattern, it should be remembered that they tell us as much about attitudes toward criminality (which in the context of this paper is the significant issue) as about objective patterns of offending.[42]

An examination of the Felons Register for Carmarthen, which records remands of those taken for serious crime between 1844 and 1871, is interesting. In the analysis presented here, I have chosen to treat "remands" as the starting point when considering patterns of offending. As the argument makes clear, not all "remands" represent different individuals, for the same person may be the subject of a number of separate incarcerations. Out of a total of 1,448 remands, only 620 are recorded as being born in the county, only 913 as having their last residence there. Some claimed to have come from very far away indeed, such as Theodore Pantcôte from La Rochelle in France[43] or Frederick Franck from Hamburg via Manchester.[44] Two prisoners gave New York as their place of birth, while three claimed it as their last residence.[45] Some 117 claimed a birthplace in Ireland. Three prisoners offered as their birthplace the unusual or conveniently vague "at sea."[46] It matters less for the moment whether they were telling the truth in that their word was, subject to what is said below, probably all the authorities had to go on.

If there is evidence of mobility in those who came into Carmarthen jail at this time, which might be seen to feed the fear of itinerant criminal, can we go further and find any support for the contemporary concern that those previously sentenced to transportation formed a serious threat to law and order? On the (again let it be said) unreliable evidence of the register it is difficult to be dogmatic. There are individual instances in both 1846 and 1849, and again in 1850, of prisoners recorded as previously sentenced to transportation, while between 1856 and 1865 a further seven are recorded as actually or "supposed" transported.[47] Of the latter category, for example, Thomas James Thomas is recorded in an entry that reveals a lack of confidence in both the prisoner's name and record as "supposed transported from Haverfordwest in the name of Cushing."[48] This use of "supposed" by Governor Stephens in completing his entry in the register here is significant. A growing sensitivity to the problems of identity on the part of the governor is apparent in the language of his records from the later 1850s, when a new caution becomes apparent. "Supposed" is one formula employed; "says" is another used to indicate the uncorrobarated nature of the information received. So, to give again but one example, in recording whether Henry and Harriet Jackson (imprisoned for stealing a pair of stockings in September 1866 and giving places of birth in Lancashire) had been in custody before, Stephens enters the words "both say no" (Figure 2).[49] Such qualification reveals both the nature of the problem and a new sensitivity toward it.

In a similar vein and no doubt for similar reasons, we notice within the register a greater concern from the late 1850s with the recording of aliases. In the data recorded between January 1844 and December 1857, some twenty-seven entries mention an alias; from January 1858 to September 1871 there are fifty-six. Nor should it be thought that all such aliases were recorded in this source, evidence from outside the register confirming its deficiencies in this respect.[50]

It perhaps should be pointed out that two different forms of "alias" may be found in the records. Some individuals are recorded as using an "alias" when what is really recorded is a nickname. In these cases the use of another name serves to reinforce rather than conceal identity (the practice is still widely used in Wales, where the prevalence of certain common names demands more precise differentiation). So James Lewis, sentenced to transportation in both 1845 and 1851, was "Jemmy Llawen" ("Happy

Figure 2: Henry and Harriet Jackson

Jemmy")[51] in a sense that involved no subterfuge, any more than is apparent in police notebooks that record familiar names for David Jones ("Jollyboy") or David Jones ("Dai Doleth") or Thomas Jones ("Sir Hugh"). These types of "aliases" however, are not the ones that caused problems, and they form a small proportion of the numbers recorded.[52] "John Phillips" or "Charles Williams," whose cases were discussed at the outset of this chapter, sought rather than fled the obscurity that inhered in a common name.

Enough has been said, I hope, to establish that uncertainty about criminal identity was a problem that, though it may be easily missed in the familiar competing discourses on the details of prison regime that rumble through the nineteenth century, was every bit as significant. Though we may detect increased official discussion of the problem in the late 1850s and the 1860s, the roots of the concern lay ultimately in more long-term social and penal changes. The problem was one that affected, and evidently gave cause for concern in, the routine practical administration of even a small local prison such as Carmarthen. What was to be done about it?

PHOTOGRAPHING CRIMINALS: ORIGINS AND PURPOSES

At some time between 11 January and 7 May 1858, the period during which its subject James Jones was confined in Carmarthen jail, Governor

Figure 3: James Jones

Stephens took the first of the photographic portraits of prisoners in his custody and affixed the tiny image to his register (Figure 3).[53] It may have been simply macabre curiosity that prompted Stephens' action, for Jones' case had proved to be something of a local *cause célèbre*. The prisoner was a weaver from Llanllwni and was described at his trial by his sister-in-law (through an interpreter) as "pretty well to do in the world, as poor people."[54] She had been the victim of a wild and apparently motiveless attack by Jones that had left her with a fractured skull, three broken ribs, and thirty to forty other wounds. Baron Bramwell, a judge not overburdened with desire to weigh the subtleties of the psychological condition of prisoners before him,[55] sentenced Jones to death on 18 March 1858, holding out little hope of a reprieve. Stephens' record, however, reads, "March 24th 1858 a respite was recorded, March 25th the High Sheriff received notice that the sentence was commuted to that of penal servitude for life. Removed to penitentiary Millbank May 7 1858." It is improbable that Stephens would have expected to see Jones again as a recidivist, nor to fail to recognize him if he did (the sentence of death was so rare in Carmarthenshire in the nineteenth century as to be almost unforgettable). A newspaper had, in any case, preserved a full verbal description of Jones, though in so doing it had displayed the very problems—the inability to escape judgment and stereotype, the failure to achieve scientific detachment and objectivity—

that, as we shall see, made photography such an appealing process to men like Stephens:

> There was hardly any expression on his face, which was pale, almost livid with hardly any whiskers upon it; but the little that were there were perfectly black like the hair of his head, which was long and combed straight down over his forehead, nearly concealing dark eyes which at times moved about restlessly and furtively glanced at the jury, but the ordinary appearance of the prisoner was that of stolid indifference and natural obtuseness.[56]

Yet whatever his reasons for photographing James Jones, Stephens obviously soon recognized a potential within photography and began to take other likenesses of his charges. From 1863 he was doing so regularly.

James Jones was certainly not the first prisoner to be photographed; the celebrated Mannings, for example, had been captured on daguerrotype by Martin Laroche in 1849. In Wales itself, photographs were taken in Newport in 1850 by Joseph Jacquier of Patrick Sullivan and Maurice Murphy and sent to their native Ireland in an attempt to discover their antecedents. A picture of the two men, based on a daguerrotype original, appeared after their execution on conviction for murder in the pages of *The Monmouthshire Merlin* newspaper.[57] In France and in Switzerland, photography seems to have been used routinely early within the penal system.[58] In England, the credit for the introduction of a regular system of custodial photography was claimed for and by Governor Gardner of Bristol, who was employing it McConville states, as early as 1852. "I was the first who introduced it and I have got it introduced into perhaps 20 or 25 gaols and they all adopt this plan,"[59] Gardner told the Carnarvon Committee. Sir Walter Crofton, the former superintendent of Irish convict prisons was another early enthusiast, telling the same committee that he had been producing stereoscopic portraits of those "whom we do not know," at the modest cost of 4d per picture amongst the penal servitude men in Ireland "for many years."[60] Whether or not these experiments were known to Stephens I do not know, though it is clear that neither in the photographic process employed nor in its presentation (albeit that this may have been to an extent constrained by incorporation in an existing register) does his approach merely mimic the pattern proselytized by Gardner.[61]

Prior to the introduction of photography, the use of written description and memory had been relied on by prison authorities in discovering the identity of prisoners. To the difficulties of using the former we have already adverted. If we again look to the Carmarthen evidence, it is clear how little practical use the limited amount of information officially retained in written form would be. Even where the record does not report the transitory ("John Phillips" is recorded as "sunburnt")[62] or tend toward stereotype (the "florid, masculine appearance" attributed to suspected cheese stealer Hannah Jones)[63] or indeed edge toward the Gothic (the "cadaverous" complexion of Thomas Davies, accused of an "unnatural offence with an heifer"!),[64] its apparently endless procession of five-foot, four-inch males with "sallow" complexions, or the like, hardly speaks to a confidence in its utility in matters of identity. As one of the inspectors of prisons, J. G. Perry, conceded in 1863; "it is a very difficult thing from a description of a man to establish his identity."[65]

Reliance on memory was also, of course, an unsatisfactory answer to the problem of recognition. Even in cases where the prisoner returned to an institution in which he had been confined before, he might not be recognized, particularly when there had been changes of staff. In instances where the offender had moved from the site of his previous incarceration the problems became all too evident. The practice of sending prison officials to "prove a conviction" against an individual charged elsewhere against whom suspicion had arisen was employed but might be infrequently used.[66] In 1847, for example, Head Turnkey William Williams of Carmarthen went to Cardiff to confirm a sentence of transportation imposed upon Thomas Powell eighteen months earlier.[67] The system, if such it can be called, was deeply flawed, however, and in the 1860s came under attack for being inadequately financed. The issue was raised before witnesses to the Carnarvon Committee, and although opinion was divided on the subject, there was some evidence to support the claim of underfunding.[68] In the debates upon the Habitual Criminals Bill in 1869, Mr. Henley raised a similar point: "the want of information in the case of previous convictions was owing in a very great degree to the parsimony of the treasury in cutting down on the expenses of gaol officials coming to give evidence on such points."[69] The experience of personal inspection by recognizing officers on admittance to jail is attested to in the accounts of former prisoners, even after photography became standard. "Captain D. S.," writing in the 1880s, speaks of some seventy or eighty recognizing officers being employed in a jail on occasion.[70] "A Manchester Merchant" tells of his experience of inspection in Kirkdale, his cell door being opened "and a tall man with a very searching glance confronted me. He told me to look him in the face and I stood staring at him in wondering amazement . . . I was afterwards told he was the chief warder of Walton Gaol in search of old hands."[71] The fallibility of human memory undermined such a process even where there existed a system of regular mutual inspection, as we shall see in operation in major population centers such as Leeds and Wakefield. Clearly, such a system could not work, save in a fortuitous fashion, where there had been any considerable movement on the part of the criminal, and the problems were exacerbated where jails were more geographically remote—Carmarthen certainly employed no such routine exchange inspections, which would have been, in any case, due to the size of the prison population and the difficulties that the absence of members of the staff would cause, an impractical extravagance. But even in the larger jails, the chance nature of recognition was a source of concern. Edward Shepherd, the governor of Wakefield Prison, expressed his concern to the Carnarvon Commission, supporting his position by providing statistics proving the prevalence of "strangers, travelling thieves and old offenders" within the prison population. Shepherd gave an illuminating explanation of the arrangements within his own prison and of their limitations, and his words are worth quoting at length:

> There is a prison at Leeds, in our immediate neighbourhood, and three days before the sessions five or six officers from Wakefield go over to examine all the prisoners for trial at Leeds and vice versa; they come over from Leeds to examine the prisoners at Wakefield and in that case many persons are detected who are known as old offenders. A month ago two persons were sent to prison at Wakefield in one day; the chaplain of the prison at Wakefield was formerly the chaplain at Portland; he came to me and said, "There are two men that you do not know, and that I know; they have been previously transported when I was at Portland; I will give you the names in confidence." A few days after, we sent a man to the Chatham prison, when he came to the Chatham prison, the authorities at Chatham knew him as having been previously at Chatham. A few days after that, a prisoner was sent from London to Wakefield for confinement, and when he came into the prison, we knew him as having been previously convicted in Manchester; and as having undergone discipline at Wakefield. A few days after that, a man came into the West Riding part of the prison, when he was inspected by the officers, he was known to have been previously convicted and sent from Leicestershire. Those are five cases all within a month; they would have escaped detection, but for accidental circumstances; and I have no doubt whatsoever that such cases are very numerous indeed.[72]

Governor Shepherd, however, set little store by photography as a means of bringing such individuals to light. He preferred the alternative identificatory technique canvassed before the Select Committee, the application of a permanent mark to the body of the convict. Shepherd's own suggestion was to mark the offender under the arm in Indian ink as the only way to ensure that the "dangerous and increasing class" of "travelling thieves" could be adequately dealt with.[73]

BRANDING: A CORPOREAL ALTERNATIVE

This alternative solution had the advantages of both permanence and familiarity. Those who worked within the prison system were aware that corporeal evidence of identity could be sought in both acquired and inflicted marks. Of the former kind, pock marks from illness and missing fingers could be useful points of reference, while of the latter, tattoos involved the conscious ascription of difference, or at least group membership, to a particular individual body. Tattoos might indicate membership of a criminal gang and were also regularly used by those in the armed services, where the desire for subcultural solidarity evident in the generality of the practice may have been influenced, in the particularity of the designs, by the desire to be identified in the event of death in battle or at sea. Marks of both kinds were regularly recorded by many but not all prisons by the 1860s. In some prison registers in which photography was employed, the prisoners sit before the camera with their hands raised before them, the better to demonstrate both disfigurement and the most immediately visible tattoos.[74] Branding was also still a familiar practice from military service, with deserters being marked with a "D" on the chest and other offenders against discipline with a "BC." An examination of the Bedford prison register, assiduous in its recording of distinguishing marks, shows a considerable number of men so branded, some more than once as well as a great many missing fingers, the results one supposes of the danger of industrial and agricultural machinery.[75] The prevalence of branded individuals in Petworth was also noted by its Governor William Linton.[76] The American penologist F. H. Wines, writing in 1895 and looking back to the Habitual Criminals Register for 1876, also observed but obviously failed to comprehend the phenomenon. Considering the record of "distinctive marks," Wines observes:

> The most common method of marking is by initials, this is noticed in 250, while 35 wear names, 7 dates, 6 numbers and one a place. The initials and names are frequently those of the person so marked, sometimes of sweethearts, or possibly, in the case of sailors, of ships. There are, in addition 44 who are marked with a D, 7 with DD and 2 with DDD on the left side; 12 are marked with BC on the right side. These seem to donate membership in some society; one prisoner shows both a D and BC as if he were doubly connected. In several instances an ineffectual attempt has been made to obliterate the D, once by a flower-pot, once by a teapot and once by a castle; obliteration can in most cases be effected only by additions to the original design.[77]

It was an extension of the process of branding that was canvassed by some witnesses before the Carnarvon Committee in 1863. Even Governor Gardner, the enthusiastic pioneer of photography, approved of the idea: "I have often thought" he said, "that just as deserters are marked with the letter D it would not do very great harm to mark a thief and I should mark him by a machine made upon the principle of a cupping machine. I would rub him over with gunpowder and water properly mixed and mark him Bristol Gaol. It might be done in one single second, without any pain or hurt."[78] Although not endorsed by the committee, the idea resurfaced in the discussions promoted by the Habitual Criminals Bill with Colonel Frazer, the commissioner of the city police advocating a system of branding that would utilize "a simple combination of alphabetical letters, similar to that employed in distinguishing postage stamps."[79]

Notwithstanding its attractiveness to at least some who had everyday experience of the penal system and the proliferation of opinions on penal matters at the time, it was, I suggest, never likely that an extension of branding would receive official sanction in the 1860s. Certainly, there were those who condemned the proposal for its lack of proportion. The journalist James Greenwood, for example, writing in 1869 attacked the commissioner's proposals vigorously: "Colonel Frazer should bear in mind that an act of criminality does not altogether change a man's nature. He is a human creature in which, perhaps through accident, perhaps through desperate, and to some extent deliberate culture, certain growths, injurious to the welfare of the commonwealth, have grown; but to brand and destroy, and crush under the heel of the said creature because of his objectionable affections, is much like smashing a set of valuable vases because stagnant water has been permitted to accumulate."[80] But it was not only its cruelty that made branding unlikely to be adopted as government policy; it was the negativity, the retrogression inherent in this "new idea" (Greenwood himself had applied the ironic quotation marks). Although the 1860s did see a clamor for the reintroduction of transportation and indeed witnessed in the panicky Security Against Violence Act of 1863 a return to the punishment of the body,[81] branding when set aside photography looked reactionary. The use of the "angel copier"[82] had an added promise, which meant that it could be promoted not simply as a more humane alternative to branding. Despite the reservations concerning photography of some who addressed the Carnarvon Committee, including no less a figure than Sir Joshua Jebb ("I do not attach much importance to it"),[83] the committee while conceding that the matter was outside its original terms of reference offered its support. Its decision to "strongly recommend the further extension of this system, which is inexpensive, effective and wholly free from objection"[84] is not surprising. Photography had an attractive quality for the policy makers of the Victorian age; it held the advantage of offering a solution to a social problem through the application of science.

PHOTOGRAPHY, SCIENCE, AND POWER

It is almost axiomatic that as the nineteenth century progressed, scientific knowledge and professionalism were increasingly seen as an appropriate foundation of criminal justice. Penology was becoming a job for experts, the prison cell itself could be urged as a laboratory for social experimentation—crank labor calibrated, the separate cell controled to exclude environmental variables, the better to administer regulated doses of deterrence or reform.[85] Alienists and forensic scientists increasingly pressed the virtues of their disciplines in the courtroom. By midcentury, as Roger Smith observes, "experimental science was entering a period of self sustaining growth in prestigious institutional settings."[86] The introduction of photography and the rejection of branding needs to be considered in this wider cultural context.

Although becoming more popular in the 1850s and 1860s and having experienced technical developments that freed it from some of the restrictions of its early years, photography remained the object of some arcane, technical knowledge. It was also, of course, much more limited in its application than it is today, its comparative novelty and scarcity increasing its social impact. As one modern commentator has observed, "its apparent integration with the cultural furniture of the late twentieth century has undermined its potency. The image is all pervasive yet devalued." Such devaluation had barely begun in mid–Victorian England.[87] The camera was a product of confidence in science and technology and in turn became its tool, possessing (this was accepted without hesitation in its early development) the capacity for objectivity so significant for Victorian notions of positivist, empirical scientific method.

It was this quality of objectivity that recommended photography as suitable for employment as "an auxiliary to the administration of justice" in an article from 1866 that also considered its utility in such areas of "pure" science as astronomy. "That it is not imaginative, that it cannot modify or omit details from its presentments becomes . . . its cardinal virtue,"[88] wrote the anonymous author. Indeed, it could be seen as combining with other technological developments to be employed in a modern scientific drive against the ancient trait of crime. Sir John Bowring, in a paper for the 1870 Congress on Penitentiary and Reformatory Discipline in Cleveland, Ohio, expressed the mood as follows:

> Modern Science has provided many new appliances, in aid of the administration of justice, for the discovery of criminals and the suppression of crime. The facilities given by the electric telegraph for the rapid communication of information have placed in the hands of the authorities an instrument of great value. Farrell, the murderer was arrested by a message through the electric wires without whose assistance he would probably have escaped. The photographic art has lately been used for the portraiture of a large proportion of habitual and professional criminals, and for enabling the magistrate to trace their previous history in the various prisons through which they may have passed. The Uxbridge seven-fold assassin was identified by a portrait taken in prison, from which he had been released just before the commission of the murders. The physiognomies of criminals, especially those of a most decided and dangerous character, have often so marked a resemblance as to be worthy of the notice not only of the speculative phrenologist, but of the practical philosopher.[89]

In a similar vein, the pioneer historian of crime, L. O. Pike, writing a few years later but in a mood of optimism nurtured by the criminal statistics regarding the problems of crime, observed:

Modern improvements in the mode of lighting towns and their suburbs following the introduction of gas must be reckoned among the most effectual preventives of robbery by night. Telegraphs aid not a little in the detection of offenders after a crime has been committed, and photography has often done most important service in proving the identity of the criminal.[90]

Such statements by Bowring and Pike suggest that, for some at least, the promise that inhered in photography was not simply that of an efficient mode of portraiture but was part of a wider belief in the onward march of science, which might be directed to the problems of crime. Upon this belief the doubts as to the practical utility of an extension of the practice that were voiced to the Carnarvon Committee by some individuals within the penal system apparently made little impact. It may be suggested that the symbolic, as well as the practical, attraction of photography was an appreciable factor in its wider adoption. Criminality might be quite literally "brought to light" by the apparatus, which could penetrate the dark mass of urban anonymity of the "criminal class" to isolate, individualize, and label. It is perhaps not absurd to see in the camera, its governor/operator standing in the dark gazing out at the criminal, an echo of the Benthamite Panopticon plan, but one that in the elimination of the limitations of time and space could outperform its architectural precursor in its disciplinary watchfulness.

Foucault's observation in relation to techniques of discipline in general is pertinent in this context in relation to the spread of photography in particular: "Disciplinary power is exercised through its invisibility; at the same time it imposes on those whom it subjects a principle of compulsory visibility . . . it is the fact of being constantly seen, of being able always to be seen, that maintains the disciplined individual in his subjection."[91]

Not only was the prisoner "captured" or "shot" by the camera objectified and isolated from his fellows; he would also be reminded of a difference in power—the cultural sophistication of those who had technology over those, increasingly regarded as the century wore on as for the most part degenerate rather than frightening, who did not. Lest it be thought that we are here abandoning nineteenth-century reality for yet more footnotes to twentieth-century theory, it may be affirmed that contemporary records confirm that prisoners certainly might find the process, for whatever reason, alarming. Governor Gardner, in answer to a question whether prisoners dreaded being photographed, affirmed that they would sooner confess their previous records than submit to the process.[92] Another pioneer, Governor Roberts of Bedford, drew attention to the significance of the prisoners' relative ignorance when he wrote in 1860, "What renders its application still more beneficial is it is distasteful to prisoners inasmuch as they invariably dread exposure, and once their photograph has been taken they are unconscious of the use that is made of it and therefore it cannot fail to have a deterrent effect to crime."[93]

Some of the advocates of photography, keen to exploit its disciplinary potential, were reluctant to await criminal conviction before capturing the image. One author, though he doubtless exaggerated the degree of exposure to the camera of a wider section of humanity than his own enthusiastic circle, and indeed who hints at the moral probity of those who had been subject to it, stresses the benefits of an increasing use of the process:

> The universality of photographic portraiture has been singularly useful. . . . There are a few men, open in any way to the sympathies of their kind, who have not at some time sat for a photograph, little dreaming of the weapon it placed in the hands of their pursuers should they at any time step into the paths of crime.[94]

As the century advanced, there is perhaps some further hint of this belief that "good citizens," those open "to the sympathies of their kind," would have voluntarily embraced and thus controlled the technology, leaving only the "criminal" classes upon whom it must be imposed. In fiction, at any rate, it might be taken as significant if a man had not been photographed.[95] Certainly, it was known that photography might reveal misconduct or imposture that had never been the subject of a court appearance. Governor Robert Roberts of Bedford, a man convinced of the utility of photography and proud of his own success with it (he notes in 1865 on the record of the prisoner Edward Carney, "alias Joseph Smith," that "The Governor through the aid of photography discovered that the prisoner was a deserter from the Royal Engineers at Chatham in the name of John Shannon 13th March 1864, also a deserter from the 4th Regiment Foot"),[96] related both his pride and his conviction to the press. He reported to the *Bedfordshire Mercury* his success in pursuing by photography the countrywide career of "the Clerical Swindler," George Henry Charles Perry, a man whose catalogue of misdeeds, which included *inter alia* the theft of a box of Manilla cigars and the fraudulent ordering of a large harmonium, had not always been attended by prosecution. Roberts had even sent a photograph of Perry to Merton College, Oxford, to expose his fraudulent claim to having graduated there.[97]

So potent was the belief in the potential of photography in some circles that the rhetoric attached to it was occasionally bizarre. It was asserted, for instance, that the image of a murderer remained preserved, as on a photographic plate, upon the retina of the victim. Although dismissed as "an absurd impossibility" in 1866, there is some evidence of a survival of the belief for some time.[98] A more interesting, if less dramatic, metaphorical invocation of the process may be seen in the writings of the Reverend Clay, a significant figure in the debates relating to penal reform. As photography isolated the prisoner from the mass, so isolation could make him sensitive to the light of reason, amenable to having a positive image developed from his negative: "A few months in the solitary cell," Clay assured, "renders a prisoner strangely impressible. The chaplain can then make the brawny navvy cry like a child; he can work on his feelings in almost any way he pleases: he can, so to speak, *photograph his thoughts wishes and opinions on his patient's mind*[99] [italics added]. Still later, Michael Davitt showed how far new technology had overruled, in its language at least, the old, when he referred in his observations on criminal typology to a verbal description of "The Bruiser" as "His Photo."[100]

In some of the jails that adopted photography there is soon evidence of an increasing sophistication in technique in its application. Governor Stephens in Carmarthen continued to use the same basic format, only varying between the shape, oblong or oval, of his images, but other supporters were more adventurous. In the late 1860s Governor Roberts of Bedford began hanging the prisoner's number from the coat buttons on the subject's chest, although it remained modestly affixed to the curtain behind female offenders.[101] He even (in a gesture that seems to preempt postmodernism!) experimented with the use, in the prison, of a backdrop of prison architecture (Figure 4), the real thing being presumably not regarded as sufficiently authentic.[102] Later still, mirrors might be employed by photographers to produce simultaneous multiple images of a kind favored by some contemporary anthropologists.[103]

Custodial photography had, by the late 1860s, a respectable pedigree of use in individual jails, an enthusiastic body of supporters, even the support of a select committee, but its introduction into the penal system had not been a uniform one. Governor Roberts argued in 1860, and supported his argument by the experience within his own jail, that malefactors "will, as far as they can avoid those Prisons in which Photography is employed."[104] Clearly a practice that relied in this way upon the old expedient of the displacement of criminality to areas that employed different custodial techniques flew in the face of the Victorian national systematic ideal. Eventually, almost inevitably, legislation was to follow that concentrated on those considered to be the most dangerous elements of the "criminal class."

LEGISLATION AND DISAPPOINTMENT

The 1869 Habitual Criminals Act,[105] a measure passed at a time of considerable social concern about the hard core of professional criminals, made only oblique reference to photography. Certainly, however, the issue of identity was well recognized as a problem in the legislation. In the introduction of the bill to the House of Lords, during which the measure was explicitly linked with the ending of transportation and the growth of "a

Figure 4: "James Knapton" alias "Spencer" alias "Madge" (courtesy of the Bedfordshire Record Office)

great army—an army making war on society,"[106] the Earl of Kimberley drew attention to the necessity of

> a complete system of communications throughout the country so as to form a complete network of supervision of criminals in every part of the country. This is obviously essential for otherwise a man convicted in the metropolis may go to some part of the country where the authorities possess no information about him so that there is no control over his conduct.[107]

The act, as is well known, established a central criminal register, and in section 6 instructed governors of county and borough prisons and chief officers of police to make returns for the purpose of the register "in such manner and at such time and containing such evidences of identity and other information" as might thereafter be directed. Unwilling perhaps to place full confidence in a system that allowed an individual to be identified by the dissemination of an image, the act spent more time detailing a rather cruder method of keeping a habitual offender's movements under supervision, namely in refusing to let him out of sight in the first place by subjecting him to police supervision.[108] A circular of November 1869 from the

Habitual Criminals Register Office that was received by the Chief Constable of the Carmarthenshire Police, Colonel Scott, provided the pattern of a form to be filled in for those convicted of particular offenses specified in the act, which, though it left a space for a photograph, made no particular mention thereof.[109] In February of the following year, however, a Home Office circular did request photographs of those convicted of offenses under schedule one of the 1869 act.[110] In May of the same year a standard form of "Album Portraits" was called for "with a view to securing an uniform system in carrying out the instructions contained in [the February] Circular."[111]

When the 1869 act was overhauled in the Prevention of Crimes Act 1871 ("an old friend under a new name," as the Earl of Morley put it, ignoring the changes that the later legislation made) photography of criminals became a matter explicitly for the statute book.[112] The act provided in section 6:

> (6) In Great Britain the Secretary of State and in Ireland the . . . Lord Lieutenant may make regulations as to the photographs of all prisoners convicted of crime who may, for the time being be confined in any prison in Great Britain or Ireland and may in such regulations prescribe the time or times at which and the manner and dress in which such prisoners are to be taken, and the number of photographs of each prisoner to be printed, and the persons to whom such photographs are to be sent.
>
> (7) Any regulations made by the Secretary of State in England shall be deemed to be regulations for the government of that prison, and binding on all persons, in the same manner as if they were contained in the first schedule annexed to the Prison Act 1865. . . .
>
> (10) Any prisoner refusing to obey any regulation made in pursuance of this section shall be deemed guilty of an offense against prison discipline. . . .
>
> (12) . . . The expenses incurred in photographing the prisoners in any prison shall be deemed to be part of the expenses incurred in the maintenance of the prison and shall be defrayed accordingly.

The movement toward the technological defeat of crime that had produced such pioneers as George Stephens and Robert Roberts, who had originally paid from their own pockets before their achievements had led to receiving both praise and reimbursement from their respective county benches, had found statutory expression.[113] With the national prison service soon to be secured, the national prisoner seemed ready to take his or her place in it.

Of course it did not work, though the details of its failure cannot be discussed here. Flaws in the system became apparent. One, which in truth had been troubling from an early period, was related to the technological crudity of the early photographic process. In the case of an unwilling subject, the difficulty of securing the necessary stasis for long exposures might be considerable, a mere jerk of the head sufficient to defeat the process, a distortion of the features sufficient to confound it. It was a matter that had arisen before the Carnarvon Committee, but Sir Walter Crofton had been reassuring: "for the first fortnight there was little else but contortions on the part of the prisoners to evade this practice, but after that time there were no faces made, and they all submitted to it."[114] In some jails the threat of punishment by deprivation of food had been used upon recalcitrant inmates even before the rather nebulous extension of the range of disciplinary offenses that we have noted in section 6(10) of the 1871 act.[115] Other governors used the expedient of a hidden camera to capture the prisoner unawares.[116] If all else failed there would even be the possibility of the resort to force, as the image of John Hewett, held down by four policemen at Farnham police station in 1898, reminds us.[117] Nonetheless, a few claimed to have beaten the system. Eddie Guerin, writing much later, reminisced: "at the time they took it I was wearing a couple of months' beard. Also, on my way to the photographer I picked up a couple of pebbles, put them into my mouth, and screwed up my face until even my own mother would not have recognized me."[118]

A mere fundamental problem became evident as photographs flooded into the records. It was impossible to sort through all the pictures to identify a particular individual.[119] While there were some successes, the utility of the resource remained dependent on a combination of memory and chance in much the same way as it had when all depended on the efforts of the recognizing officers of individual jails. As one commentator in the 1880s put it quite succinctly:

> Photographs are undoubtedly a great aid in establishing the identity of the criminal. But it is very difficult, almost impossible, to find in a large collection the picture of a person without knowing his name. A photograph is valuable in *verifying* the identity of an individual, but it is altogether impotent to help you *discover* the identity if you have no other means but your eyes to search for the photograph among the thousands in an ordinary collection.[120]

An idea that had seemed so promising when practiced irregularly was exposed as deficient when employed as routine. Changes were introduced in the practice of central registration in consequence of the fact that the Register of Habitual Criminals "was soon swamped by its completeness." As part of the same revision of procedures, the contents of the register were circulated to local authorities. The means of identification that these volumes (which contain no photographs) recommend is by utilization of physical anomalies and tattoos, for which purpose an accompanying Register of Distinctive Marks was issued yearly along with the register. Thereafter, a photograph might be obtained from the governor of the prisoner's previous jail to confirm the identification, although even then this process is referred to as an option[121]—other (undisclosed) "means of identification" or "the assistance of a person acquainted with him" also being mentioned.

In the course of time, other methods that allowed more sophisticated techniques of sorting material but also, as knowledge of photography became more popular and less arcane, continued the role of the esotericism of science in the drive to control crime, were gradually developed. In the process, the approach to the body to establish identity has gradually become closer, more physically invasive—anthropometric measurement, fingerprinting, and now DNA testing. For all its failures and for all its cozy familiarity to the late twentieth-century individual, photographed from bearskin rug to geriatric birthday, the camera once offered a similar promise to the criminal justice system, but one perceived of as even more significant by virtue of the novelty of the enterprise.

NOTES

I am reluctant to enter on to a recital of gratitude that reads like an Academy Award acceptance speech, but many people deserve mention here. I did much work on this chapter while a McCarthy Tetrault visitor at the University of Victoria in 1993, where conversations with Hamar Foster, John McLaren, Tom Johnson, and David Flaherty were invariably as illuminating as they were enjoyable. Without the extraordinary cooperation of all at both Carmarthen and Aberystwyth Record Offices the work would never have been possible. Bedford Record Office, in particular Mr. Nigel Lutt, provided much appreciated help. I am grateful to Claire Breay for her splendid work on the computer and to Dr. Stevenson for allowing reference to his unpublished Ph.D. thesis. Thanks, too, Lilian Stevenson and Christine Davies. Helen Palmer deserves the credit for, amongst many other things, interesting me in the project initially. This work arises out of a wider and still ongoing investigation into the inmates and administration of Carmarthen Gaol in the nineteenth century.

1. Carmarthenshire Record Office (CRO) *Felons Register* (acc. 4916, hereafter *F.R.*) 1076. See also 463.

2. CRO *F.R.* 1108. See also 411.

3. CRO *F.R.* 1109.

4. "Reality" in this respect is not an unproblematic concept. Compulsory registration of births, a measure that is of significance within the context of the arguments to be developed in this chapter, only began in 1837 and may not always have been complied with. Moreover, what a person is called in life, whether it be, as we shall see later, a nickname or an assumed name, may support a greater claim to "reality" than that recorded at birth. That we should automatically accept the "official" as the "real" tells us more about our own age than about the past.

5. This is not the time or place to enter into a discussion of nineteenth-century penal historiography in general, and the debate between what we might label the "traditionalists" and "revisionists" is well known. I would observe simply that the recent widening of the discussion to consider local practice and a wider range of criminal conduct than the gravest of offenders is welcome. Works such as Margaret de Lacy's *Prison Reform in Lancashire 1700–1850* (Manchester, 1986) and Lucia

Zedner's *Women, Crime and Custody in Victorian England* (Oxford, 1991) demonstrate the merits of careful local study. Sean McConville's recent work, *English Local Prisons 1860–1900* (London, 1995), was published after this chapter was accepted. This excellent book contains much of value. For the most part, I have been able here to incorporate reference to it only in footnotes.

6. See Christopher Harding, William Hines, Richard W. Ireland, and Philip Rawlings, *Imprisonment in England and Wales: A Concise History* (Beckenham, 1985), 37.

7. See John Styles, "Sir John Fielding and the Problem of Criminal Investigation in Eighteenth-Century England," *Royal Historical Society Transactions* 33 (Fifth Series, 1983): 127 et seq.

8. For an illuminating discussion see Martin J. Wiener, *Reconstructing the Criminal, Culture Law and Policy in England 1830–1914* (Cambridge, 1990). Wiener's important thesis, part of which argues for a dominant model of the criminal as calculating moral individual at midcentury is, I suggest, supported by the arguments concerning the ascription of individual identity advanced here.

9. The most significant text exploring this theme and forming the basis for subsequent discussion and controversy is of course Michel Foucault's *Surveiller et Punir*, translated as *Discipline and Punish* (Harmondsworth, 1979). For a full discussion of the literature on the subject see Philip J. Rawlings in William Hines, ed., *English Legal History: A Bibliography and Guide to the Literature* (New York, 1990), chap. 5. For a recent reappraisal of the position in France see Richard M. Andrews, *Law, Magistracy and Crime in Old Regime Paris 1735–1789*, vol. I (Cambridge, 1994), especially 409–12.

10. See, for example, Leon Radzinowicz and Roger Hood, *A History of English Criminal Law and its Administration from 1750*, vol. 5 (London, 1986), chap. 14; David Smith, "The Demise of Transportation: Mid-Victorian Penal Policy," *Criminal Justice History* 3 (1982): 21–45.

11. Radzinowicz and Hood, *History of English Criminal Law*, 5: 465–66.

12. Assize of Clarendon 1176, c.1 and see Richard W. Ireland, "First Catch Your Toad: Medieval Attitudes to Ordeal and Battle," *Cambrian Law Review* 10 (1979): 50–61 at p. 52.

13. Leon Radzinowicz and Roger Hood, "Incapacitating the Habitual Criminal: The English Experience," *Michigan Law Review* 78 (1979/80): 1305–89 at 1308.

14. Ibid. On the garotters see Jennifer Davis, "The London Garotting Panic of 1862: A Moral Panic and the Creation of a Criminal Class in Mid-Victorian England," in Victor A. C. Gatrell, Bruce Lenman, and Geoffrey Parker, eds., *Crime and the Law: The Social History of Crime in Western Europe since 1500* (London, 1980), 190–214. But note the risk of overstating the importance of one manifestation of a general fear, and see Simon J. Stevenson, "The 'Criminal Class' in the Mid-Victorian City: A Study of Policy Conducted with Special Reference to those made subject to the Provisions of 34 & 35 Vict c. 112 (1871) in Birmingham and East London in the Early Years of Registration and Supervision" Ph.D diss., University of Oxford, 1983). Recidivism had been in the system for many years; alcohol and the vagrancy laws made Carmarthen's notorious Mary Ann Awberry a recidivist long before the Penal Servitude Acts. (For Awberry see Richard W. Ireland, "Eugene Buckley and the Diagnosis of Insanity in the early Victorian Prison," *Lla-*

fur 6 (1993): 5–17 at 14. Moreover, when transportation de facto frequently had meant no more than incarceration in the hulks offenders had been released into domestic society. The possibility of the transport's return, from whatever his destination, long had been recognized as a possibility. See, for a literary example, the Justice's taking Roderick Random for the transported Patrick Gahagan using imposture: "yes, yes, here's an old acquaintance of mine—you have used expedition . . . in returning from transportation; but we shall save you the trouble for the future—the surgeons will fetch you from your next transportation at their expense." (*The Adventures of Roderick Random* [1748], chap. xxvii, in *The Works of Tobias Smollett*, ed. David Herbert [Edinburgh, 1885], 74–75.

15. "What is to Be Done with Our Criminals," *The Economist* 5 (1847): 835, as quoted in Radzinowicz and Hood, "Habitual Criminal," 1310.

16. For patterns of criminality in Wales see David J. V. Jones, *Crime in Nineteenth Century Wales* (Cardiff, 1992).

17. Henry Mayhew, *London Labour and the London Poor*, 4 vols. (London, 1861), 1:2–3 as quoted and discussed in Wiener, *Reconstructing the Criminal*, 31–33.

18. Quoted in Radzinowicz and Hood, "Habitual Criminal," 1309.

19. Note the transitions in meaning of the words "character" and "personality," today taken as primarily signifying personal attributes. The latter term had a far more universal connotation before the nineteenth century, the former retained a meaning within that century as an employer's reference—"character," that is, could be given by another rather than possessed exclusively by oneself.

20. Sir Walter Crofton, "The Irish System of Prison Discipline," in *Transactions of the National Congress on Penitentiary and Reformatory Discipline*, ed. Enoch C. Wines (Albany, 1871), 71. The Congress was held in Cincinatti, Ohio.

21. On Crofton's role, see Stevenson, "Criminal Class," chap. 1, and see Crofton's evidence to the Select Committee on Prison Discipline, 3246–62.

22. Select Committee on Prison Discipline 1863 (I.U.P. Parliamentary Papers Reprint, Shannon, 1968). Hereafter CC. Minutes para. 4957.

23. Michael Davitt, *Leaves from a Prison Diary* (1885; reprint Shannon, 1972), 139.

24. Tom Taylor, *The Ticket-of-Leave Man: A Drama* (London, 1863), 57. This splendid piece undoubtedly should be revised for performance!

25. Henry Mayhew and John Binney, *The Criminal Prisons of London* (1862; reprint London, 1968), 295.

26. *Diary of P. C. David Williams*, 1857–58 (CRO Mus 112), see e.g., entries for 26 December 1857, "Also about 11.30 p.m. there was a row between some Irish lads and the *Whites* of under the bank. I went there and seen all to their lodgings"; 27 December 1857, "There was also a little noise with the Irish at Kidwelly fach"; and 30 June 1858, "I prevented a row near the Horse and Jockey between some Cornish Miners. . . . I patroled the beat regularly during the night there was two weddings with the Irish under the bank there was no row there."

27. For an illuminating consideration of the conditions and demography of the area in the first half of the century see David J. V. Jones, *Rebecca's Children* (Oxford, 1989), chap. 1, and for the population movement and impact of the railways after the 1840s see 364–68. And see Pat Molloy, *And They Blessed Rebecca* (Llandysul, 1983), 20–7.

28. On which, see Jones, *Rebecca's Children*, chaps. 1 and 5. Note also that elements of obfuscation of identity, not only in the crowd but also in the use of disguises, had made the Rebecca and other popular disturbances both alarming and difficult to combat.

29. The earliest railway in the county was, in fact, very early indeed; the Carmarthenshire Railway opened for freight in 1802. Trains reached Carmarthen itself in September 1852 (the South Wales Railway). Works for the Carmarthen and Cardigan Railway were carried on in 1858 and 1859, and it was opened in 1860. See William Spurrell, *Carmarthen and its Neighbourhood. Notes Topographical and Historical* (Carmarthen, 1879), 152–53; T. L. Evans, "How Ganymede Came to Carmarthen." *Carmarthenshire Historian* (1974): 55. The telegraph arrived in 1853, ibid., 61. Since this piece was written, I have considered the effect of the railway on criminality in more detail. See R. W. Ireland, "An Increasing Mass of Heathens in the Bosom of a Christian Land: The Railway and Crime in the Nineteenth Century," *Continuity and Change* 12 (1997): 55–78.

30. See, for example, the case of Henry Stringer, who offers only a card for his name and refuses to give an address. Witness deposition, 6 May 1874, CRO QS Box 18 (1874).

31. See, for example, the many convictions in CRO QS Box 16 (1873), obviously part of a concerted effort, though cases are to be found frequently at other times.

32. There are many of these to be found in any of the Quarter Sessions records of the 1860s and 1870s.

33. CRO *F.R.* 586, Daniel Jones, convicted of embezzlement in February 1854, and Francis Sherlock Griffiths, convicted of forgery and embezzlement at Assize, 17–18 March 1858.

34. CRO *F.R.* 1405, George Jones, convicted along with another (John Davies), a railway porter, of stealing two quarts of beer on the railway in August 1871.

35. For example, the three Irishmen convicted of passing 6d. in counterfeit money in January 1852, Cornelius Sullivan, John Hoare and John McNamara, CRO *F.R.* 391, 392, 393. In the records of the Felons Register, twenty-four people have their occupations specifically related to employment (of all sorts) on the railway, though in the case of laborers it may not always be specifically mentioned. In addition, six individuals are described as "engine drivers" and one as a "fireman."

36. See, for example, the exploits of the famous David Davies ("Dio Penllys") alias "William Hall" alias "Walter Evans" alias "James Harrison" alias "Richard Evans" chronicled in A. Scriven, *The Dartmoor Shepherd: 50 Years in Prison*, (Oswestry, n.d.), especially 85.

37. For Birmingham's history in respect to counterfeiting, see Peter J. Cook, "Flash Money and Old England's Agent in the Early Nineteenth Century," *Cambrian Law Review* 24 (1993): 12–44, and note p. 27 for an early Welsh case. Not all coiners need have been from so far afield; Jones (*Rebecca's Children*, 169) mentions the trade at Haverfordwest.

38. The chief constable's accounts include many records of rail travel. See, for example, that presented to Quarter Sessions in October 1869, CRO QS Box 11, which also includes a reference to recompense for "Travelling in Warwickshire and apprehending David Morgan, stealing a mare." Standard forms for recovery of train

fares for PCs and prisoners are printed—see e.g., the forms from Summer 1872 in CRO QS Box 16.

39. *Diary of P. C. David Williams*, 24 March 1858.

40. *Gaoler's Diary* (CRO Acc. 4916), 11 September 1850 et seq. Journeys were not always so quick; one in May of the same year by the steam packet took ten days (Ibid., 4 May 1850 et seq).

41. CRO QS Box 1. Much ale and "grog" was taken on this trip!

42. It must be conceded that there is no apparent growth in the proportion of "outsiders" jailed for felony in the period examined. Jones *Rebecca's Children*, (162 et seq.) posits a largely local origin of crime in the first half of the century, though he cites only one year of the register evidence. His observation about the difference between "isolated country districts" and the towns (p. 164) should be noted, however, as should his observations on the changes witnessed in the second half of the century (see chap. 7).

43. CRO *F.R.* 1216 (29 November 1867). The governor remarks, "Can only speak French, sent to French Consulate, Swansea."

44. CRO *F.R.* 1044 (24 September 1864).

45. CRO *F.R.* 254, 485, 534 (Charles Brown, no place of birth recorded), 535 (Samuel Welsh, born in "Poland, Dantzic"), and 536 (Christian Johnson, born in "Denmark"). These last three were sailors charged with robbing a wrecked vessel.

46. CRO *F.R.* 888 (George Davies, a railway labourer whose place of birth is recorded as "supposed at sea"), 1360, 1379 (these latter two were sailors).

47. CRO *F.R.* 140, 232, 332 (James Lewis, or "Jemmy Llawen"), 615, 633 ("now on ticket of leave"), 658, 832, 1076 ("John Phillips"), 1078, 1081.

48. CRO *F.R.* 615.

49. CRO *F.R.* 1164.

50. See, for example, a prisoner of 1869 who appears in the register (no. 1272) simply as Jane Kelly. On the indictment, however, she is named as "Anne Miller, otherwise Jane Kelly, otherwise Anne O'Brian." The indictment also records a felony conviction against her in the borough of Aberystwyth in neighboring Cardiganshire in the previous year. (Indictment of 12 November 1869, in CRO QS Box 12.)

51. CRO *F.R.* 332 and also 68 and 72.

52. See the aliases kept by P. C. Williams' Diary 1859–60 (CRO Mus 113), at the rear of which he records a "List of Persons of Suspicious Characters with their Names and Aliases and Residences and Remarks Alphabetically." The record is obviously linked to the new series of Criminal Statistics dating from 1857. See Radzinowicz and Hood, *History*, 98.

53. CRO *F.R.* 708.

54. *Carmarthen Journal*, 19 March 1858.

55. For Bramwell see Wiener, *Reconstructing the Criminal*, 88–89.

56. Supra, n. 54.

57. For these early cases, see Bernard V. Heathcote and Pauline F. Heathcote, "The Custodial Photograph," in *Shadow and Substance: Essays on the History of Photography in Honour of Henry K. Henisch*, ed. Kathleen Collins (Michigan, 1990), 115–17.

58. For France (1841), see Heathcote and Heathcote, "Custodial Photogra-

phy," 115, for Switzerland (1852), see Camfield Wills and Deidre Wills, *History of Photography: Techniques and Equipment* (London, 1980), 142.

59. James Gardner, *CC* 3590. See generally Gardner's evidence, paras. 3582–95, and note his use of the apparatus for "those whom we do not know, railway thieves and strangers to the city, who are taken up for picking pockets at the railway stations and in railway carriages" (*CC* 3584). S. McConville, *Local Prisons*, 177, nn. 112, 128, 135.

60. Sir W. Crofton, *CC* 3246.

61. Stephen's *inter alia* was using the newer "true" photographs rather than daguerrotypes. McConville, *Local Prisons*, 128, n. 135 refers to the role of prison inspectors in spreading Gardner's idea.

62. CRO *F.R.* 1076.

63. CRO *F.R.* 1173.

64. CRO *F.R.* 1133. For an interesting exploration of the relationship between the Gothic form and "scientific" criminological record, see Robert Mighall, "The Brigand in the Laboratory: The Strange Haunting of Nineteenth-Century Medico-Legal Discourse," *Cambrian Law Review* 24 (1993): 45–58.

65. J. G. Perry, *CC* 768, cf. Anon "Photography: Its History and Applications," *British Quarterly Review* 88 (1866): 379. "Written descriptions were rarely found sufficiently precise for identification."

66. See, for example, the remarks of the governor of Maidstone, Major C. W. Bannister *CC* 4405–72. See McConville, *Local Prisons*, 393. For Du Cane's views on the procedure and its defects see ibid., 397–99.

67. *Gaolers Diary*, 4 January 1847.

68. See the remarks of the governor of Petworth, W. Linton, which refer to a warder being 3/-out of pocket (*CC* 4276), and cf the views of Governors Musson (1863–70), Shepherd (3157–62), and Bannister (4405–10). See also McConville, *Local Prisons*, 399.

69. *Parliamentary Debates*, House of Commons, 4 August 1869, paras. 1276–77.

70. Quoted in Philip Priestley, *Victorian Prison Lives* (London, 1985), 12.

71. *Kirkdale Gaol: Twelve Months Imprisonment of a Manchester Merchant*, quoted in priestley, *Prison Lives*, 12.

72. Edward Shepherd, *CC* 3152.

73. Ibid., 3144–52.

74. This was the practice at Pentonville in the 1880s. See the illustrations in David Hawkings, *Criminal Ancestors* (Stroud, 1992), 232.

75. Bedford Record Office, QGV 10/4. Hereafter Bedford Gaol Book.

76. *CC* 4277.

77. Frederick H. Wines, *Punishment and Reformation* (Boston, 1895), 239–40. Wines does note the identificatory value of tattoos in case of death, ibid., 238. Stevenson, *Criminal Class*, 361 takes "B.C." to mean "Before Convicted," but Governor Linton in 1863 seems to understand it as "Bad Character," *CC* 4277.

78. *CC* 3596, cf. the views of other witnesses to the committee, paras. 1294–1318 (Jebb), 2363–2387 (Everest), 3145–3152 (Shepherd), 4277–4280 (Linton), 4558 (Keene), 4951–57 (Colvill).

79. Quoted in James Greenwood, *The Seven Curses of London* (1869; reprint

Oxford, 1981), 62. The book was written while the Habitual Criminals Bill was being debated.

80. Greenwood, *Seven Curses*, 62–63.

81. 26 & 27 Vict. c.44, see Radzinowicz and Hood, *History*, 692–93. Note the condemnation of branding in France in 1832 as the "odious debris of barbarism," Peter Gay, *The Cultivation of Hatred* (London, 1994), 143.

82. The description given to the camera, "an angel copier; a God-like machine of which light and sunshine is the animating Promethean fire," in (1859) *Journal of the Photographic Society*, quoted in Christopher Pinney, "The Parallel Histories of Anthropology and Photography," in *Anthropology and Photography*, ed. Elizabeth Edwards (London, 1992), 74.

83. CC 1319.

84. *Report*, XV.2.

85. Cf. Foucault, *Discipline and Punish*, 203.

86. Roger Smith, *Trial by Medicine* (Edinburgh, 1981), 41.

87. Edwards, *Photography*, 4.

88. Anon., "Photography: Its History and Applications," 379.

89. Sir John Bowring, "The Proper Purpose of Prison Discipline" in Wines, ed., *Transactions*, 92.

90. Luke O. Pike, *A History of Crime in England* (1873–76; reprint Montclair, 1968), vol. 2, 467. Note also Charles Dickens' observations in *Barnaby Rudge* (1851) (Harmondsworth, 1973 ed.), 177, about the danger of unlit streets in former times. It is unfortunately not possible within the scope of this paper to pursue the neglected connection adverted to by Bowring between the rise of photography and the construction and ultimate demolition of a discourse of positivist criminology. It is, I think, significant that Lombrosianism should have its *origin*, as well as its decline in the age of photography. On this see Allan Sekula, "The Body and the Archive," in *The Contest of Meaning: Critical Histories of Photography*, ed. Richard Bolton (Cambridge, Mass., 1989), 342–89. I became aware of this interesting piece only after this paper had been accepted for publication. Contrast Radzinowicz and Hood, *History*, 262. The use of photography in anthropology is also a significant parallel that merits further discussion than is possible here.

91. Foucault, *Discipline and Punish*, 187, and see also the observations relating photography to this argument in Pinney "Parallel Histories," 76.

92. CC 3954.

93. *Report* of Governor Roberts, 16 October 1860, Bedford RO:QGR 1/43.

94. Anon., "Photography," 382–83.

95. See Robert L. Stevenson's comment on Dr. Jekyll's (and science's) criminal alter ego: "He had never been photographed; and the few who could describe him differed widely, as common observers will," *The Strange Case of Dr. Jekyll and Mr. Hyde* (1886) (Ware, 1993 ed.), 21. On criminal photography and the detective novel see now Ronald M. Thomas, "Making Darkness Visible: Capturing the Criminal and Observing the Law in Victorian Photography and Detective Fiction," in *Victorian Literature and the Victorian Visual Imagination*, ed. Carol T. Christ and John O. Jordan (Berkely, 1995), 134–69, which was published after this chapter had been accepted for publication.

96. Bedford Gaol Book no. 109, 23 December 1865.

97. Bedford Gaol Book no. 125, 30 December 1865. For the account of Roberts' actions see *The Bedfordshire Mercury*, 17 March 1866.

98. One source records the dissection of the eyes of a Whitechapel "Ripper" victim for this purpose. Lionel Rose, *Crime and Punishment* (London, 1977), 70.

99. Reverend John Clay, in Walter L. Clay, *The Prison Chaplain, Memoirs of the Reverend John Clay* (1861), quoted in Michael Ignatieff, *A Just Measure of Pain* (Harmondsworth, 1989), 197–98.

100. Davitt, *Prison Diary*, xii.

101. See e.g., Bedford Gaol Book no. 157, 28 January 1868; and no. 184, 8 February 1872.

102. See e.g., Bedford Gaol Book no. 72, 22 March 1864, James Knapton, alias "Spencer" alias "Madge."

103. See e.g., the illustration in Richard Whitmore, *Victorian and Edwardian Crime and Punishment from Old Photographs* (London, 1978), no.11.

104. Roberts, *Report, supra*, n.94.

105. 32 & 33 Vict.c.99. For habitual criminals legislation generally, see Radzinowicz and Hood, "Habitual Criminal," and for a detailed investigation of its working see Stevenson, *Criminal Class*. Space forbids discussion of other material from around the same period that is significant in the context of the arguments advanced in my argument, in particular the "individualization" of prostitutes under the Contagious Diseases Acts and the increasing use of photography with respect to young offenders (see e.g., the admission registers of Calder Farm Reformatory School, using photographs from 1871, Wakefield R.O. RTI/73) and in the records of Dr. Barnardo from 1874 onward (Stevenson, *Criminal Class*, 401).

106. Earl of Kimberley, *Parliamentary Debates* (H.L.), 26 February 1869–338.

107. Ibid., 341.

108. s.8. For a recognition of the fact that photography was an alternative to "dogging" by the police, see Sir Walter Crofton, *CC* 3252. Note also the fascinating case from as early as 1824 that involved the precursor of photography, the Camera Obscura, through the instrumentality of which a pickpocket apparently had been apprehended in Glasgow. The device was commended as a supervisory agent. "By this means, the necessity of sending out emissaries to reconnoitre the conduct of the lieges would be superseded, since everything would then take place, as it were, under the eyes of the police." *The Glasgow Mechanics Magazine*, no. xxxii, as quoted in *Pandemonium 1660–1886*, ed. Humphrey Jennings (London, 1985), 164.

109. Circular of 30 November 1869, CRO.QS Box 12.

110. Circular, 9 February 1870, P.R.O., HO/158/8, 8459 OC.

111. Circular 9 May 1870, P.R.O., HO/158/8, 8549 OC. The circular provides, "I am . . . to request that the Photographs to be supplied may be Album Portraits, 3¼ inches long, 2½ inches wide (assuming the Prisoner to be seated) and show the figure to the knees and that the measurement of the face may be nearly one inch long. It is desirable also that Prisoners should wear their own clothes when their likennesses [*sic*] are taken."

112. 34 & 35 Vict.c.112, for Morley's comment see second reading in the House of Lords, 4 July 1871, *Parliamentary Debates*, 1082.

113. The Carmarthen bench gave Stephens £10. His actual expenditure had been £8 on the camera and a "glass house" he had erected to take the pictures. The Inspector of Prisons had approved of Stephens' photographs, though the ones he

retained were not in the form specified by the Home Office Circular (*supra* note 111). See *The Welshman*, 21 October 1870: 5 and *The Carmarthen Journal*, 21 October 1870: 5. For Roberts see the praise displayed at Quarter Sessions, *Bedfordshire Mercury*, 4 July 1859. For the grant of £20 for past expenses and £7 per year subsequently and the sum of up to £25 for the construction of a room for the purpose see the Quarter Sessions minutes for Easter 1861 (Bedford R.O. QSM 1861, 153). The notorious parsimony of the Carmarthenshire Bench is eloquently attested by the disparity.

114. Crofton, CC 3246.

115. "One governor informs us that he generally contrives that the operation shall take place just before dinner, and refractory sitters are informed that no dinner will be dispensed until the portrait has been obtained, a practical argument, the force of which is generally recognised." Anon., "Photography," 381.

116. Ibid., and see Gardner, CC 3592.

117. See the picture reproduced in Whitmore, *Crime and Punishment no. 10.* The legality of force was addressed after the report of a Committee on Identification of Habitual Criminals in 1894, see McConville, *Local Prisons*, 408, n.62.

118. *Crime: The Autobiography of a Crook* (1928), quoted in Priestley, *Prison Lives*, 14. Such facial contortion formed the subject matter of the early short film, *Photographing a Female Crook*, shot in New York on 13 January 1904, as was the similar *A Subject for the Rogues Gallery.* See Jay Leydon, ed., *Before Hollywood* (New York, 1987), 127. I am indebted to Robert Ireland for this cinematographic reference.

119. See Radzinowicz and Hood, *History* 262–63; Stevenson, *Criminal Class*, chap. 2, and note his comment on p. 127: "Before the age of the finger print, the criminal registry remained a philosopher's stone for certain penal and judicial 'alchemists' in search of order."

120. *A. Bertillon's Instructions for Taking Descriptions for the Identification of Criminals and Others by the Means of Anthropometric Indications*, trans. G. Muller (Chicago, 1889), 6.

121. See the preface to the *Register of Habitual Criminals England and Wales.* The quotations here appear in the extant copies in Carmarthenshire Record Office for the years 1889 and 1891, CRO CDX 243. For a full discussion of the problems and later history, see McConville, *Local Prisons*, 393–408.

"Private Policing and the Workplace": The Worsted Committee and the Policing of Labor in Northern England, 1840–1880

Barry Godfrey

'Thah lives like a lord o' the fat o' the land
An wod giv nowt but skilly to a poor fact'ry 'and;—
Nowt but skilly an bran, and t'ahse o' correction;
An that comes o' thee an thi wark ov inspection—
Poor kimmers and weyvers—tha'd starve 'em to deeath
An if thah could help it, they muddent ev breeath.
Ah knaw thee ov old. Ah sal allus hate thee,
For t'troubles tha's browt on mi naybors an me.'
—John Room, Worsted Inspector, mid–nineteenth century.[1]

In recent years, historians and social scientists have begun to emphasize the episodic nature of publicly funded police forces, with the inference that the private organization of policing will prove more durable than publicly funded organization.[2] Indeed, the modern constabulary is now viewed by some as merely a lengthy "experiment" in public policing that is now returning again to the "traditional" organization of prosecution and apprehension forces that operated before the New Police. As Nigel South said in 1987, "The modern police are indeed a"new police" and in some important respects it is they and not the modern phenomena of agencies within the private security sector that are out of step with the historical lineage of policing forms."[3] By this he meant that the borough and county police forces created in the nineteenth century were only the most recent option in a wide range of policing services. This range of control agencies included the borough watches, poor law officers, and inspectors of nuisances and factories in the public sector and the many subscription-funded policing agencies in the private sector.[4] The most important of these policing options for textile employers was the Worsted Committee and their Inspectorate.[5]

In examining this particular agency, this chapter will challenge some established theories concerning the emergence of the New Police in Yorkshire and analyze the relationship between public and private policing in the mid– to late nineteenth century. Specifically, this chapter will pose four questions. First, how was the Worsted Inspectorate organized in the West Riding, and how did it operate in a way that enabled it to curb appropriation from the factory? Furthermore, what was the interaction and relationship between the "official" police forces and the Inspectorate, and how did this change over the 1840–80 period?

The history of the Worsted Inspectorate in this period falls into two distinct phases. The first period stretches from 1840 to the midcentury, when the factory system was thriving in parts of the West Riding and increasingly appeared to be the dominant production system for the textile industries. In 1853, the Worsted Inspectorate underwent substantial organizational changes in response to a financial crisis that engendered a period where the Worsted Inspectorate operated at a reduced level. This phase ended in 1870, when the Inspectorate was reanimated by the employers in response to their self-perceived needs and fears. This chapter will examine the reasons for the 1870 renaissance and, indeed, follow the progress of the Inspectorate from 1840 to 1880.

In 1777, when the Worsted Acts were passed, a regulated system of peripatetic inspectors was seen by manufacturers as necessary for the control of embezzlement among unsupervised domestic workers. When the factory system developed and spatially dispersed employees were gathered together in centralized production areas complete with a supervisory staff to guard against fraud, the *raison d'être* of the committee seemed to have been removed. From the study of Worsted Committee records, it is apparent that the Inspectorate in the nineteenth century was not merely a superfluous relic of an "under-policed" society. How could it be when between 1844 and 1876 it forwarded approximately 3,000 cases to the West Riding courts?[6]

Although the Worsted Acts covered Lancashire and Cheshire as well as Yorkshire, the Inspectorate was mainly active in the West Riding and the worsted producing regions of the Pennines. Each of these districts was patrolled by an inspector who reported his actions at each quarterly meeting of the committee, which also checked the accuracy of the inspector's recording of prosecutions and convictions. The caution shown toward the entries in the inspectors' books was due to the misbehavior of the inspectors in the eighteenth and early nineteenth centuries, who had made false entries to boost their conviction rates.[7] By 1840, however, there had been a conscious effort to raise the standards of behavior in, and the standards of entry to, the Inspectorate, and inspectors who made false entries or were slack in their duties could be suspended by the member of the committee responsible for his district. This effort to increase the internal discipline of the organization was largely successful and aided by the high salaries offered. The raising of the inspectors' salary to the equivalent of a chief constable's wage in 1852, for example, enabled the committee to recruit a higher caliber of candidate than ever before.[8]

Notwithstanding the high salaries, some inspectors in this period left to join the borough and county police forces, as it was a more secure and pensioned occupation,[9] and a few higher ranked policemen journeyed in the opposite direction to join the Inspectorate.[10] This was inevitable, as the two agencies recruited from the same pool of labor and appointed similar types of men. Both agencies attracted men, throughout the period, who were able to perform detective duties in the field and to act as prosecutors on behalf of victims in the court rooms. However, aspects of this part of their role sometimes were challenged. For example, the legitimacy of an inspector to act as both witness and prosecutor was challenged by a defendant's advocate in 1844. The advocate stated that the bench would never consent for an attorney's clerk to conduct a case, and they should not allow the prosecutor's servant to act as witness, prosecutor, and advocate for the prosecution case. The magistrates discounted this view and directed the case to proceed but were further interrupted by a senior lawyer who was in the court at the time. He asserted his opinion that the defending advocate was correct in the first instance, and the inspector was ordered to leave the court. Extraordinarily, it appears from the press report that the bench then acted as surrogate prosecuting advocates.[11] Criticism was brushed aside, however, and the inspectors continued their practice of acting as both witness and prosecutor unabated, but professional counsel were also employed by the committee.

Outside the courtroom, the operation of the Inspectorate in the mid– to late nineteenth century "in the field" remained unchanged in many respects from that of the late eighteenth century. Since appropriated cloth often was stored temporarily in a worker's house or shed before being sold or was used by the worker to decorate or repair his household furnishings, the homes of factory workers were searched as assiduously in this period as the houses and workshops of domestic workers had been. Inspectors had merely to obtain a warrant signed by two magistrates before searching the house of a suspect, often accompanied by police officers and the suspect's employer.

The inspectors also continued to have few dealings with the direct supervision of the production process, although they often placed agents inside the works in order to gain information.[12] Only once was an inspector recorded as acting as an agent himself. For obvious reasons, inspectors took every effort to conceal their operational methods, and this case only came to light because of a very public denunciation of this method of detection by a prominent employer. Inspector Yewdall's decision to act as a "spy" inside Lister's Mill was bitterly criticized in court by Mr. Murgatroyd, the defending advocate. His criticism was rebutted in the correspondence column of the *Bradford Observer*. "If Mr. Murgatroyd," wrote the clerk to the committee, "would only tell our detectives how to discover offenders without using vulgar espionage, they would no doubt be duly grateful." Yewdall went on to say that the employer "ought to know as a magistrate that detectives must use various means to discover the tricks of thieves, both wholesale and retail, and he knows that I got most of my information from his own men."[13]

Agents also were placed in locations frequented by workmen and where appropriators sold or exchanged "stolen" goods. Inspectors were, therefore, keen to find informers who worked in public houses. It is not clear whether such persons would exchange information for money on an ad hoc basis, or whether a more formal relationship existed as an inspector's report that "an eating house keeper has been working under my instructions for two months endeavouring to catch a party in this neighbourhood" implies.[14]

If many of the inspectors' operational methods remained unchanged, the rise of the factory system, however, did introduce one major change in their modus operandi. The organization of the factory introduced a physical point at which searches could be conducted, and offenders apprehended—the factory gate. Surprisingly perhaps, only a seventh of the searchers conducted by the Worsted Inspector and/or a constable that led to prosecution took place at the factory gate[15] (although this would have been the most beneficial place in terms of the prosecution proving an intent to steal in any subsequent court case). Nevertheless, the proportion of people apprehended at the gate together with those apprehended inside the premises (50 percent) makes it clear that the factory authority structure and physical organization did allow for the successful apprehension of appropriators. The authority of the foreman, and his subsequent testimony in court, was obviously sufficient to override the problem of whether appropriated property could be said to have been "stolen" if it had not left the premises.

The factory system, with its physical control on the entry and exit of personnel, altered both the physical point and also the point on the route to court at which the policing agencies were introduced to control appropriation, and the Inspectorate adopted a more reactive than proactive stance. The speculative searching of houses and the regular checks on the wares of waste dealers continued and yielded good results, but in many cases the initiation of action now came at the request of the foreman, who was of course the head of the internal supervisory structure. As quarter sessions show, the workers who were arrested inside or just outside their workplace, were usually first questioned by the foreman, and only later questioned and arrested by a police officer.[16] Petty sessions records, had they survived, may have indicated a greater involvement by the inspector in the arrest. Quarter sessions depositions can overemphasize the role of the police officer, since the constables always provide a witness statement and are not shy of outlining their involvement to the exclusion of other interested parties. Even so, the witnesses mentioned that the inspector was present at the arrest of the suspect in 20 percent of cases, and involved in questioning the suspect after his/her arrest in 29 percent of the cases at quarter sessions between 1840–45, and although in the 1870–75 period the inspector only apprehended 4 percent of the suspects, in 45 percent of cases an inspector and constable worked together to apprehend offenders.

If the inspector was not involved either in the detection process or the arrest of the suspect, he was still integral to the decision to prosecute. By using his specialist knowledge and experience of the legal system through interviewing the suspect, the inspector assessed the likelihood of conviction and could advise the employer as to whether a prosecution should be prepared. Such advice was welcome. The laws that could be applied to appropriation were numerous, detailed, and intricate.[17] Thus legal opinion sometimes was sought even by the committee to clarify points of law or in order to prepare test cases to establish a legal precedent.[18] Inspectors, too, mindful of their conviction rates, sometimes decided that cases that were too complicated could be abandoned. For example, the employee who was found with 260 bobbins in his house declared he was keeping them back until he received his wages. His employer, who had already had the man in court once and now was being sued for false imprisonment, admitted owing him wages but wished him locked up regardless. The inspector clearly did not relish having this intricate and confused case on his hands, and he gladly entered in his ledger that he had withdrawn from the case.[19]

This example does not prove a general rule. Inspectors were not eager to exercise their own discretion. Although they occasionally withdrew from cases, they were anxious to emphasize that all of the suspects they caught would be charged. Indeed, the prosecution procedure was initiated even if the evidence against the accused was inconclusive. This served two purposes. First, by uniformly prosecuting those they suspected they hoped to avoid accusations of corruption. Turning a blind eye in return for small bribes must have been both an ever present temptation for inspectors and a constant concern of the committee.

Second, the suspect had time, while awaiting trial, to settle with his employer and recompense the committee's expenses, and thus the intention to prosecute offenders where the evidence was insufficient to gain a conviction became a device to raise revenue.[20] Cases sometimes were delayed in order that the offender could raise the money by selling furniture or receiving help from relatives, either to settle with his employer, or to pay the twenty-pound fine when convicted. The committee had no wish to see the offender languish in jail when he could become a source of revenue through the reallocation of a proportion of the fine to its coffers.

The committee was able to wage war against appropriation because it could call on a variety of financial sources. The committee was funded mainly by a tax remittance on the soap duty paid by manufacturers.[21] A considerable amount of soap was used in the preparatory processes of cloth production, such as scouring and willying, and as a concession to manufacturers the government allowed them to draw back a third of all duty paid. The Worsted Committee was entitled to a portion of this drawback, which remained a major contribution to the committee's finances until 1853.[22] Three other sources of revenue existed—the share dividends from investments they made in the Leeds to Liverpool Canal Company,[23] from the sale of seized goods that were believed to be embezzled but were unclaimed by the owner[24] (although this never amounted to a significant sum), and a proportion of any fine imposed on convicted embezzlers by the magistrates up to ten pounds. Before 1784, the cost of the prosecution was borne by the individual inspector, and his costs were reimbursed out of the fine imposed. This system was changed when the committee realized that the inspectors were only prosecuting cases when conviction was certain. Thereafter, the costs of the prosecution were paid by the committee. Of the committee's portion, a certain amount was passed to the successful inspector. Therefore, when Inspector Kaye stated at Huddersfield petty sessions that "he had no pecuniary interest in the convictions as he uniformly handed over the penalties he received . . . to the treasurer of the Association,"[25] he was only telling half the truth.

As is the case today, financial limits controlled the level of police action, and the committee was keen to preserve and expand all of their sources of income. Accordingly, their services were advertized in the *Bradford Observer, Leeds Mercury, Manchester Guardian*, and newspapers in other textile areas. The clerk of the committee also sent details of successful prosecutions to the local newspapers (if they had not sent a reporter to the court that day) to ensure that they were published, especially if the case established a precedent, illuminated the scale of appropriation, or revealed a new method of embezzlement that would worry employers into calling in an inspector to investigate possible frauds. The reporting of the inspectors' successes helped to maintain a consensus that manufacturers should continue to fund the committee's activities. Furthermore, any case that resulted in a severe penalty could be used as a warning to the workpeople, as is made explicit in this entry from the Worsted Committee Minute Book: "In the conviction which was for taking Rovings from the Mill where she had been working and knitting stockings with the same, I collected sufficient evidence to make a case of Felony against her and she having several former convictions proved against her the court ordered her to be kept in penal servitude for seven years. I then consulted as to the desirability of giving publicity to this case in the newspapers in order to deter others from doing the same."[26] These advertisements served to make the Inspectorate well known to workers and employers alike, and the range and extent of their activities made them an obvious choice for manufacturers who wished to control or eliminate appropriation. The committee encouraged this view by delineating clearly its area of jurisdiction and expertise. By concentrating its operations within well-defined geographical and legal areas, it established a moral authority in pressing its right to police the industry, and was able to dissuade other agencies from interfering. For example, when the Silk Trade Protection Society wrote to the committee in 1852, offering to co-join in prosecutions where the inspector found silk mixed with other purloined materials, the expenses of the cases being shared, it received a courteous but dismissive reply. This compact with a fellow trade prosecution agency would have been profitable, especially in the western regions where cotton and silk production existed alongside that of worsted, but the committee resented the *lese majesty* of the Lancastrian society, and this led it to reject the proposed plan.

Besides other nascent trade policing organizations, the borough and county police were also held at bay, though this was an easy task, at least until the mid-1850s. The 1838 guidelines issued to the Leeds borough police talked of patrolling streets, thoroughfares, and houses. The factory was not suggested as an area that needed supervision. It remained the duty of a constable to arrest anyone he saw committing or suspected of having committed a felony. Appropriation, however, mostly occurred within the workplace, and while inside the factory, an offender was unlikely to be caught red-handed by a passing bobby. Indeed, the constable was unlikely to have the right to freely patrol inside the factory perimeter fence. A number of the Bradford chief constable's reports, for example, stated that the police had no responsibility for the numerous thefts taking place in the warehouses and manufacturies, since they had no right of access. Bradford's chief constable blamed the robberies on the inattention of factory supervisory staff and suggested that the responsibility for catching the perpetrators lay with private security forces and not his men.[27] The police officer was unlikely to be involved in the detection of theft within the factory and was only called upon to exercise the power of arrest at the instigation of the foreman or Worsted Inspector.[28]

Until the midcentury, the Worsted Inspectorate was indisputably the main force for combating illegal appropriation. Aside from relying on the police to arrest offenders, it remained the supreme external agency for the control of embezzlement. However, in 1853, the number of general inspectors was reduced from eight to three, and by 1859 there remained but one inspector in service. This situation did not arise because the factory had eradicated fraud or because the practice of illegal appropriation had ended, "on which distant day," Heaton speculated, "lawyers, magistrates and worsted inspectors may find their occupations gone."[29] The committee was forced to cut back on its activities, not because the need for their services had disappeared, but due to a financial crisis.

The committee had used its influence with Parliament to maintain, and periodically increase, the allowance for drawback, which was the life blood of the committee. That life blood was drained away by the Chancellor of the Exchequer, William Gladstone. The government in which he served had pledged to repeal the drawback on soap, and this they did in July 1853.[30] The consequences of Gladstone's budget appeared to be catastrophic and prompted inquiry as to whether the committee could continue its work. The decision to go on turned on the fact that they considered "the new improved system of Police insufficient for enforcing the Worsted Act,"[31] and it was decided that rationalization and cost cutting would ensure the committee's survival to continue working at a more circumspect level.

Rather belatedly, the committee had foreseen the possibility of the withdrawal of soap drawback and had hastily attempted to preempt the revenue crisis by attracting many new subscribers. Handbills and statements were issued, and inspectors visited manufacturers to advertise their services and attract new patrons.[32] The recruitment of new members was slow work, however, and the committee was never again fully able to police the districts as they had in the 1840s and early 1850s.

Why did the manufacturers not make financial provision for the Worsted Inspectors to continue their work after the drawback remission was withdrawn? If the Worsted Committee were so influential in protesting their interests, why did the manufacturers not pay voluntarily what had previously been involuntary—a levy or subscription? The answer lies in the principle of collective security. Out of the money due to the manufacturers as a rebate on their soap duty, the treasury kept back a proportion that was sent directly to the committee. Heaton explained the utility of a policing system funded in this manner: "All masters who prepared their wool for weaving were affected by this drawback, but at the same time all were to benefit by the activities of the worsted inspectors. Therefore let the cost of the police system be defrayed out of the drawback which the clothiers received. This was the arrangement established by the Worsted Act."[33]

Manufacturers were unwilling to fund a policing system that was provided for the benefit of all, but not funded by all that benefited. Many of the larger employers believed that smaller-sized competitors were able to undercut them by buying cheaper (embezzled) raw materials. For the smaller manufacturer, this could be the only advantage it had over its large specialized and mechanized neighbors. It was, therefore, not in the interests of every manufacturer to subscribe to the committee.

The reduction of the Inspectorate and the withdrawal of the inspectors from various areas in 1853 had left something of a vacuum. Ready to step into the space were the borough police forces. However, as will be seen, they were only willing to partially fill the void.

The Bradford borough force was established in 1848, some years after the Leeds force had been formed in 1836.[34] Both borough forces grew rapidly, as did their reputation for efficiency,[35] and by the late 1850s they were confident enough in their field of operations to launch an offensive against "every species of ruffianism," dog-fighters, prize fights, street games, prostitution, and pawnbrokers.[36] The pursual of workplace appropriators would not have been out of keeping with this moral crusade. However, if the inspectors had left the field, the police forces were disinclined to pick up their swords. As before, they rarely involved themselves with appropriators while they remained within the factory unless they were called in by the foreman or Worsted Inspector to exercise the power of arrest. The police simply lacked the expertise and inclination to usurp the Worsted Inspectorate's specialist policing functions.

It may be that appropriation continued unhindered by the attentions of the lawful authorities, or, alternately, that the factory system gradually but steadily reduced the amount of embezzlement due to strong internal controls. In any case, the Inspectorate was not reanimated until 1870, when its role was extended from one primarily dealing with appropriation to one that encompassed appropriation, work discipline matters, and other duties on behalf of the employers. The duties performed by inspectors between 1870 and 1880 need not concern us here, and will be considered only insofar as they affected the relationship between the police and the Inspectorate.

On 23 June 1870, the leading manufacturers in the West Riding met to discuss the possibility of reestablishing the Worsted Committee by raising regular subscriptions from manufacturers and employing two more inspectors.[37] This section explores two possible reasons why the employers breathed new life into the Worsted Committee at this time. The first possibility is that the manufacturing elite perceived a general and relative decline in the level of policing in the West Riding, and that they took steps to bolster the agents of order in the manufacturing districts.

In the late 1860s and early 1870s, many new mill chimneys were seen on the West Riding skyline, and the new factories brought thousands of new workers into the industrial townships. Were the police facing a crime wave resulting from the increase in population that prevented them from patrolling the manufacturing districts effectively?

The Bradford police statistics indicate that the numbers of those prosecuted summarily escalated from 2,000 in 1867 to 3,400 in 1870; mainly these were cases of vagrancy and drunkenness.[38] This is a prestigious rise of 70 percent over three years, especially given that the numbers of policemen employed in Bradford rose by 16.4 percent between 1869 and 1870, and similarly, the Leeds force only increased by 16 percent over the same period. However, it has already been established that the police had a limited role in the control of embezzlement, and the manufacturers agitated for more Worsted Inspectors, not policemen, so it appears that the elite industrial class of Bradford had no *extraordinary* fears about lawlessness in the borough at this time. They may have been concerned about vagrancy, burglary, and drunkenness, but their concern did not translate into agitation for reform of the police, increased men on the beat, or a call for police to patrol inside factory perimeters. The manufacturers seem to have been responding to a different need in calling the Worsted Committee again to arms.

The second reason why employers may have wished to reanimate the Worsted Committee is that economic conditions in the 1870s prompted the manufacturers to take action, both to preserve profits and to minimalize losses. A natural enough reaction to a period of trade depression, but was there also an intent to defeat labor militancy in the boom years?

As Karl Ittmann noted "From 1850 to 1872, the number of powerlooms in the Bradford district increased by almost 120 percent and the number of spindles by over 140 percent and entrepreneurs constructed more than 1,000 mills and warehouses in the borough. The mid-Victorian era was a golden one for textile manufacturers. Between 1856 and 1867, the level of assessed profits in Bradford shot up 250 percent."[39] The good times did not end there, with the period between 1868 and 1873 being particularly rosy. This made the following slump seem both unexpected and severe. From 1873 through to the early 1880s, the worsted trade experienced a deep and profound depression due to the increased competition from woolen manufacturers. A fall in the price of wool had made woolen products affordable to more people, and the demand for worsted products dried up. Manufacturers, as they had always done under the "Bradford system," attempted to minimalize lost profits by shedding labor, reducing wages, using cheaper materials, and promoting tighter work discipline among the workforce.

The extreme periods of fast economic growth (1868–73) and contraction (1873–80) had many implications for the relationship between Capital and Labor. In the boom period, workers were better able to negotiate wage increases, for example. If wage demands were not met, employees were able to find employment easily at another mill. Accordingly, the manufacturers' attempts to use master and servant, and threat and persuasion, to keep their employees from being tempted away by other millowners were unsuccessful, and many workers left to take better-paid jobs with rival manufacturers. At the same time the manufacturers were faced with wage claims by those workers that remained, which were increasingly being articulated through trade society mouthpieces. Although the worsted and especially the woolen industries had been retarded in their growth of workers' collective organizations, several societies came into being in the 1860s and 1870s that represented the skilled and supervisory workers.[40]

The hegemonic control over employees that had long been exercised by the Bradford manufacturers therefore was being challenged by intraindustry competition for labor, rising prices, and the challenge of organized labor. The employers' reaction was twofold: First, they formed employers' societies that would oppose by common cause the demands of the nascent trade unions,[41] and second, they turned again to the Worsted Committee as an effective power for the enforcement of contractual obligation, as much as for the control of appropriation. It was to this end that manufacturers met to reanimate the "sleepy" if not yet "sleeping" giant.

After 1870 the committee reestablished its authority over the detection and prosecution of suspected embezzlers, not that this authority had been challenged seriously by the police force.[42] The borough police forces and the committee consciously redefined their roles, confirming that felony cases and embezzlement cases were dealt with separately by the respective forces. This separation of duties was strictly enforced on the committee's side, and even the suggestion that inspectors were involved in cases where the Worsted Acts could not be applied was quickly pounced upon. Yewdall, for instance, was censured for stating in his report that he had not convicted anyone of "felony."[43] He quickly explained that, "Whenever I get any such information I at once report such cases to the Chief Constable or Superintendent of Police where they properly belong,"[44] and by so assiduously moving such cases over to the police, the inspectors were able to regain their moral authority to root out appropriation.[45]

The new inspectors hired by the committee, however, were not of the same quality as those of the earlier period, and lower salaries reintroduced the temptation of corruption—embezzling subscription money or accepting bribes from apprehended suspects, for example.[46] As the older inspectors left or died off, the Inspectorate became a deprofessionalized force, much to the exasperation of longer-time servers. The difference in quality between the old and new Inspectorate became evident in its work. As previously stated, the inspectors had always been responsible for presenting the prosecution's case in the courts. This situation, which in itself had been barely tolerated by the legal profession, was now made almost impossible by the low caliber of the new inspectors. The defending solicitor who described a new Worsted Inspector as "a man having been appointed to an office for which he appeared not to have the slightest personal ability or qualification" was wrong, however. The inspector *was* qualified to bring suspects to trial but not to conduct the prosecution with all the intricate legal knowledge that required.

If the inspectors were of less use in the courtroom, they became more useful as enforcers of work discipline within the factory. As part of their role as a general "employers' protection service" they performed several types of duty. First, they prevented the free movement of labor and attempted to dissuade employees from initiating industrial action: "Many petty disputes between Employed and Employer most especially between weavers in most of which my explanation of the Laws and gentle persuasion have had the desired effect."[47] Where gentle persuasion or intimidation did not work and industrial action could not be avoided, the inspectors would summon the strikers for neglecting their work. Notices were sent out first by the committee to the workers who had made themselves absent, informing them of the penalties of infringing the Worsted Act clause regarding "neglect."[48] When they did not return to the factory, prosecutions followed.[49] In the case of walkouts or strikes, only the spokesmen needed to be threatened with legal proceedings for the point to be made to the mass of the strikers. "I put an end to a strike at Shaws," boasted one inspector, "by serving twenty of the leaders with notices to complete work, consequently 350 returned to work."[50] When faced with such evidence, it is easy to understand the huge impact the Worsted Acts and their enforcers could have on industrial relations in the textile areas.

A second duty performed on behalf of the employers was the defense of their subscribers in court actions. One of the first cases fought by Inspector Yewdall after the committee was reborn involved the successful defense of a manufacturer in a claim for wages he owed to a worker.[51] "We have to defend our Manufacturers for refusing to pay wages," stridently asserted an inspector in January 1875. Only those who subscribed to the committee were defended in these cases, but occasionally it seems that manufacturers were able to subscribe after they had been summoned for nonpayment of wages.[52] The inspectors also protected their subscribers from factory safety legislation, such as the Employers Liability Act. An inspector in self-congratulatory mood described the circumstances of a case in 1883: "A boy having been killed while engaged in repairing a belt. The Father sued for about £100 compensation, when on the case being heard the lad's father unfortunately, through me, missed his way—the case being dismissed."[53]

It is an indication of how far the Worsted Committee and its Inspectorate had moved along the road from embezzlement control to general employers' aid that they were sometimes involved in negotiating wage agreements on the employer's behalf. The "painstaking care, tact and delicacy" exhibited by an inspector negotiating a new wage agreement at Temperance Mill was commended in a letter written by the millowner to the committee.[54] Tact and tactical use of the threat of litigation could achieve much for the employers on these occasions, as can be seen from this inspector's report: "I got six of them (the striking workers) in the office and told them that the masters had taken the order at such a price that they (the masters) could not possibly give any more, therefore I should take proceedings if they did not return and work up the warps . . . they said they would come back for 3d. per piece advance, Mr Sichel and the Manager consulted and agreed the advance."[55]

It must be remembered when studying the new duties of the inspectors that they may not have imbibed completely the new philosophy of the committee, and they may have continued to view the prosecution of embezzlement as their primary function, rather than preventing strikes and so on. However, it is evident that the enforcement of work discipline and the new subscribers that work attracted to the committee, brought in funds that were essential for the continuation of the struggle to control illegal appropriation. Cases of embezzlement therefore continued to be regularly brought before the courts by the inspectors throughout this period and beyond.[56]

The employers' most faithful servants survived the 1853 crisis and a couple after that to continue their work until their final dénouement in the second half of the twentieth century. In the length of their service, they were an atypical prosecution service—they were still prosecuting offenders in the second half of the twentieth century—unusual too was the extent of their duties, pursuing the suspect from the point of crime until the final judgment of guilt or innocence was delivered in court. Even in its depressed period between 1853 and 1870, the committee made an impact, prosecuting over 800 cases. It must be concluded that this employers' police, empowered by law to coerce and intimidate the workforce, was the most dynamic private policing agency seen in England in the last three centuries.[57]

A private policing agency as dynamic and regionally important as the Worsted Committee must have had an impact on the development of policing in Yorkshire, if not England. Since this area has been relatively ignored by historians, it is worth briefly outlining four questions raised by this study. First, how well accepted were private police forces compared to the New Police? Second, how well supported were the New Police by manufacturers? Third, what effect did models of private policing have on public policing in the West Riding? Last, is the classification of policing agencies into "public" and "private" sound?

As Storch has shown, the police were seen as intruders into workers' lives.[58] He gives the situation in Colne as an example of the bitter feuding that sometimes occurred between police and the occupants of the northern industrial districts. How much more bitter might this "war of attrition"[59] have been expected to be for the Worsted Inspectors as they stopped workers in the streets, searched their house with no warning for scraps of cloth, searched their lofts, dustbins, and outhouses, and questioned their families—and yet there is little evidence of resistance.[60] The attitude of the textile workers may be summed up in one case remembered by Inspector Room. He described the scene when an old widow had been acquitted at petty sessions for the possession of embezzled worsted waste: "The tender lamb of the flock had been delivered out of the teeth of the spoiler, and I was prayed for and against as a Phayroh, a Senna Cherrib, a Nebby Chad Nayzer, a Phillistian, an Amlakite . . . Satan transformed into an angle of light. . . . They were the heroes of the night, the champions of the poor combers, the victors of the battle for the working man's rights. The worsted manufacturers were anathematised as tyrants, bloodsuckers, who wished to rob the working man of his just rights, and hired a bloodhound to hunt him down."[61]

The outcome of the case was obviously of some irritation to the inspector, but the widow's supporters' party was also the most serious challenge to his authority that the inspector could remember, and yet there was no direct confrontation, physical attack, or even threat of violence issued. This accords with the experience of other inspectors. There are few cases of assaults against inspectors recorded despite the committee's keenness to prosecute in all cases of assault, both to protect their inspectors and to defend the legitimacy of their methods. "The Committee takes proceedings to make a proper example of such offenders," it was stated,[62] but there are no cases of inspectors being attacked in the 1840–80 period. Compare this to the hostility shown to policemen in Colne or Bradford, to take another example, where well over a thousand cases of assault on Bradford policemen were recorded between 1869 and 1879. Policemen, of course, had to deal with drunks and vagrants, but even so, there seems to be a vast difference in the number of assaults on representatives of each law enforcement agency. So real was the threat of violence that until 1856 the police did not dare venture into some industrial areas of Leeds,[63] and yet the Worsted Inspectors patrolled these areas apparently without fear. It may be assumed that the Worsted Inspectors were disliked, even hated, but they were not seen as *alien* to the working-class districts in the same way as police constables were.

Of course, police history has been concerned not just with the resistance of those who were "policed," but also with the identification of the groups calling for more efficient forms of policing. As is well known, the relationship between industrialization, urbanization, and the development of formal policing agencies in the nineteenth century is usually represented as a causal one. The theory that the threat to public order caused by the increasing numbers of workers crowding into the manufacturing districts, together with the rise of industrial militancy, provoked the middle and upper classes to call for a uniformed and disciplined body of men to act as a locally controlled police service is well known and does not need to be rehearsed here.[64] However, strategically important to this view is the belief that the northern borough forces were supported politically and financially (through taxation) by the industrial elite, and that the police in turn provided services for the manufacturers. These duties included not only the protection of the millowner and his property in the street, in his house, and in his factory but also the protection of his commercial interests when they were threatened. Thus the legal and operational requirement to preserve the public peace necessitated police governance of strikers' actions in times of labor disputes, for example.[65] It has been suggested that for this reason, the working classes resisted the introduction of the police, while the urban and industrial elites welcomed them with open arms.[66]

These assertions can be challenged, however, notably on the question of policing industrial disputes. The first problem is that of "class sympathy." Most members of the borough forces had previously held agricultural or industrial laboring occupations. The sympathies of a police force drawn from the same social background and living in the same communities as those people on strike may have undermined the loyalty they held to the law.[67] Conversely, policemen drawn from a higher social class may have "exacerbated" rather than mollified class violence.[68] Seemingly, the use of policemen drawn from both within or without the community may have handicapped the control of striking workers. This, however, was not the opinion of those northern millowners who testified to the Constabulary Force Commissioners.[69] This is unsurprising; the commission was after all designed by Chadwick to find evidence that a national police force would be beneficial to many sectors of society. With this in mind, they concluded that for "the want of an efficient preventative force, the peace and manufacturing prosperity of the country are exposed to considerable danger."[70] Those manufacturers who testified were not from the West Riding, however. Was this because the millowners in that region already had control over a preventative force that acted directly to protect millowner's property? The borough force's duty was to control labor disputes when they reached the streets, but the truly effective work of dissuading employees from leaving their work already had been achieved by the Worsted Inspector. Naturally, manufacturers were loathe to contribute financially for policing services they did not need, or for a duplication of services.[71] They were also in a dominant position to affect the development of the borough forces. A quarter of the Watch Committee that oversaw the introduction of Bradford's borough police were Worsted Committee members, and two-thirds were manufacturers eligible to subscribe to their services.

Rather than acting as a positive model for the new police, the Worsted Committee and its Inspectorate acted as an obstacle to the development of the Bradford borough force in the period up to 1853. It was an efficient and competent force, as one police historian admitted,[72] but its example had not led to agitation for a similar force but had acted as a constant reminder that privatized police agencies were more efficient, cheaper, and *easier to control* than official police agencies. Manufacturers in areas patrolled by the Worsted Inspectors did not gleefully welcome ever increasing legions of the blue-coated workers; rather, they saw the police as a necessary evil to be tolerated. No doubt, in areas where private police agencies were absent, manufacturers desired a strong police presence in times of industrial tension.[73] However, in areas patrolled by the Worsted Inspectors, there was clearly an ambivalent attitude toward the police forces. For example, at a meeting of Halifax ratepayers, Inspector Seed (the Halifax Worsted Inspector), together with prominent businessmen, formed a committee to express local discontent with the Halifax borough force. They declared that "all policemen are evil; but they were a necessary evil, and the dire anarchy that would reign if they were done away with would be infinitely worse than having to pay for the police out of the rates."[74] This cannot be taken as a ringing endorsement. Clearly, police historians should at least recognize the differences in attitude toward the police between those industrial areas that had established private police forces and those that did not.

It has not been the intention of this chapter to examine in detail the reasons why certain manufacturers may have favored the introduction of borough and county forces, and why others did not. Nor has the chapter attempted to evaluate in depth the impact private policing had on the development of formal policing in the nineteenth century. This study of the Worsted Committee merely has suggested some inconsistencies in the theory that links industrialism and policing. Until historians address these inconsistencies, a complete explanation of the relationship between public and private forms of policing and industrial capitalism is impossible.

NOTES

I am grateful for the comments of Professor Clive Emsley and Professor Peter King at an earlier reading of this chapter.

1. Rev. J. Room, *Notes from the Log Book of a Late Worsted Inspector* (Keighley, 1882), 129–38.

2. See N. South, "Law, Profit and 'Private Persons'; Private and Public Policing in English History," in P. C. Stenning, *Private Policing* (California, 1987); L. Johnston, *Rebirth of Private Policing* (London, 1992). In his discussion of the "Golden Age" of policing, Reiner has also tended to this view, see *The Politics of the Police* (Harvester, 1985), chaps. 1 and 2.

3. South, "Law, Profit," 72.

4. See David Philips, "Good Men to Associate and Bad Men to Conspire: Associations for the Prosecution of Felons in England, 1760–1860," in D. Hay and F. Snyder, eds., *Policing and Prosecuting in Britain, 1750–1850* (Oxford, 1989); and P. King, "Prosecution Associations and their Impact in Eighteenth-Century Essex," in the same volume. These subscription-funded agencies dealt with the retrieval of stolen property and the prosecution of the suspected thief and were present in both rural and industrializing areas. However, some social scientists, such as Spitzer and Scull, have suggested that private policing was a requirement of nineteenth-century industrial capitalism. Unfortunately, they have not examined the operation of any private agency in detail. See S. Spitzer and A. Scull, "Privatization and Capitalist Development: The Case of the Private Police," *Social Problems*, 25:1 (1977). Little and Sheffield have examined the membership and operation of Halifax Prosecution Association in their comparative study of private policing in late eighteenth-and early nineteenth-century England and the phenomena of vigilantism in America. See C. B. Little and C. P. Sheffield, "Frontiers and Criminal Justice: English Private Prosecution Societies and American Vigilantism in the Eighteenth and Nineteenth Centuries," *American Sociological Review* 48 (1983). This agency

did exist in an industrial, if not factory, district and continued until the end of the nineteenth century. Research could be usefully undertaken to determine the level of activity of this agency in the latter stages of Halifax's industrialization in order to test Spitzer and Scull's assertions concerning the relationship between private policing and industrial organization.

5. For the early history of the Worsted Committee, see R. Soderlund, " 'Intended as a Terror to the Idle and Profligate.' Embezzlement and the Origins of Policing in the Yorkshire Textile Industry, c.1750–1777," *Journal of Social History* 31 (spring 1998): 3.

6. Worsted Committee Registers, 1844–1876, West Yorkshire Archives: Bradford (*WYAB*), 56D.88/4/2–3. See also B. Godfrey, *The Impact of the Factory on Workplace* (1999), and for an explanation of the gendered nature of factory policing, see B. Godfrey, "Workplace Appropriation and the Gendering of Factory 'Law': West Yorkshire, 1840–80," in M. Arnot and C. Usborne, eds., *Gender and Crime in Modern Europe* (London, 1999).

7. See J. Styles, "Embezzlement, Industry and the Law in England, 1500–1800," in M. Berg, P. Hudson, and M. Sonenscher, eds., *Manufacture in Town and Country before the Factory* (Cambridge, 1983), and R. Soderlund, "Law, Crime and Labour in the West Riding of Yorkshire, 1750–1850" (Ph.D. thesis, University of Maryland, 1992).

8. 5 April 1852, Worsted Committee Minute Books (WCMB), *WYAB*, 56D.88/1/4. The general inspector's yearly salary was, on average, £167 between 1847 and 1870, as compared to an average salary of £223 for the chief constable of Bradford between those dates, £69 for police detective officer, and £46 for a borough constable. Worsted Committee Account Books, 1847–76; Borough Watch Committee records, Bradford, 1847–65, *WYAB*, BBC1/2.

9. Cheesebrough, for example, becoming an inspector in the West Riding force in 1854. 26 September 1854, WCMB, *WYAB*, 56D.88/1/4.

10. 10 April 1876, WCMB, *WYAB*, 56D.88/1/6.

11. 6 June 1844, *Bradford Observer*.

12. In January 1888, an inspector placed an agent inside the works in order to find the man who had been stealing patterns from the mill. After identifying the man, the inspector placed an advert in the Bradford Observer stating that he was a new manufacturer looking for patterns. The unsuspecting suspect sent the patterns along with a request for a job. WCMB, *WYAB*, 56D.88/1/6.

13. 12 May 1864, *Bradford Observer*.

14. January 1876, WCMB, *WYAB*, 56D.88/1/6.

15. Fourteen percent, West Riding quarter sessions courts, 1840–45, West Yorkshire Archives: Wakefield (*WYAW*), QS1.

16. The suspect could be released through lack of evidence on the advice of the constable or Worsted Inspector. This did not prohibit the foreman from initiating informal disciplinary sanctions.

17. To give but one example of the complexity of the law, the act of appropriation, as defined by law, could be prosecuted either as Larceny by Servant, Simple Larceny, Larceny under 5s. Larceny under the Worsted Acts, or Grand Larceny. Therefore appropriation could be prosecuted at either indictable or summary level.

18. Taking the opinion, for example, of the solicitor general in 1843, and dropping a case on his advice. 10 April 1843, WCMB, *WYAB*, 56D.88/1/4.

19. 3 April 1882, WCMB, *WYAB*, 56D.88/1/6.

20. 21 September 1880, WCMB, *WYAB*, 56D.88/1/6.

21. 27 Geo.III c.56.

22. June 1841 and September 1851, WCMB, *WYAB*, 56D.88/1/4.

23. Heaton suggests these investments were ill-advised. They did, however, provide an income of £70 p.a. between 1840–56, and £134 p.a. between 1857–62, before falling back to £48 p.a. after that date, and the money brought in from this source tided the committee over some very straitened times. See H. Heaton, *The Yorkshire Woollen and Worsted Industries* (Oxford, 1965), 437.

24. 27 Geo.III c.56 stated that any material found by the court to be embezzled must be returned to its rightful owners. If, however, the material remained unclaimed, or if the cloth had no identifiable markings, the material could be sold publicly for the benefit of the committee.

25. 10 December 1846, *Bradford Observer*.

26. 17 January 1870, WCMB, *WYAB*, 56D.88/1/5. These cases sometimes reached a wider audience than those that read the report in the *Bradford Observer*. Messrs. J. and J. Craven of Keighley had copies of this case printed and posted down in their "Rooms in their Works for their workpeople to see." 17 January, WCMB, *WYAB*, 56D.88/1/5.

27. Bradford Chief Constable's Reports of 1863, 1869, and 1873, *WYAB*, BCC1/2.

28. The police were concerned with the exterior of the factory, however. 4 October 1864, John Crossley and Co., Directors' Minute Book, 1864–66, West Yorkshire Archives Centre (*WYAC*) MIC:21/1.

29. Heaton, *The Yorkshire Woollen*, 437.

30. The cabinet debated budgetary considerations over a number of days in April 1853. From Gladstone's rough notes it appears that some members, such as Lord Lansdowne and Sir Charles Wood, advocated a reduction in soap duty by half, but in the end the cabinet decided to completely remove duty on soap. British Library Add. MS. 44778 ff. 84–7, 98–105.

31. 26 September 1853, WCMB, *WYAB*, 56D.88/1/4.

32. Five thousand copies of the Worsted Acts, for example, were distributed by inspectors in January 1853.

33. Heaton, *The Yorkshire Woollen*, 423–24.

34. The Borough of Leeds had a uniformed police in 1836. R. D. Storch, "The Plague of Blue Locusts: Police Reform and Popular Disturbances in Northern England, 1840–1857," *International Review of Social History* 10 (1981): 98.

35. The Bradford force, for example, grew by 60 percent between 1848 and 1858, and by 70 percent between 1859 and 1870, Bradford Watch Committee Minute Books, 1848–58, *WYAB*; Chief Constables reports, 1859–70, *WYAB*.

36. For example, Bradford police first patrolled visiting fairs and circuses in 1852 and started to attend cricket matches in 1853; see Borough Watch Committee Minute Book, 1852–56, *WYAB*, BBC1/5/2. Johnston states that policemen were also encouraged, in this period, to replace factory inspectors, which would have brought them physically into the arena of normative policing within the workplace. See L. Johnston, *Rebirth*, 5.

37. 23 June 1870, *Bradford Observer*. The inspectors were installed in Halifax and Keighley two days later, 25 June 1870, *Leeds Intelligencer*.

38. 1861 Chief Constables Reports, *WYAB*, BBC/1/2–5.

39. K. Ittmann, *Work, Gender and Family in Victorian England* (London, 1995), 14–15.

40. There were 7 woollen and worsted workers' societies created before 1860 and 8 between 1860 and 1875, for example.

41. As Irene Magrath stated, it was only when the employees began to organize that the employers felt the urge to join together to oppose their workers. Magrath also writes of the congruence of interests of employers being undermined by intraindustry competition. "The relationships between employers," she notes, "were fluid." This is to say the least. See I. Magrath, "Protecting the Interests of the Trade: Wool Textile Employers' Organizations in the 1920s," in J. A. Jowitt and A. J. McIvor, eds., *Employers and Labour in the English Textile Industries, 1850–1939* (London 1988), 44–64.

42. See entries for January 1881 and 11 April 1881, WCMB, *WYAB*, 56D.88/1/6.

43. The decision as to which cases could be handled by the inspector and which should be referred to the police officer was taken either by the inspector when the theft was detected or later by the committee in the time between the suspect's arrest and his/her appearance in court. As previously stated, the Worsted Acts could be interpreted in a variety of ways, and the inspector's judgment was not infallible.

44. 26 March 1877, WCMB, *WYAB*, 56D.88/1/6.

45. This system seems to have been reciprocated by the police, and when detectives realized than an offense came under the Worsted Acts, the arrested person was handed over to an inspector. See entry for 3 April 1882, WCMB, *WYAB*, 56D.88/1/6.

46. June 1879, WCMB, *WYAB*, 56D.88/1/6.

47. 5 January 1880, WCMB, *WYAB*, 56D.88/1/6.

48. Designed to enforce the speedy completion of work by domestic workers, this clause allowed the prosecution of anyone who failed to complete work allocated to him as part of his normal work load.

49. April 1871, WCMB, *WYAB*, 56D.88/1/5.

50. June 1887, WCMB, *WYAB*, 56D.88/1/6.

51. 21 June 1870, *Bradford Daily Telegraph*, 21 June 1870. Further entries in the minute books for the 1870s and 1880s detail the inspectorate's role in defending employers from claims of owed wages, wrongful dismissal, and other claims under master and servant actions initiated by the employees.

52. 28 September 1885, WCMB, *WYAB*, 56D.88/1/6.

53. 1 January 1883, WCMB, *WYAB*, 56D.88/1/6.

54. Letter dated 29 October 1884, Correspondence to the Committee, *WYAB*, 56D.88/1/6.

55. 3 April 1882, WCMB, *WYAB*, 56D.88/1/6.

56. See Printed Circular of the Worsted Committee, *WYAB*, 56D.88/5/7; and Deposition of Worsted Inspector, *WYAB*, 56D.88/5/9.

57. Although with the plethora of private forms of policing currently blossoming today, and a more pluralistic system of policing emerging, one cannot rule out the possibility that factory police forces may once again reappear.

58. See R. D. Storch, "The Plague," and "The Policeman as Domestic Mission-

ary: Urban Discipline and Popular Culture in Northern England, 1850–1880," *Journal of Social History* 9 (1976).

59. Storch, "The Plague," 100.

60. In Colne, which Bob Storch takes as an example of the intransigent opposition of industrial workers towards the police, the Worsted Inspector was never physically prevented from going about his work. As previously stated, the problem with the Colne district was the indiscipline of the inspector, and not the people he was prosecuting.

61. Room, *Notes from the Log Book*, 110.

62. 5 April 1819, WCMB, *WYAB*.

63. Pudsey and Armley in the South and West of the City, see Storch, "The Plague," 104.

64. See A. Silver, "The Demand for Order in Civil Society: A Review of Some Themes in the History of Urban Crime, Police, and Riot," in D. J. Bordua, *The Police, Six Sociological Essays* (London, 1967).

65. Living in the towns and cities as they did, "the new manufacturing and merchant urban bourgeoisie lacked certain protections against crime which the rural gentry enjoyed. They did not have the ecological safeguards of large estates and lack of proximity to the 'dangerous classes.' " M. Brogden, " 'All Police Is Conning Bastards': Policing and the Problem of Consent," in B. Fryer et al., eds., *Law, State and Society* (London, 1981), 49–50. It was therefore necessary, so the theory goes, to create a force that would protect the factories and also the homes of factory owners so as to have a police force that was in other words, "a weapon of the employers," as Storch termed them. Storch, "The Plague," 93.

66. Storch, "The Plague" and "The Policeman."

67. R. Reiner, *The Politics*, 22; J. Foster, *Class Struggle and the Industrial Revolution* (1974), 56–61; and Storch, "The Policeman," 89, 92–93.

68. A. Silver, "The Demand for Order In a Civil Society: A Review of Some Themes in the History of Urban Crime, Police and Riot," in D. J. Bordua, *The Police*, 10.

69. See Storch, "The Policeman," 92–93, for an interpretation of this evidence.

70. *PP* [*Parliamentary Papers*] 1836 Constabulary Commission Report, 181.

71. D. Hay, "Property, Authority and the Criminal Law," in Hay, Linebaugh et al., eds., *Albion's Fatal Tree* (London, 1975), 59. The Bradford watch committee was always seeking to reduce the costs of policing the borough, and many entries record their resistance to increase in policemens' wages. They went so far as to regularly commission surveys of other comparative forces to ensure that they paid the very lowest rates of pay. See Borough Watch Committee Minute Book, 1862, *WYAB*; again in 1871, the survey revealed that the chief constable of Bradford received the lowest salary of all chief constables controlling forces of over a hundred men.

72. G. Smith believes that the inspectors helped the burghers of Bradford to decide to establish a professional force of policemen but offers no evidence for his theory. G. Smith, *Bradford's Police* (Bradford, n.d.).

73. Witness the fears of Charles Napier in Manchester. W. Napier, *The Life and Opinions of General Sir Charles Napier*, vol. 2 (London, 1857), 146.

74. 22 July 1876, *Bradford Observer*.

Street, Beat, and Respectability: The Culture and Self-image of the Late Victorian and Edwardian Urban Policeman[1]

Mark Clapson and Clive Emsley

> Our police force . . . has a status and position different from all other official bodies, civil or military. It is not merely a great human mechanism, perhaps the greatest of its kind. It is a body of men who, though distinctive in their character from all others, as the members of any public service must necessarily be, are yet related to the people whom they serve by ties of intimate personal association which are not to be found in any other country in the world.
>
> —*The Times*, 24 December 1908.

Until recently the English "bobby" was lionized by both his contemporaries and his historians, both of whom tended to affirm his muscularity along with his reserve and his unarmed honesty in dealings with the criminal and not-so-criminal classes. Moreover, the public face of the policeman was also a professional one, wherein social duty and a specific monopoly of lawkeeping were and still are combined. Yet recent historical research has argued persuasively that he spent at least some of his official time enforcing so-called bourgeois codes with the edge of his truncheon or the back of his hand. He was, after all, the only official of the state authorized to employ a degree of force in his day-to-day dealings with his fellow citizens. Similarly, sociological enquiry in the 1970s and 1980s has exposed a canteen culture among English policemen that is aggressively male, sexist, and racist.[2] This does not fit with the traditional image of the policeman, as established in the Victorian years, which found its most effective and popular portrayals in cinema films and television fiction series in the 1950s and 1960s.[3]

This chapter will explore aspects of the self-image of the late Victorian and Edwardian policeman. The sources for this are autobiographies, police personnel registers, and the force's trade newspapers, especially the *Police Review*. We have also used the meticulous empirical work of Charles Booth's survey of the *Life and Labour of the People in London*; this combined a systematic approach to the changing social and economic structures of London in which Booth graded streets according to their levels of wealth and residential tone. Booth's investigators wrote down their own observations on the households they assessed and held a number of interviews with police, religious, and other worthies; we have also drawn upon these.

Primarily, we are concerned with the relationship between self-discipline, self-help, and self-respect, as measured against those who had fallen by the wayside: the unrespectable and, in Booth's late Victorian terminology, "the vicious and semicriminal poor." Fundamental to this value system was the Smilesian notion of self-help, with its incremental, respectable, and stolid ethos. The notion had a double resonance for the hierarchical institution of the Victorian police, first in the promise it offered to recruits, and second in the way that it encouraged personal identification in contrast to others. By self-help a police recruit could, in theory, pull himself up from constable third class to head constable of a borough force. He could not, of course, transcend his class origins. The command of the Metropolitan Police of London, the largest city forces, and the county constabularies, that is, the most prestigious forces, remained the preserve of gentlemen and often former military officers. Moreover, the continuing perception of the borough policeman as a municipal servant answerable, in the final analysis, to the local worthies on the Watch Committee, ensured the maintenance of the working-class aura even among borough head constables. The emphasis on upward mobility was reflected in the longevity of many individual police careers, as will be demonstrated below. It also encouraged an ambitious member of the working class to place upon himself the uniform of respectability, to live in a respectable area, and to define his social value against the residuum, that element of the poor deemed idle, incompetent, and deviant.[4] While few members of the respectable working class had much to do with this element, the residuum was precisely that section of society with which the policeman was in daily contact and which he was expected to control. The way in which he went about this reflected the imperatives of the force, but also his personal values: The Victorian and Edwardian policeman was not simply the conduit for, and enforcer of, alien or "other" values on the streets.

There is little doubt that the pursuit of a long-term incrementally upward career is reflected in the origins of many policemen and in the length of many police careers. In all forces, the majority of these recruits were relatively young men in their early twenties. In the Metropolitan Police, for example, the average age of recruits was twenty-two or twenty-three in the decades from 1870 to 1914[5] Most joined young, and increasingly they appear to have had the intention of growing old as policemen. Policemen came from a wide variety of working-class backgrounds, mostly semiskilled and unskilled manual, a pattern that changed gently but significantly from the mid-Victorian years until 1914. In this, the recruitment profile of London's police reflected city forces elsewhere in England. For example, between 1880 and 1914, the percentage of "laborers," a catch-all term including agricultural and a wide variety of urban manual work, declined from a little under 60 percent in the Metropolitan Police to below 20 percent. In Leeds the decline was from 55 percent to a little over 10 percent over the same period, and in Hull, the decline was similar: from almost 70 percent to 35 percent. The other most common trades represented in recruitment to these urban forces were baker, the brick trades, butcher, carpenter and joiner, clerk, painter and decorator, and the railway. Such trades were increasingly represented as the number of laborers declined. It is no coincidence that as the period progressed men with better educational qualifications tended to be recruited. This was more than just a consequence of the Education Acts of 1870 and 1902: It also reflected the increasing appeal of the police force as a career,[6] a major theme of this chapter.

Military experience also fed into the recruitment of the civilian, uniformed working class. Over the second half of the nineteenth century and into the Edwardian years, the number of police recruits who gave their "trade" or "calling" as "soldier" was small: just under 1 percent of recruits to the Metropolitan Police and just under 2 percent in Leeds. However, this obscures the growing number of recruits who had military service but who did not consider such as their "trade." For example, the percentage of recruits to the Metropolitan Police with army service doubled from 10 percent in 1860 to 20 percent by 1910. In Leeds the increase was from 15 percent to 25 percent over the same time span.[7]

The following data on length of service is drawn from the divisional registers of the Metropolitan Police. It illustrates strongly that the majority of recruits viewed the force as a long- to middle-term career, or else made up their minds quickly that the police was not for them. Resignations, whether voluntary or compulsory because of a misdemeanor, and dismissals generally occurred early in the careers of the majority of policemen. Thus, of 1,820 entries in the divisional registers for the years 1880 to 1914, 548 (30 percent) had resigned within one year, 140 (8 percent) within two, and 113 (6 percent) in their third year of service. Or to put in another way: 52 percent of all resignations occurred in the first three years of service. Dismissals were heavily located in the first years of service, too. Of 593 men dismissed in the period with which we are concerned, 283 (48 percent) had less than one year of service, and 97 (16 percent) were dismissed during their second year. To put it another way: 380 men (64 percent) were dismissed before two years of service were completed, and some 209 men (35 percent) were dismissed between three to twenty-five years of service; the statistics give single figures for dismissals of men after ten years of service.

Transfers reflect a high degree of mobility between divisions, and this may in some part be a consequence of the residential preferences of policemen, but transfer could also be a means of punishment. Moreover, some men moved as a result of promotion. The pattern revealed in the warrant books again was for transfers to occur most often in the early years of a policeman's service, and to fall off considerably after ten years, suggesting settlement and perhaps the exigencies of the policeman's family life cycle and the arrival and bringing up of children. Of a sample of 2,489 transferees, 818 (33 percent) were transferred within the first two years of service. Between and including three and six years of service, transfers numbered 578 out of 2,489 records (22 percent). Between seven and ten years of service 374 were transferred (15 percent). Thus over two-thirds of all transfers for recruits took place before a decade of service years was completed. We may conclude from these findings that the large majority of recruits objectively fulfilled their superiors' specifications for them. Recruitment patterns strongly support the picture of a stable working class with its eyes on a steady job with a pension at the end. Some, too, pursued a modicum of upward mobility.[8]

Such findings can be emphasized by an exploration of subjectively inspired social and economic action, too. Choice of housing and residence, also, were inextricably bound up with career, but accommodation costs could be a drain on earnings. The biggest towns and cities had "police barracks" or "section houses" for young and unmarried men. These were often run by a serving officer and his wife or by a pensioned officer.[9] In London, most single policemen lived in such accommodations for which half a crown per week was charged for everything but food in the early 1890s, thus "avoiding the pressure of high rents."[10] Young, unmarried men also stayed as lodgers in the homes of fellow policemen, probably contributing to the household income. At 4 Hotspur Street, West Lambeth, lived a policeman and his wife: "Rents the house. has another policeman, a single man lodger, with them." Furthermore, at 14 Romilees Street, Westminster, one policeman with three children leased his house and sublet to "single policeman lodgers."[11]

As the nineteenth century wore on and as more and more recruits tended to stay longer in the police, many men found wives. Indeed, there were some commentators who considered that married policemen were to be preferred. Richard Mayne, one of the first commissioners of the Metropolitan Police told a parliamentary select committee in 1834 that he considered married men to be steadier. For one thing, they were less likely to succumb to the temptation of "the women of the town."[12] Over half a century later, J. D. Pennington, arguing for a pay rise for the Manchester

Police, declared that ["the policemen's] ideas of duty for one thing act more forcibly upon him when he is [married]; his behavior towards women and children requiring his assistance, is likely to be much more gentle and human if he has a wife and children of his own."[13]

Married men made up three-quarters of the Metropolitan Police in 1890.[14] They had to find their own accommodation, and where they sought it reflects three factors: first, the requirement by the force that a policeman lived near to his station within his subdivision; second, that "the policeman must choose his dwelling in a neighbourhood untainted by any suspicion of criminality"; third, the desire of the married policeman to move his family to affordable yet respectable accommodation.[15] We can see the consequences of this in the movements and domestic conditions of the police family as illustrated by the Booth materials.

Following his house-to-house surveys of the East End of London and his more impressionistic surveys of the streets of South, West, and Northern London and their inhabitants, Booth and his team divided the streets into the following categories:

The streets of the vicious, semicriminal poor, and the very poorest. The popular contemporary term was the "residuum." Many social reformers, including Booth and even later Herbert Morrison, who was to become leader of the London Labour Party and a Cabinet Minister from 1940, were in favor of carting these improvident or thieving wretches off to labor camps, in order to remove them from the mainstream and respectable working class. These were streets colored black on his *Descriptive Maps of London Poverty.*

The very poor and the feckless. These were streets colored dark blue.

The poor. These were still under Booth's poverty line. They lived in streets colored light blue on Booth's maps.

Mixed class. Could include those just above, below, or on the poverty line, and varying shades of respectability or otherwise. Purple on maps.

The respectable working class and lower middle class, usually above the poverty line. These lived in streets colored pink on the maps.

The middle class, professionals, small businesses, etc.: red streets.

The wealthier middle class and landed wealthy: orange.

A sample of 181 streets from Booth's *Poverty* notebooks (Table 1) gives vivid confirmation of the relationship between earning power and the institutional requirements for the police to embrace a higher residential tone:

Table 1: Police Households by Color of Street in "Life and Labour" *Poverty* Notebooks

Black	0	0%
Dark blue	1	0.5%

Light blue	8	4%
Purple	37	20%
Pink	103	57%
Pink–Red	12	7%
Red	12	7%
Orange	8	4%
Total	181	99.5%[16]

These streets are drawn from a random sample of all the *Poverty* notebooks and include all the boroughs of London that Booth and his team studied. It is clear that there is a bias toward the respectable and, to a lesser extent, the mixed streets. Those "in the pink" make up well over half of the total. In the pink streets generally, the occupational descriptions vary, from laborers to artisans, cabmen, or coachmen to shopkeepers, but the predominance of such broad categories as clerks, mechanics, cabmen, artisans, laborers, servants, and porters is marked. Policemen living in mixed ("purple") streets but who would, except perhaps for the vagaries of the family cycle, have been above the poverty line, are about one-fifth of the total. Taken together, this amounts to over three-quarters of police households residing in those respectable working-class streets that were palpably above the classic slum areas but below the classic wealthier suburbs.

Equally significant is the very low number of police households living among the poor and very poor. There are considerably more amongst the wealthy middle class. This, as is revealed from the following examples, represents either the achievement of rank, or a promotion to or preference for proximity to the uniformed service class: those looking after the premises or property of the state or businesses. Policemen in these "orange" streets were rarely far from servants. In Regents Park, for example, lived a park constable," a superintendent of the botanical gardens, and servants.[17] In Egerton Gardens, Chelsea, the notebook refers to "caretaker police."[18] In St. Georges Square and Eccleston Square, Westminster, lived "police caretakers, &c."[19] And, to take another example, in Wynell Road, Greenwich, colored red for the map, lived "a police inspector as caretaker."[20]

These colors rested upon Booth's scale of eight classes, into which he placed the inhabitants of each street by household. Class A was the lowest, class H the wealthy professionals and landed gentry. Police households in purple and pink streets were mostly to be found in classes E and F, the regularly employed uniformed and artisanal working class. Together, classes E and F comprised 51.5 percent of the population of London.[21] In Booth's economic definition, eighteen to twenty-one shillings was a sufficient and regular income but one that provided the bare essentials for the maintenance of good family health. Those below this were in poverty, and working class occupations above it were "comfortable," earning anywhere between twenty-three and thirty shillings a week. Their residential location was, above the purple streets, broadly homogeneous.

There is, of course, a chicken-and-egg problem here. Families were mobile, and housing districts can improve and decline. Doubtless the police opted to live in the better class of street, yet the movement of respectable police families into a street might have an effect on its status. Furthermore, the problem of finding accommodation in the right place was not always easy. Booth's survey recognized "the extreme difficulty of obtaining houseroom within the bounds [of the subdivision]" and found that a few married men tended to have quarters at police stations "but this is exceptional," as the major preference for married men was "to be stationed in the suburbs so that they may benefit by the cheaper rents and increased space for their families."[22]

Chief Inspector Littlechild, a Metropolitan Police detective, told the Departmental Committee on Superannuation that the policeman's home was required to be more respectable than those of the class of men from which he was drawn, "because he has to show an example round about him, and he feels that it is incumbent upon him so to do." Other witnesses to the committee stressed how rents cut deeply into police pay, even when accommodation was not in the best areas. The situation was aggravated by the fact that, unlike most other artisan groups, the policeman's wife was forbidden from carrying on a trade and, thus, eking out the family budget.[23] This repudiation of extra earnings from the informal economy of the local district was another marker of the moral distance that was supposed to be held between police and the local poor, even if it caused economic problems.

John Monk had very positive ideas about the residuum and the "rough elements" of the working class, having spent much of his early police career in tough districts of the metropolis. When he found himself transferred to F Division in Kensington in the 1890s as an inspector, the tenor of his work changed with the residential tone: "The chief work of the station seemed to be that of dealing with ladies who came to report the loss of a dog, a purse, or to complain of some trivial matter; cabmen were also coming to deposit property left in their cabs."

But if the policing tasks were easier, finding accommodation was difficult, and Monk took himself and his family to a suburban address, in keeping with Booth's findings: "I could not find a house for my growing family near to the station, so eventually had to take a three years lease on one in West Kensington in T' Division. After paying the relatively high rent and rates, despite my promotion, I found I was 2/-a week worse off than I had been at West Ham."[24]

G. E. Arkell, one of Booth's investigators, reported that in the more crowded districts of central London, the police family's choice was "almost limited to the better class of block dwellings." He instanced a large block near Charing Cross that was home to a total of 156 families: "of the heads of these families forty-eight were police officers."[25] In a separate published volume of the Booth survey, Octavia Hill, of the Charity Organisation Society, described such dwellings as free from the residuum:

> where the tenants are the quiet, respectable, working-class families, who, to use a phrase common in London, "keep themselves to themselves," and whose well-ordered, quiet little homes, behind their neat little doors with bright knockers, nicely supplied with well-chosen appliances, now begin to form groups where responsible, respectable citizens live in cleanliness and order.[26]

It was the task of the wife in the respectable working-class family to ensure this cleanliness and order and to make the children look presentable. Wives played a key role in creating the family image in this way, and it was the aim of the respectable artisan to support his wife so that she did not have to undertake paid employment, and could devote herself to this role.[27] The restrictions on the policeman's wife, which prohibited her from working, may not have helped the family budget but probably did help contribute to the respectable image.

However, whatever the aspirations, some police families were compelled to live at least for a while in the poorer dwellings. Katharine Buildings in the East End was one such place. There were 628 family rooms, excluding the top floor, where the poorest lived; at the time of Beatrice Webb's assessment for Booth in the early years of his enquiry, three of these were occupied by police families. The wife of P. C. Thomas Robbins was a difficult person who "used to borrow from everyone who would lend and speak evil of most." She appears also to have considered the buildings beneath her family and took it upon herself "as a policeman's wife" to inform on her neighbors, some of whom were evicted. When P. C. Robbins moved his family to Royal Albert Buildings early in 1886 there were rejoicings among all the neighbors.[28]

Unrest in the Metropolitan Police and other large urban forces over increasing rents and the resulting problems of finding adequate accommodation that the men considered suitable for the position prompted agitation in the correspondence columns of the *Police Review*,[29] letters to the *Times*, and a succession of questions in Parliament at the turn of the century and again immediately before the First World War. Shortly after the Home Secretary agreed to a rent allowance for the Metropolitan Police in 1901, Claude Hay—the independent Conservative MP for Hoxton, who took a keen interest in working-class housing and the Municipal Movement—was concerned that some policemen and their families were compelled to seek accommodation in building erected for the poor.[30] It may have been an effort for constables to afford rents in some of the better streets, but they had little desire to be associated with the poor, and kept well away from the residuum. Herbert Morrison's parents, for example, lived in a small "two down, three up" in the Victorian working-class dormitory area of Brixton. This was toward the edge of London, superseded only by the suburbs of the wealthy beyond, and removed enough from the "warrens" of poverty further north.

Herbert Morrison, who in many respects diverged from his father's values, was his father's son when it came to status. The job of a policeman, he wrote, "was respectable because the standard of character demanded was very high and the uniform was an envy of service for the Crown. . . . The modest Morrison home was the envy and admiration of the neighbours, though with little reason on the grounds of practical considerations."[31]

The real reasons, as Morrison knew, were the sureness of work in "a steady job with one's future clearly mapped. There was a pension. In those days few of his class could expect as much."[32] Moreover, securing the pension had been a struggle for policemen. All forces had begun with superannuation schemes collecting a small amount from the men's pay for this. But it was one thing to be collecting for such schemes when a force was new and its ranks were filled with young recruits; as time progressed and more and more men became eligible for a gratuity or a pension, many of the schemes began to founder.

The problem was compounded in the eyes of the police themselves by the fact that the gratuities and pensions were discretionary. In his report for 1872 W. J. Elgee, Her Majesty's Inspector of Constabulary for the Northern District, warned of the necessity of putting superannuation on a firmer footing if good men were to be retained. Captain Edward Willis, the Southern District inspector, agreed and considered that superannuation had "much to do with influencing men to enter and continue in the police service."[33] A Commons Select Committee recommended that pensions should be a right after twenty-five years service in 1877,[34] but it was another thirteen years before the Police Act of 1890 guaranteed such a pension. Even then there were disputes. In 1894, William Wood Cant took the Lancashire Police Authority to court when they refused him his full pension on the grounds that he had begun his police career in the Roxburghshire Constabulary and that there was a gap in his service between leaving Scotland and moving to Lancashire. Cant's claim was successful, but he was greatly assisted by the *Police Review*, the police trade paper established in 1893, which organized both his case and the subscription for his legal fees.[35]

The *Police Review and Parade Gossip* was the second of the most significant police trade papers, but under its enthusiastic and forceful editor, John Kempster, it rapidly eclipsed its nearest rival, the *Police Chronicle*.[36] It set out to be the mouthpiece for the respectable, educated working man who served as policemen and had rights as a citizen. It also evinced a strong sense of professionalism in its mediation between public service, private self-improvement, and the career structure. Its first leader proclaimed:

> The policeman is not to be regarded as a mere chattel or machine: he is a man and a citizen. The Force is now being daily recruited from the ranks of those who have shared the advantages of our modern Board Schools. Policemen, as a class, are thus increasingly educated, and do not fall intellectually below their fellow men. It is the more needful that there should be opened to them healthy sources of information upon matters especially bearing on their useful and honourable career.[37]

Here was typical encouragement for the autodidactical working-class man and policeman. The *Review* began to develop its own educational section with notes on grammar, composition, dictation, and mathematics. A regular feature was the biography of a serving or recently retired officer. These might be the chief constables drawn from the gentry, but they were also policemen in the news, such as William Wood Cant,[38] and the Smilesian self-help ethos, with its insistence upon thrift, sobriety, and deferred gratification, was especially evident when the subject was a working man who had risen to a significant rank. John Fisher, who became chief constable of Grimsby in 1899, aged only thirty-eight, offers a prime example:

> He received his early education at the village school, but was called upon to commence the battle of life at an unusually early age. When only eleven years old he was working regularly in a coal mine, and from that time until he reached the age of twenty three he followed the same occupation. Always strictly temperate in all his habits, and being of a studious disposition, and a literary turn of mind, he took every opportunity of educating and preparing himself to make his way in a new sphere of life, which he had already made up his mind upon, namely, the Police Force.[39]

Richard William Steggles was forced to leave school at twelve years, when his parent's business failed, but "his constant habit of utilising every opportunity of continuing by diligent study the education that had been interrupted at so early a date" enabled him to rise to the rank of superintendent in the Metropolitan Police. Detective Inspector George Harvey, also of the Metropolitan Police, was "a life abstainer . . . proud of the fact that he has never tasted intoxicating drink of any kind."[40]

In 1894, the *Police Review* was instrumental in organizing the Police and Citizen's Association, which aimed at improving the education of constables, offering them legal advice and assistance, and ensuring a fair system of promotion.[41] Before the General Election of 1900, the *Review* contacted parliamentary candidates on behalf of the association, and posed five questions relating to these aims. The names of the candidates who responded sympathetically, with a precis of their comments, were then printed in the

Review. There were also six candidates named as special friends of the police: C. E. Schwann, Captain Cecil W. Norton, E. H. Pickersgill, H. J. Wilson, John Burns, and John Wilson.[42] Burns and Wilson are interesting for their own origins in working-class self-help and trades unionism. Burns had known the police as an opponent in his days as a trade union activist and member of the Social Democratic Federation. His brother Alec, perhaps significantly, was in the Metropolitan Police.[43] Wilson had originated among the miners of County Durham, and as M.P. for mid-Durham, he had been one of the first two members of Parliament to join the committee of the Police and Citizens Association. The *Review* had praised his "intelligence, integrity and force of character," which had brought him from the coal mine to Westminster. It further explained that he joined the association "as a Worker's representative to show his sympathy with a class of brother workers."[44]

Did the police themselves readily identify with their "brother workers"? If so, with which groups particularly? Police witnesses before the Departmental Committee on Superannuation, while all drawn from the senior ranks of the Metropolitan Police, saw the policeman as superior to other members of the uniformed working class. There was, for example, no comparison between the police constable and the postman, and police tasks were more responsible and delicate than those of railway servants. Moreover, railway companies allegedly were prepared to take men refused by, or dismissed from, the police.[45] Chief Inspector Littlechild discussed the wage and prospects of the policeman in comparison with "a good operative" like a carpenter, but noted: "the operative does not have to look as respectable as the policeman, at least in my opinion. The policeman gets a little bit more ambitious with regard to that sort of thing."[46]

The officers recognized and accepted that police pay was lower than that of the civil servant because the latter needed a higher standard of education. However, they also stressed that the policeman needed better physical qualities and fitness, and that his job was more grueling, more dangerous, and likely to lead to a man being physically broken after twenty-five years; in consequence, they argued, policemen needed better pensions than civil servants.[47]

At some stage any work organization is likely to witness dissatisfaction over pay and conditions. The police were no exception. During the Victorian period there was a degree of ad hoc union organization among urban police forces in certain instances. There were strikes in Hull and Manchester in the 1850s, and among London's policemen in 1872, 1889, and 1890. During the latter unrest, meetings of police delegates were held in workingmen's clubs and even on the premises of the Social Democratic Federation. There were also links with socialists and trade union leaders,[48] though it is impossible to assess the extent to which police activists shared their ideology.

In some respects, the *Police Review* assumed many of the organizational characteristics of a national trades union. It spoke the language of Victorian trades unionism: self-help, fair treatment, and improved conditions of work, and not a little sectionalism, perhaps placing the police in a unique position between two stools. Its language and the ethos within it reflected, on one side, an artisanal status consciousness without the measure of radicalism that had characterized the organized tradesmen and skilled workers of the metropolis. On the other, the newer instrumentalism, the "bread-and-butter" insistence of unskilled workers, with an, at best, subpolitical orientation, is also strongly in evidence.[49] Following on from this, it is possible to view the police as part of those sections of the working class who departed the central zone of the city for the near suburbs, the working-class dormitory sprawls. Their ideology is one that is pertinent both to the consciously "respectable" and to what has been described recently as "the integrated working class." This is characterized by its difference from the "marginal working class." "[The integrated working class] is more likely to belong to homogenous residential communities, to be employed in large enterprises, and thus to be working alongside other manual workers on the shop floor, and to be relatively stable with respect to geographical and social mobility."[50]

If we remove the reference to manual and substitute the beat for the shop floor, this is a particularly apposite description for the majority of lower-ranking policemen. There is certainly a considerable subjective and objective distance between the organized working class and the marginals of the very poor, and the marginality of the individual aspirant who is allegedly beleaguered and isolated at the intersection of the upper working and lower middle classes: a poor suburbanite. Such a fate did not befall the policeman or the card carrying trades unionist. Thus, there was, perhaps, more in common between men like Larry Meath, the fictional autodidact and trades unionist in Walter Greenwood's *Love on the Dole*, and the policeman who caused his death through a blow on the head, than there was between Meath and the poorest of his slum in Salford, who felt he was, like the police, not of them.[51]

However, police trades unionism, while it could become agitated by poor conditions of service and inadequate wages, was rarely radical, and rarely politicized. The government's refusal to recognize police unions in the late Victorian and Edwardian eras because they would undermine discipline misunderstood the power of self-discipline in the ranks, as well as that instilled by the codes of the force. Police trades union consciousness was then and has remained primarily that of a wage earner in a hierarchical occupational system. Even in the troubled conditions of 1919, the strike by several large urban forces for union recognition can be seen as a strike for *incorporation*, as a desire for acknowledgement of their worth with the reward of a trades union, moreover, a trade union defined by a rather conservative and instrumental solidarism.[52] The police willingness to take up truncheons against Bolshevism in these years lends further support to this perspective. Moreover, Richard Hyman has argued that at this level, all trade unions can be seen as essentially integrative mechanisms for capitalism, as collective strategies by workers to be accepted into bargaining structures and the normative culture which shapes them, rather than as challenges to it, police unionism would seem to fit with this perspective.[53]

The occupational community of the police, while ostensibly riven through by hierarchy, was integrated significantly by its shared sense of self-help and the long-term commitment of most policemen to a future with the force. For some, this was leavened, too, by the element of temperance and Christianity. It gave policemen a sense of identity across different forces and encouraged them to take pride in their calling. But while its organ, the *Police Review*, permitted discussions in the correspondence columns of whether or not the police should unionize themselves, Kempster broke with the infant Police Union in December 1913, primarily over its insistence on the right to strike, and refused to accept any advertisements for it.[54]

While not always popular with chief constables—especially the gentlemen in the counties, who, increasingly after 1856, were men with a military pedigree—Kempster and his *Review* had a clear idea of the respectable, self-disciplined, autodidact who made the ideal bobby. This concept was not that dissimilar from the one advocated by officialdom, and the *Review*'s advocacy of such characteristics doubtless contributed to the policeman's self-conception as a respectable career man, a notion central to a professional and integrated system dependent upon human capital. At the same time, the policeman could draw upon the structural, hierarchical police organization and the promise of future promotion, or at least a pension, for his own sense of personal security and individual and social worth. Thomas Smethurst recalled, "At the age of twenty one, I, a tall, slender built but muscular young man, full of life, energy and high spirits, after careful thought and consideration as to whether the life of a policeman was better than the life of a miner earning his living in the bowels of the earth, came to the conclusion that the former was better, and so decided to join the Force."[55]

Policing was a tough occupation. The police trade press, and probably also many of the autodidacts in the service, disliked the often humorous portrayals of constables that appeared to play down the demands and dangers of the job. The *Police Guardian* quoted, with evident satisfaction, a passage from the *Daily News* in 1884:

> In the rough localities of London police officers are often seriously knocked about, and do daring deeds, which if performed by a soldier would receive distinct marks of approbation. The police officer, however, labours under the disadvantage of being considered a humorous person, derided by the clown in the pantomimes, and

suspected of yearnings for cold mutton. But all who have seen him really at work will recognise his genuine pluck and power of quelling the "rough" when he happens to come his way.[56]

Table 2: Assaults on Metropolitan Policemen, 1867

Numerical strength of police	6,999
No. of police assaulted	2,229
No. temporarily off work because of assault	191
No. killed or discharged	4
No. pensioned as a result of injury on duty	20

Table 3: Assaults on City of London Policemen, 1867

Numerical strength of police	668
No. of police assaulted	190
No. temporarily off work because of assault	3
No. killed or discharged	0

P.C. John B. Nobbs of the Liverpool Police penned a series of Kipling-like ballads about "the Bobby" for the *Police Review*, reflecting these points:

> Who is that one, at whom you sneer
> And oftentimes will cheek and jeer,
> What do you call him far and near?
> Why, 'bobby.'
> Yet, when there comes a vicious fight,
> Or when mad dogs begin to bite,
> Whose coming hail you with delight?
> Why, 'bobby.'[57]

Most patrolling was done at night and it had to be done whatever the weather, something that contributed to a significant sick list. G. E. Arkell, drawing upon police medical evidence, noted that diseases resulting from exposure, such as bronchial and lung disorders, caused the largest proportion of sick cases.[58] Also, the police were "liable to accidents and malicious injuries not found in other callings."[59] In 1875, Captain William Congreve, the chief constable of Staffordshire, suggested that these assaults made the life of his policemen more dangerous than that of the soldier: "The other day in Birmingham we had a man killed; not a week passes in the Black Country but what a man is almost killed; a soldier may be in the army for 20 years and never be hurt, but the policemen in the Black Country are liable to be hurt every day; certainly they would not go five years without being hurt."[60]

Table 4: Return of the Number of Police Injured Whilst in thc Execution of Their Duty during the Years 1903, 1904, 1905, and 1906[61]

Year	Assaulted by prisoners or injured when making arrests						Assaulted by persons who were not apprehended			When dispersing disorderly crowds			Total			Total	Number of officers who were incapacitated for further service from injuries received
	By drunken persons			By other persons													
	Not placed on sick list	On sick list less than 7 days	On sick list 7 days or over	Not placed on sick list	On sick list less than 7 days	On sick list 7 days or over	Not placed on sick list	On sick list less than 7 days	On sick list 7 days or over	Not placed on sick list	On sick list less than 7 days	On sick list 7 days or over	Not placed on sick list	On sick list less than 7 days	On sick list 7 days or over		
1903		1,830			828			80			2			2,730		2,730	4
1904	1,529	81	144	822	43	117	43	5	15	7	-	1	2,421	109	277	2,807	9
1905	1,361	76	173	859	41	130	48	5	10	5	-	-	2,273	121	313	2,708	7
1906	1,188	91	198	812	39	111	37	1	9	9	2	4	1,746	133	320	2,199	7

One of Booth's poverty notebooks for Bethnal Green, dated October 1887, provides a glimpse of an ex-policeman, by then a dock laborer, who had descended into Booth's class D: "Policeman who was injured by a burglar and being incapacitated from work was pensioned. gets 18/-a week and his salary from Dock."[62]

As Tables 2, 3, and 4 indicate, there was an overall decline in the statistics of assaults on the police between the late 1860s and into the Edwardian years, but the trial statistics at least suggest that this decline (64 percent) was not as great as the decline for all assaults (71 percent). Nevertheless, the superintendent to H Division, covering the rough working-class district of Whitechapel, estimated that 40 percent of his men were assaulted in 1889 and that half of these were obliged to go on the sick list. Some 12,000 people were being tried summarily each year of the 1890s for assaults on police.[63]

Given the incidence of these assaults, police constables needed to be fit and strong. Many police autobiographies suggest men taking a pride in masculine fitness and toughness. "I was young," recalled John Monk of his early years in the Metropolitan Police, "weighed 14st. 9 lbs. and kept myself in the pink of condition and carried no spare flesh: in fact, in some quarters I was jocularly known as 'tin ribs.'[64] James Bent and Richard Jervis joined the Lancashire constabulary when the violence against the police was at its midcentury peak, and Bent himself was badly assaulted with red-hot irons at a steel works in Newton Heath. The autobiographies note the decline in violence in the second half of the century yet revel in the toughness required of them as individuals to hold their own and subdue opponents. Jervis, for example, writes of the "fun, excitement and broken heads" of election disorders.[65] Tom Divall, who joined the Metropolitan Police at the Deptford station in 1882, recalled being asked by a duty inspector, "Can you fight?" and when he replied that he could the inspector responded, "That will just do for us."[66] Some constables also fought amongst themselves to settle arguments and to "put men in their place," and police barracks commonly resounded to the rough horseplay of young men.[67]

Together with this rough masculinity went the swagger engendered by a uniform that set the policeman apart from those he policed. Thomas Smethurst, who joined the Bolton and Stalybridge force in 1888, was on the beat the day after his appointment ceremony:

> I have secured the appointment, received my clothing and accoutrements, obtained suitable apartments, and am now ready for the fray. About 9.30 pm the following night, dressed in a tight fitting tunic with a broad belt round my waist, a heavy lamp hanging on my left side, a thick piece of wood in the pocket on the inside of my right trouser leg, a heavy helmet on my head, and a cloth cape over my shoulder, I set out on my journey.[68]

Timothy Cavanagh remembered feeling very peculiar when he first put his uniform on: "I thought everyone I passed had a humorous eye on me. I never felt so uncomfortable in all my life."[69] But Cavanagh, unlike many other recruits, had no experience of wearing a military uniform, and while it was continually asserted that the policeman was a civilian rather than military officer, throughout the Victorian and Edwardian years policemen were given military drill to ensure discipline and smartness and to combat "slouching habits."[70] John Monk recalled, for example, how his first three weeks in the Metropolitan Police in the winter of 1881 were spent at Wellington Barracks "learning what I thought was boring and rather useless drill."[71] There is, furthermore, autobiographical evidence that life in the armed forces had engendered a distinction within the ranks of subsequently serving policemen, between those who were "as hard as nails" and could "take it" and those who could not.[72]

Tough masculinity and the swagger associated with the uniform probably helped to foster self-importance and a reluctance to have personal authority questioned. The policeman was expected to keep his temper and to remain cool under provocation. Often it would seem that he did, especially in his dealings with his social superiors, yet there were occasions when a constable's "officiousness" could even wound a member of the middle class.[73] Lashing out at those whom he perceived as undeserving wretches from the residuum and "troublemakers" could provide the constable with a way of asserting his sense of personal esteem and social superiority:

> Frederick John Edwards, coal porter, stated he was saying "Goodnight" to four friends at the corner of New Church Street and Jamaica Road. A Sergeant of Police came over and said to him "get out of it." As he was moving away he was struck a blow on the side of the face with the Sergeant's cape. One of Edward's [*sic*] friends said "that wasn't asked for," and the Sergeant said "if you don't clear out you'll get the same." This statement is corroborated by two people in the employment of the Anglo-American Cold Storage Company, and by two carmen. On the part of the Police, several officers were called who were on duty at or about the time mentioned. Their evidence is to the effect that no such incident took place . . . I am of the opinion that some such incident must have taken place; it is impossible to believe that all these persons can have conspired together to fabricate a false charge of this description.[74]

The dangers to policemen in so-called "rough" districts may have prompted some constables to get their retaliation in first. Punishment inflicted on the spot obviated the need for a long wait in court after a long night on the beat; it also avoided handing decisions over to magistrates who might not share the policeman's point of view. Violence also could be justified and rationalized unofficially by policemen as a means of achieving their principal aim: the prevention of crime.[75] Physical chastisement was accepted as a legitimate punishment for certain petty offenses by the Victorian and Edwardian working class. Policemen, as a subgroup of the respectable working class, might consider a summarily administered "clip round the ear" as a way of dissuading a juvenile offender, or even a potential offender, from taking the road to becoming a "habitual criminal." Stan Gibson, brought up in London's East End at the beginning of the twentieth century, remembered:

> One Christmas time we was looking in the Post Office at the top of the road, and it had Christmas goods in it. And we was looking in there, both of us, my friend and I was looking in it most intently and all of a sudden, oh we had a clip round the ear 'ole. It was a cold night and the lobes of your ear was frozen and this copper had a knack of—most coppers did in those days—had a knack of flicking their gloves onto the lobe of your ear. I very nearly cried out of pain.[76]

The incidence of such behavior by individual policeman is impossible to assess. Poor people had little opportunity or facility for making complaints; such action was not going to be noted in police records, and as in the case of Frederick Edwards quoted earlier, policemen were inclined to back each other up and deny accusations of wrongful conduct.

Mutual support to deny wrong-doing and to confront complaints was a corollary of, on the one hand, the creation of an *esprit de corps* by the police authorities and, on the other, the sociability of the work experience. The uniform symbolized both, as is evident in the following example. In June 1887, P.C. Bowen Endacott, on special patrol duty in Regent Street, arrested a young seamstress, Elizabeth Cass, on a charge of soliciting. The case became a *cause célèbre* with questions asked in Parliament. Endacott claimed that he knew Cass to be a prostitute and had witnessed her soliciting in the past as well as when he apprehended her. But Cass had arrived in London only recently and could produce witnesses to the effect that she hardly ever had gone out alone. The case against Cass was dropped; Endacott was suspended and charged with willful and corrupt perjury. Members of the Metropolitan Police petitioned the Home Secretary for permission to start a subscription for Endacott's defense. Permission was granted, and Endacott was able to employ an effective counsel, who, when his trial came on at the Old Bailey, launched a vigorous assault on Cass's morality. No evidence was deployed to prove that Endacott's accusations were correct, and, aside from her meetings with a married man before she came to London, meetings of which the defense made much, Cass could bring forward witnesses to support her own case. Without Endacott being called as a witness, the judge dismissed the case; Endacott was restored to his rank and entrusted with the supervision of the British Museum. The *Police Review* believed that the subscription for Endacott's defense demonstrated the *esprit de corps* of the Metropolitan Police. This might also be illustrative, like Endacott's assertion that he knew Cass as a prostitute, of the belief that the policeman's professional intuition should remain impervious to criticism from nonexperts.[77] More than ten years after the Cass affair, a woman long associated with the rescue of the "fallen" commented in a letter to an M.P. that "the police are prone to take the bad character of women who are out at night very easily for granted."[78] The police, it appears, considered themselves as the experts who knew who offenders were, and who should be trusted to police them. Commentators on the "criminal classes" were stressing police expertise in this area by the 1850s,[79] and by the close of the century, police bureaucrats were emerging who employed a variety of new scientific techniques for maintaining a surveillance of criminals.[80]

The extent to which this masculine culture of the police involved a sexist attitude toward women is also difficult to assess. Sexual attitudes were not the kinds of issues commonly discussed in Victorian and Edwardian autobiographies. However, evidence from a slightly later period is suggestive. C. H. Rolph, who joined the City of London Police in 1921, found his new workmates "among the most sex-absorbed body of men in the country," indulging in group discussions on sex and boasting about their prowess. Harry Daley, who joined the Metropolitan Police four years later, was ridiculed and abused by some constables for his homosexuality.[81] Stories of the way in which the police enforced the Contagious Diseases Acts in the last third of the nineteenth century, while difficult to substantiate, suggest that even the "respectable" Victorian bobby had an overdeveloped interest at least in the sight of unclothed women and the use of obscenities.[82] Indifference, too, signified male uniformed protest at women speaking out: during the 1872 election campaign for Pontefract, a meeting held in a hayloft by women opposing the Contagious Diseases legislation was torched, and the women threatened with fists, while the police looked on.[83]

On the surface, there would appear to be contradictions in the relationship between police self-image, their modes of intervention, and the institutional emphasis upon probity and fairness. On the one hand there was the sedulously cultivated, respectable public face of the policeman—an earnest autodidact, polite and controlled—and, on the other, the man who was swaggering and streetwise, who was not averse to overly physical tactics, and who stood by his colleagues whatever their faults and offenses. The Victorian and Edwardian police contained representatives of both extremes, and probably a majority who personified both to varying degrees according to circumstance. Policemen may have been deployed against trades unionists on occasions, yet their own aspirations were often much closer to those of unions than has been commonly allowed. Policemen possessed the prejudices of the respectable male working class, and their job put them in a position where they could ensure that those prejudices had an impact on those whom they identified as stereotypical members of the residuum: the habitual criminal, the vagrant, the juvenile delinquent, the prostitute. These supposed contradictions were compatible elements in the value system of the policeman: public respectability, private machismo, and sometimes violence on behalf of law and order were not mutually exclusive. Beneath the professional imagery of the police force lay a set of interdependent personal strategies that united the goals of the force with those of the policeman. This did not mean, however, that when the organization was seen to be reneging on working conditions or pensions the policeman was quiescent. Again, police criticism and strike action, while ostensibly repudiating the force's emphasis upon discipline, also demonstrate a sense of long-term commitment to their jobs.

In *The Rise of Professional Society: England Since 1880*, Harold Perkin says nothing of the police force. Of course, the wider model of professionalization has its roots in the liberal professions, among well-educated individuals with particular skills developed by specialist training. The educational requirements of police recruits at the end on the nineteenth and beginning of the twentieth centuries were minimal, and the bulk of police training was acquired while carrying out the job, possibly under the tutelage of a seasoned constable. Police constables did not relate to the public or, specifically, the working class in quite the same way as doctors or lawyers, for example, related to their clients or the class community from whence they came. Nevertheless, over time, and beginning in the late Victorian period, the police increasingly insisted on their status as professionals.[84] In many respects, as we have indicated, they were perceived increasingly as experts in crime fighting and law and order maintenance. Just as doctors were increasingly concerned, through legislation by the state, in the prevention of illness through sanitary inspection and vaccination, as well as in controlling and combating disease through their specific skills, so the police were concerned with the prevention of crime and the control and supervision of "degenerates" and the residuum. Moreover, the pension, the regular fixed wage, and the necessity of respectability set them aside from many, perhaps most, of their class. Thus, during the Victorian and Edwardian years, the police were seen and saw themselves as having a central role as the professional bulwark of an orderly capitalist society. In its hierarchy, its sense of public service, its emphasis upon the values of self-help and self-respect, and fundamentally, in its sense of moral superiority as the justification for its interventionism and regulatory role, policing was and remains the apogee of public-sector professionalism.[85] It also expressed the emphasis upon human capital and a distinctive monopoly of specific functions that are central to Perkin's definition of professionalism, and its growing pervasiveness from the 1880s.

It was the very act of intervention that crystallized the training, self-image, and, for the policeman, the social expectation of his role as keeper of law and order, as the defender of respectable values. These were the values that he felt he personified. Thus the scale and nature of intervention reflected the individual and institutionalized codes of the police, and continue to do so. Jennifer Davis has illustrated how Jennings Buildings, a rookery of mid-Victorian London, and Broadwater Farm, a poor council estate in Tottenham, London, and a bastion of brutalist planning in the mode of 1960s comprehensive redevelopment, were viewed by affluent residents nearby as containing the dangerous classes, a term that signified further racial and class prejudices given the prominence of ethnic minorities and the residual poor (or "underclass") in both estates. The junior ranks of the police force, in both cases, manifested a willingness to judge the estates upon such terms, and to adopt a "bring in the cavalry" approach that heightened hostility between the residents and the police force.[86] Our findings illustrate that, in this sense, the police mediated between specific communities that they perceived as alien to their personal set of values, and this influenced the strategies they adopted on the beat. The social construction of these values was as much from within the ranks as from the top down.

NOTES

1. An earlier version of this chapter was read to the Canadian Learned Societies conference, Calgary, Alberta, June 1994. Our thanks to the British Academy and the University of Luton for financial assistance toward our participation. We also would like to thank those who gave helpful comments at this presentation and at a presentation of this paper at the University of Warwick, 12 November 1994. We are grateful to David Englander, Haia Shpayer-Makov, and Barbara Weinberger who generously commented on a previous draft. Also, we would like to thank the ESRC and the Research Committee of the Open University for grants that made possible the research for this paper.

2. Robert Reiner, *The Blue-Coated Worker: A Sociological Study of Police Unionism* (Cambridge, 1978).

3. The classic film is, of course, *The Blue Lamp* (1949) and the television series it spawned, *Dixon of Dock Green.*

4. For the debate upon the late Victorian residuum see Gertrude Himmelfarb, *Poverty and Compassion: The Moral Imagination of the Late Victorians* (New York, 1991).

5. Clive Emsley and Mark Clapson, "Recruiting the English Policeman, c. 1840–1940," in *Policing and Society* 3 (1994): 269–86, at 283. There is evidence from the urban force of Middlesborough in the Victorian period shows similarly that the bulk of recruits were from semi- and unskilled occupations, with a growing number of skilled men seeking "regularity of employment." See David Taylor, "The Standard of Living of Career Policemen in Victorian England: The Evidence of a Provincial Borough Force," *Criminal Justice History* 12 (1991): 107–31, at 120, 128–9.

6. Emsley and Clapson, "Recruiting the English Policeman," 283.

7. These statistics are drawn from the Open University Police Database, compiled by Ian Bridgeman and Mark Clapson under the guidance of Clive Emsley. Our methodology and findings are discussed in Emsley and Clapson, "Recruiting the English Policeman." The statistics above are on 272–74.

8. Emsley and Clapson, "Recruiting the English Policeman," 282.

9. Charles Tempest Clarkson and J. Hall Richardson, *Police!* (London, 1889), 140–41.

10. Charles Booth, *Life and Labour of the People in London*, British Library of Political and Economic Sciences (BLPES) Booth Collection, Industry series, manuscript folios by George Arkell for *Life and Labour* &c., Second Series, Vol. 4, Chapter III: Folios "Soldiers and police," 14.

11. Charles Booth, *Life and Labour of the People in London*, British Library of Political and Economic Sciences (BLPES) Booth Collection, Poverty series, notebook B72, 175, B55, p. 58.

12. *Parliamentary Papers* (hereafter PP) 1834 (600) xvi, "Select Committee on the Police of the Metropolis," qq. 148–49.

13. *Police Review* (12 April 1900): 175.

14. PP 1890 (c. 6075) lix, *Departmental Committee on Metropolitan Police Superannuation*, qq. 348–51, 658 (hereafter PP).

15. BLPES, Booth Collection, Industry series, Arkell manuscript folios "Soldiers and Police," 13–14.

16. Please note: the figures do not add up to 100 percent as all have been rounded up or down to the nearest whole number except for the statistic for dark blue streets, which is rounded up to 0.5 rather than down to zero or up to one.

17. BLPES, Booth Collection, Poverty series, notebook B65, 80.

18. Ibid., notebook B66, 85.

19. Ibid., notebook B67, 20, 40.

20. Ibid., notebook B69, 43.

21. Michael Cullen, "Charles Booth's Poverty Survey: Some New Approaches," in *The Search for Wealth and Stability: Essays in Economic and Social History presented to M. W. Flinn*, ed. T. C. Smout (London 1979), 162.

22. BLPES, Industry series, Arkell manuscript folios "Soldiers and Police," 14.

23. PP 1890 (c. 6075) lix, *Departmental Committee on Metropolitan Police Superannuation*, qq. 2404, 654–55, 913–20, 949–50, 2407.

24. Metropolitan Police Archive MS 844.85, *The Memoirs of John Monk, Chief Inspector*, 48; in Nov. 1889 Superintendent William Huntley of the Metropolitan Police was asked by the *Departmental Committee on Metropolitan Police Superannuation* what was the attraction of the police for recruits. He replied: "The hope of a pension." PP 1890 (c. 6075) lix, *Notes of Evidence . . . before the Departmental Committee*, q. 657.

25. Booth, *Life and Labour of the People in London, Second Series, Industry: Public, Professional and Domestic Service*, 2nd ed. (London, 1903), 53.

26. Booth, *Life and Labour of the People in London, First Series, Poverty: Blocks of Buildings, Schools and Immigration*, 2nd ed. (London, 1903), 31.

27. Ellen Ross, " 'Not the Sort that Would Sit on the Doorstep': Respectability in pre World War 1 London Neighbourhoods," *International Labor and Working Class History* 27 (1985): 39–59.

28. BLPES, Booth Coll. Misc. 43, *Ledger of the Inhabitants of Katharine Buildings, 1885–1890*. Our thanks to Rosemary O'Day for this reference.

29. See inter alia, for the Metropolitan Police, *Police Review* for 1900: 16 Feb., 76; 30 Nov., 567; 7 Dec., 579; 14 Dec., 591; 21 Dec., 603; 1901: 22 Feb., 87. For other cities in 1900: Manchester, 12 April, 175; Hull, 20 July, 339; Liverpool, 21 Sept., 448.

30. *Hansard*, cviii (1908) col. 1051; and see also lxxxviii (1901) col. 1043, cxxiv (1903) col. 255, cxxxi (1904) cols. 1241–42 cxxxix (1904) cols. 981–82, lxiii (1914) col. 573; *Times*, 27 Oct. 1900, 8, 9, 14, and 25 Jan. 1901, 8, 9, 12.

31. Lord Morrison of Lambeth, *Herbert Morrison: An Autobiography* (London, 1960), 12.

32. Ibid.

33. PP 1873 (1) xxxi, *Report of HMIC for 1872*, p. 7; PP 1875 (1) xxxvi, *Report of HMIC from 1874*, 212; see also, inter alia, PP 1890 (345) xxxvi, *Report of HMIC for 1889*, 129.

34. PP 1877, xv, *Select Committee on Police Superannuation Funds*.

35. *Police Review* (26 Jan. 1894): 45–46; see also 2 Feb. 54. The Cant case did not resolve all of the problems about the transfer of pensionable service from one force to another. Ten years later questions were still raised in the semiofficial journal *Justice of the Peace* lxvi (1902), 636; lxvii (1903), 393, and lxviii (1904), 373–74.

36. The *Police Chronicle* had begun life as the *Police Service Advertiser* in February 1866, changing its name to the *Police Guardian* in Jan. 1873, and then back to the *Chronicle* in 1888.

37. *Police Review* (2 Jan. 1893): 1.

38. Ibid. (16 March 1893): 127–28.

39. Ibid. (23 Feb. 1900): 90.

40. Ibid. (12 Jan. 1894: 19, and 27 April 1894): 199.

41. Ibid. (2 March 1894): 102.

42. Ibid. (28 Sept. 1900): 462–63; 5 Oct. 475–76 and 2 Nov., 524–26.

43. For Alec Burns see Metropolitan Police Archives, *Memoirs of John Monk*, 13.

44. *Police Review* (15 June 1894): 282.

45. PP 1890 (c. 6075) lix, *Departmental Committee on Metropolitan Police Superannuation*, qq. 81–82, 240, 659–62.

46. Ibid., q. 2390.

47. Ibid., qq. 366, 708.

48. Clive Emsley, *The English Police: A Political and Social History* (Hemel Hempstead, 1996), 95–99.

49. On the decline of artisan radicalism in London, and the "remade," less politicized working-class culture, with which the trades unions of the unskilled were coincident, see Gareth Stedman Jones, "Working Class Culture and Working Politics: Notes on the Remaking of a Working Class" in *Languages of Class: Studies in English Working Class History, 1832–1982*, ed. Gareth Stedman Jones, (Cambridge, 1985), passim.

50. A. F. Heath and Sarah-K. McDonald, "Social Change and the Future of the Left," in *Divided Nation: Social and Cultural Change in Britain*, ed. Linda McDowell, Philip Sarre, and Chris Hamnett (London, 1989), 36.

51. Walter Greenwood, *Love on the Dole* (1929; reprint Harmondsworth, 1980).

52. Reiner, *The Blue-Coated Worker*, 274–76; Barbara Weinberger, *Keeping the Peace? Policing Strikes in Britain 1906–1926* (Oxford, 146. For the French comparison, reflecting similar solidarities and problems, see Jean-Marc Berlière, "Quand un métayer veut être bien gardé, il nourrit ses chiens: la difficile naissance du syndicalisme policier: problèmes et ambiguitiés (1900–1914)," *Le Mouvement Social* 164 (Juillet–Sept. 1993): 25–51.

53. Richard Hyman, *Strikes* (London, 1972), chap. 4 on the institutionalization of conflict.

54. Emsley, *The English Police*, 99.

55. Thomas Smethurst, *Reminiscences of a Bolton and Stalybridge Policeman 1888–1922* (Manchester, 1983), 6.

56. *Police Guardian*, 25 Jan. 1884.

57. *Police Review*, (9 Jan. 1893): 16. See also 20 Feb., 96, and 27 Feb. 113.

58. BLPES, Industry series, Arkell manuscript folios "Soldiers and Police," 18.

59. Ibid.

60. PP 1875 (352) xiii, *Select Committee on Police Superannuation Funds*, q. 1614.

61. Tables 2–4 adapted from PP 1867–68 (89) lvii, *Return of Number of Metropolitan and City Police*, 1867; PP 1908 (c. 4156) i, *Royal Commission on the Duties of the Metropolitan Police*.

62. BLPES, Booth Collection, Poverty series, notebook B50, 1.

63. V.A.C. Gatrell, "The Decline of Theft and Violence in Victorian and Edwardian England" in *Crime and the Law: The Social History of Crime in Western Europe*, ed. V.A.C. Gatrell, Bruce Lenman, and Geoffrey Parker *Since 1500* (London, 1980), 288–89 and App. Table 5; PP 1890 (c. 6075) lix; *Departmental Committee on Metropolitan Police Superannuation*, qq. 924–26.

64. *Memoirs of John Monk*, 13.

65. Superintendent [James] Bent, *Criminal Life: Reminiscences of Forty Two Years as a Police Officer* (London, 1891); Richard Jervis, *Lancashire's Crime and Criminals* (Southport, 1908), 52–53.

66. Tom Divall, *Scoundrels and Scallywags* (London, 1929), 12–13, 17.

67. Ibid., 24; Chief Inspector James Berrett, *When I was at Scotland Yard* (London, 1932), 64.

68. Smethurst, *Reminiscences*, 7.

69. Timothy Cavanagh, *Scotland Yard Past and Present* (London, 1893), 37–45.

70. Emsley and Clapson, "Recruiting the English Policeman," 273.

71. *Memoirs of John Monk*, 6.

72. The uniform had this effect on early recruits. For a naval example from the interwar years, see Bill Naylor, *Lancashire Leatherneck* (Manchester, 1985), 11–12.

73. "The Metropolitan Police System," *Westminster Review* 45 (1874): 31–56, esp. 39–40.

74. PP 1912–13 (297) xlvii, Cd. 6367: "Transport Worker's Strike: Report by Mr. Chester Jones on Certain Disturbances at Rotherhithe on June 11th 1912, and Complaints against the Conduct of the Police in Connection Therewith," p. 5. On

the conduct of the police during strikes in the Edwardian years see Weinberger, *Keeping the Peace*. On police violence in general see Clive Emsley, " 'The Thump of Wood on a Swede Turnip': Police Violence in Nineteenth Century England," *Criminal Justice History* 6 (1985): 125–49.

75. The "prevention of crime" was declared to be the main duty of constables of the Metropolitan Police when the force was first established in 1829, and the idea became central in the directives issued to other forces; Emsley, *The English Police*, 24, 67. For a comparison and contrast between the English obsession with prevention and the experience of the French police see Clive Emsley, "Police et prévention: une perspective historique," *Les Cahiers de la sécurité intérieure* 14 (août-oct. 1993): 37–47.

76. Stephen Humphries, *Hooligans or Rebels? An Oral History of Working-Class Childhood and Youth, 1889–1939* (Oxford, 1981), 147.

77. *Hansard*, cccxvi (1887), cols. 1796–1823; *Central Criminal Court Sessions Papers*, cvi (1887), no. 1053; *Police Review* (28 Dec. 1900): 614.

78. *Hansard*, lxxxv (1900), col. 1545.

79. [J. H. Burton], "Our Convicts—Past and Present," *Blackwood's Magazine* 83 (1858): 291–310, at p. 299; [Andrew Wynter], "The Police and the Thieves," *Quarterly Review* 99 (1856): 160–200, esp. 171, 180.

80. Stefan Petrow, *Policing Morals: The Metropolitan Police and the Home Office 1870–1914* (Oxford, 1994), Chap. 4.

81. C. H. Rolph, *Living Twice* (London, 1974), 57–58; Harry Daley, *This Small Cloud: A Personal Memoir* (London, 1986), 101, 112–13.

82. *PP* 1871 (408–1) xix, "Report from the Royal Commission on the Administration and Operation of the Contagious Diseases Acts 1866–9," qq. 9193–99, 12,585–98, 19,893, 20,300.

83. Susan Kingsley Kent, *Sex and Suffrage in Britain, 1860–1914* (London, 1990), 72.

84. Barbara Weinberger, "Are the Police Professionals? An Historical Account of the British Police Institution," in *Policing Western Europe: Politics, Professionalism and Public Order, 1850–1940*, ed. Clive Emsley and Barbara Weinberger (Westport, Conn., 1991).

85. Harold Perkin, *The Rise of Professional Society: England Since 1880* (London, 1990), 378–80.

86. Jennifer Davis, "From 'Rookeries' to 'Communities': Race, Poverty and Policing in London, 1850–1985," *History Workshop Journal* 27 (spring 1989): 77.

French Police, German Troops, and the Destruction of the Old District of Marseille, 1943

Simon Kitson

On 12 November 1942, in a carefully prepared counter to the Allied invasion of North Africa four days before, German tanks and camouflaged lorries poured into Marseille through the Porte d'Aix, turned down the boulevard d'Athènes and the Canebière into the Vieux Port and the city center amid the bewildered looks of the local population, most of whom were catching their first glimpse of these mouse-grey uniforms. Marseille was occupied for the first time since 1815. While the dreaded police force, the Gestapo, set up shop in a villa in the rue Paradis, the soldiers of the Wehrmacht took up residence in the *lycées* and filled the cinemas and bars.[1] The invaders had to adapt to a different environment and the particular culture of Marseille. Although they had much to learn about local culture, they brought with them a solid prejudice against this city, which was judged as a "repaire de criminels internationaux" ("den of international criminals"), "un chancre pour l'Europe" ("a canker for Europe"), and a French version of Hamburg.[2]

They were not alone in making disparaging assertions about the city. It had become customary for successive French governments to view Marseille with suspicion. In the seventeenth century, the Marseillais had sided with La Fronde against the young Louis XIV, and as a punishment, the Sun King conquered the city and in 1660 built the forts of St. Nicholas and St. Jean, less to protect Marseille than to keep watch on it.[3] In the eighteenth century, the Marseillais had been prominent in the ranks of the early revolutionaries and after having learned the marching song of the army of the Rhine from a delegation of Montpelliérains stationed in the rue Thubaneau, had given their name to the national anthem by being the first to sing it in Paris. But in 1793, the Marseillais backed the Girondins against the Jacobins. Defeated by the Jacobin troops of Carteaux, the city was stripped of its name and for a period of three months became *"la ville sans nom"* ("a town without a name"). Fréron, the representative of the Convention, ordered the destruction of a number of buildings suspected of harboring counterrevolutionaries, such as the Église des Accoules, and declared the city *"incurable à jamais, à moins d'une déportation de tous les habitants et d'une transfusion des hommes du nord"* ("forever incurable, at least without a deportation of all the inhabitants and a transfusion of men from the north").[4] More recently, the assassination of Alexander I of Yugoslavia on the Canebière in 1934 and the street fights of the 1930s had given Marseille the reputation of a European Chicago. Moreover, since the armistice, the influx of refugees into the city had caused the fascist writer Lucien Rebatet to nickname it "*Marseille la Juive.*" ("Marseille the Jew").[5]

Both French and German criticism focused particularly on the *quartier de l'hôtel de ville* (district of the townhall), also known as the Vieux Quartiers or quartiers napolitains. Situated to the immediate north of the Vieux Port, much of this *quartier* dated back to 600 B.C. and the original Greek settlers, although a number of buildings, particularly the hotels, had been added between the fourteenth and seventeenth centuries. It was populated essentially by minor civil servants, small-time traders, sailors, fishermen, and dock workers, many of whom were of Italian or Corsican extraction. It was this combination of the origin of its inhabitants and the age of its buildings that was at the base of the district's reputation. Even authors sympathetic to the *quartier* have underlined the uniqueness of its noises and smells. Louis Blin, writing in 1941, described the misnamed Grand'rue. Scarcely three meters wide and built before the invention of automobiles, it had become too narrow to fulfill its modern role as one of the city's main thoroughfares.[6] The frustrated outbursts of drivers blocked by the street's welter of activity were drowned out by the cacophony of radios and gramophones competing to make known the songs of Tino Rossi or Rina Ketty. The odor of pizzas baking in its pizzerias or *chichi-frégis* frying in the street mingled with the smell of cheap perfumes in popular hairdressers' shops. The bright colors of the laundry hanging above the street on pulley ropes like so many flags gave the *quartier* an appearance of constant festivity.[7] But the district was also noted for its black market activity. The *Préfet délégué à l'administration de la ville* (prefect dedicated to the town's administration), installed in the town hall, complained about such activity in the place de Lenche, but police inquiries consistently drew a blank.[8] Anti-government activity also was denounced, and letters of complaint were sent to Pierre Laval.[9] There long had been talk of razing the whole *quartier* to the ground, and a project, the infamous *plan Baudouin*, was drawn up to this effect.[10]

Historians have been unable to establish a direct link between this project and the German-inspired operation to destroy the district at the beginning of 1943, but it is certain that the French obsession with the seediness of the Vieux Quartiers lent credibility to German prejudice. The Nazi authorities were worried that the narrow streets of this *quartier* could form the stage for street combats, that resisters could escape all too easily using the secret underground passageways linking these old buildings to each other and that a number of German deserters may have found shelter here. The significance of these concerns was amplified by a lack of faith in the local police. When Vichy police chief Bousquet met the German generals Oberg and Daluege in Paris in December 1942, the latter brought up this question, underlining that a demonstration of 14 July 1942, where the Marseille police had sided with the demonstrators, had shown where police sympathies lay.[11]

The feeling that German troops were unprotected by the local authorities seemed confirmed, first by attacks against the requisitioned Hôtel Astoria on the Canebière and a military vehicle on the Cours St. Louis on 2 December 1942[12] and then on 3 January 1943 by what the Germans described as an "*explosions d'explosifs lourdes de conséquences*" ("explosions of explosives severe in consequences") carried out by the communist resisters and aimed at a German brothel in the rue Lemaître and the requisitioned Hôtel Splendid.[13] In the hours following the attacks of 3 January the regional prefect, Joseph Rivalland, was summoned to the Hôtel Noailles, where the German general staff instructed him to draw up a list of hostages who would be shot in the event of further incident. In application of a government circular of 7 May 1942, Rivalland refused and, taking a courageous attitude, added that the only hostage he would name was himself.[14] The Germans, irritated by the prefect's intransigence, declared a state of siege and announced that the Marseille police were to pass under direct SS control.

The following ten days were marked by a series of negotiations. On 5 January, Bousquet met Oberg in Paris. At this meeting it was agreed to return the police to French control.[15] It is not clear what Bousquet offered in return, but it is not unreasonable to make a connection between this meeting and the replacement of Prefect Rivalland by Prefect Lemoine three days later. On 13 January, a group of senior Nazi officials, including Oberg, met the senior echelons of the local French administration together with Bousquet, in the villa Ben Quillado, in the Roucas Blanc district. The German plans to destroy the Vieux Quartiers and to make 40,000 people homeless were countered by the suggestion of the most senior local police official,[16] raised at a meeting the following day, that the French police, acting in complete independence, should carry out an operation aimed at purging the city of its criminal element.[17] The Germans accepted the French plan but refused to renounce their own project, although they did agree to reduce the perimeter of the area to be destroyed. The decision to allow French forces such a prominent role and, indeed, a complete independence in the whole operation, with the exception of the sealing off and actual destruction of the Vieux Quartiers, must be explained by four factors:

- the arrests throughout the city were entirely of French inspiration, conceived as a bargaining counter to save the buildings of the Vieux Quartiers;
- the operations were to be supervised personally by René Bousquet, who still enjoyed complete German confidence;
- the unreliability of the Marseille force would be diluted by the participation of other police services from outside the city;
- the Germans could not have undertaken such an operation on their own and, indeed, Himmler had insisted to Oberg that during the preliminary negotiations, the latter should play on the French desire to maintain a semblance of sovereignty to persuade them, not only to provide the manpower necessary but also to believe that in so doing they were being offered a major concession.[18]

Henceforth, there were to be two operations in Marseille, a German operation (called "Sultan") to seal off and blow up the Vieux Quartiers and a French operation to carry out vast police operations throughout the city and to perform the evacuation of the district to be destroyed by the Nazis. The new prefect insisted on the separateness of these measures.[19] In fact the police operations throughout the city were to run from January 22 to 29 and involved home visits, roundups in the street, and identity checks in public places such as cafés or cinemas.[20] The targets of the operation were listed as the following: habitual criminals, pimps, vagabonds, vagrants, anyone without a *carte d'alimentation* (ration book), all Jews [both French and foreign], illegal immigrants, and anyone who had been out of work for more than a month.[21] The operations were to be the largest in French history, not only by their duration, but also by the size of the forces mobilized and the number of identity checks carried out. Beyond the entire mobilization of the local police, Bousquet had ordered the drafting in of all available personnel from forces throughout the country. Their exact number is not clear, but estimates vary between 7,000 and 9,000 officers brought in to supplement the local force (and the 5,000 German troops present).[22] These reinforcements were drawn from the Groupes Mobiles de Réserve (GMR), urban police forces, the gendarmerie, and the garde. André Sauvageot has described how "*on n'aperçoit de tout côté que casques luisant au soleil et faisceaux de mousquetons à proximité de groupes en alerte*" ("on all sides one only saw helmets gleaming in the sun and clusters of muskets near to units on alert").[23] The scale of the operation is underlined by its results, which the prefect summarized as follows.[24]

Number of identities checked:	400,000
Number of individuals apprehended:	5,956
Number of individuals freed after verification:	3,997
Number imprisoned:	30
Number sent to Center for the Concentration of Foreigners:	13

Number interned:	294
Number sent by a special train to Compiègne:	1,642
Number retained as suspect or dangerous by the Vetting Commission in Frejus:	600

The 1,642 persons directed to Compiègne represented a convoy sent in the early hours from the gare d'Arenc and made up of about 1,300 individuals sent to the Baumettes prison in Marseille for verification of their identity between 22 January and the next evening, together with 300 or so arrested during the night of 23 January, and sent directly to the Commissariat Central. The French authorities had little time to vet these individuals, and their figures must be seen as approximate, because the vetting commission set up in the Baumettes by the senior local police official, the *intendant de police*, was only able to operate during a few hours before its registers were seized by the Nazis and instructions were issued to send the internees on to the gare d'Arenc.[25] Serge Klarsfeld has been able to establish that 782 of those taken that evening were Jewish.[26]

The responsibility of Vichy in these deportations was manifold.[27] A letter from a woman in the boulevard d'Accès whose two sisters and aunt had been taken in the roundup of 22 January was addressed to Pétain in desperate tones, pleading with him to find out what had happened to her relations. There can be no denying the sense of betrayal in her request.[28] Vichy's insistence that all Jewish identity cards comply with the law of 11 December 1942, whereby they were to be stamped with the word Jew, was one more stage in the process of exclusion that now made such citizens easy targets for police roundups.[29] Moreover, all those transferred for deportation on the morning of 24 January had been arrested during the French initiated operations and without exception they were arrested by the French police. The German operations which destroyed 1,400 buildings, making 25,000 people homeless, did not begin until later that day, although the evacuation of the *quartier* defined by the Nazis was to account for a number of the 600 people later transferred via Fréjus.

Vichy's responsibility was also an expression of the naiveté of its police chiefs, who seriously believed they were gaining some concessions in their negotiations with the Nazis. The morality of a trading off of roundups of suspect individuals against the limitations of the destruction of buildings was, to say the least, dubious. It is not difficult to find examples of callousness in the attitude of the police hierarchy in this affair. The photograph of René Bousquet smiling while surrounded by Nazi officers during the negotiations is very well known.[30] No historians have yet quoted a Resistance report (whose precise inside knowledge of the details of the operation suggest it originated with a police resister), which described the director of the Sûreté, Buffet, as particularly keen to take back to Vichy a living souvenir of his excursion to Marseille and as the one who instructed a commissaire and number of locksmiths to open up abandoned houses in order to find a parrot. The Resistance report regretted that the bird found was unable to speak and hence "*n'a pu élever aucune protestation et ne pourra davantage témoigner*" ("wasn't able to put up any objection and wouldn't bear witness besides").[31] Even amongst the senior hierarchy, however, there were examples of protest. Although it was the *Intendant de Police* de Rodellec du Porzic's suggestion to carry out the dragnet operation throughout the city, it was this same civil servant who protested the most vigorously against the destruction of the Vieux Quartiers. Following the negotiations of 13 January, de Rodellec had suggested that the French authorities should use the intermediary of a neutral embassy to alert world opinion as to what was about to happen in Marseille. Shortly after the operations were terminated, de Rodellec resigned his post of *Intendant de Police* in protest.[32]

As could be expected from an operation mobilizing several thousand police officers, reports concerning their attitude contain wide divergences. In order to assess more accurately the attitude of police officers during these operations, it is necessary to distinguish between the measures taken between 22 and 29 January, which targeted categories of outcasts and particularly Jews, and the operations of the night of 23–24 January, which aimed at the evacuation of the population of the Vieux Quartiers.[33]

As with the deportations of Jews in the summer of 1942, there was no mass rebellion of police officers.[34] A Resistance report seemingly of police origin, spoke of uniformed officers who had little choice but to execute orders and esteemed that their rank eliminated all possibility of initiative.[35] Obedience was encouraged by the fact that in most cases policemen were divided off into pairs containing officers from different branches and from different towns, obliging potential police resisters to make hasty assessments of the opinions of their companions if they wished to avoid denunciation for any act of Resistance. The presence of commissaires outside buildings, noted by a number of witnesses, opened up the possibility that the thoroughness of the search could be the subject of immediate verification by hierarchical superiors. Both the possibility of agents provocateurs amongst the potential victims and the general sense of urgency in these operations could serve as deterrents to initiative.

If these hierarchical pressures made resistance difficult, it certainly did not render it impossible, as the very existence of a (limited) police Resistance to these measures testifies. It was more than anything a question of plucking up enough courage.[36] Often the attempts to help were too half-hearted or couched in ambiguous tones. Roxanne Matalon remembers that the police officers who arrested her father in their home in the rue Glandèves offered him the chance to go back and fetch some cigarettes, an offer which she interprets as an invitation to escape but which her father, believing that the regularity of his situation would be a sufficient protection, failed to act on.[37] There were examples of more active resistance. Before the roundups, Ignace Doboin received the visit of an officer, whom he had befriended during their period of military service in 1939–1940, who now tipped him off as to the imminence of the operations.[38] In another case, a potential victim was accompanied to the station and put on a train by a commissaire friend of his.[39] But the personal acquaintance of a police officer was not always sufficient protection once the operations got under way. Simone Beraha, who was fourteen in 1943, remembers that one of the two policemen who knocked at her family's door, 9 rue Vacon, was well known to her father and even addressed him by his first name when asking for his identity papers; this did not stop them from loading him onto a police truck.[40] This is not to say that there was no help from police officers during the operations. Victor Algazi recalls that the inspector who called on his family told them to lock their door and to answer to no one. When another officer began banging at their door, the inspector called out "*ici, c'est fait, ils sont descendus*" ("here, it's done, they have gone down"). Algazi attributes this act to the fact that the inspector was acquainted with his mother's birthplace—Smyrna (Asia-Minor)—and had fond memories of it. It is far more likely that his initiative was prompted by the fact that he had entered the Algazi flat unaccompanied.[41] Following the arrests, there were examples of police resistance at the Baumettes prison, the immediate destination of a number of those rounded up. Sarah Aboaf remembers how a police officer took her and her mother off to one side while the other Jews were loaded up for transfer to the gare d'Arenc and, once the departures were completed, put them on to a bus for Mazargues with the words: "*nous sommes tous des êtres humains*" (we are all human beings").[42]

This last incident illustrates the series of choices police officers were making. The officer who helped Sarah Aboaf and her mother did so despite watching a number of other Jews being taken out for transfer. Like many of his colleagues, he worked on the logic that by participating in the operations he could save a few people, even if this meant standing by and watching or even helping as others were loaded up. There was no room in this logic for a questioning of whether the Germans really had the capacity to carry out the operations themselves and what they would have done in the event of mass defections from the police. It was the policy of the "*moindre mal*" ("lesser harm") that in the event proved so disastrous. This series of choices was encouraged by the instructions given to police officers at a conference in the run-up to the operations. Bousquet and his director of the Sûreté, fearing that their policy might be misconstrued by the rank and file, had addressed two large gatherings of officers assembled in the Centre d'hygiène Mentale and the Intendance de police. Bousquet had claimed that "*l'intervention de la police française ne se justifiait que parce que nous avions voulu éviter une action directe de l'armée allemande*" ("the intervention of the French police was only justified because we wanted to avoid direct action by the German army"). He presented the situation of the administration as a choice between leaving the Germans to carry out the operations *"avec le risque pour la population française d'avoir à en souffrir terriblement"* ("with the risk that the French population would have suffered terribly") and working with the Nazis and, thereby, achieving concessions. The head of the political branch, the Renseignements Généraux, in Marseille remembered that *"dans l'ensemble les personnes présentes avaient emporté une impression favorable de cette conférence"* ("on the whole the people present had taken away a favorable impression from that conference"), thereby implying that whatever their general hostility to Vichy, they had accepted the essence of the choices Vichy was making.[43]

The high proportion of Jews amongst those arrested in the operations suggests that there was a trading off of the arrest of Jews for the nonarrest of Aryans. Even within the Jewish community, the police made a certain number of distinctions between those they would and those they were more reluctant to take. Rabbi Israël Salzer has described as *"de très rares exceptions"* ("very rare exceptions") the cases where *"un policier moins malveillant a laissé chez elle une mère avec un petit enfant, emmenant tout de même le père et les enfants plus âgés"* ("a less malevolent policeman had left at home a mother with a small child, all the same taking away the father and the older children").[44] To claim that this practice was rare contradicts the evidence left by a number of witnesses and victims.[45] Of course, the value of their accounts must be set against the fact that a large number of those arrested could not leave any record of their suffering as a consequence of their almost immediate deportation. But it is clear that a considerable gender and age bias existed in arrests. This is not to say that there was not a large number of cases where whole families were taken or much more exceptional ones where both parents were arrested while the children were left unaccompanied, but it was certainly not unusual for the father and elder children to be taken while the mother was left tending the younger children. This brutal application of traditional gender stereotypes goes some way toward explaining why, of those Jews who were included in the convoy of 24 January, there were 517 men and 228 women. The decision to leave the children in a number of cases was a reference back to the shock many police officers had experienced in the summer of 1942 when confronted with the horror of the separation of children and parents prior to deportations of Jews or, subsequently, when children themselves began to be deported.[46]

Similar shock had been experienced the previous summer as regards the deportation of sick people, and this shock was to have some overspill onto the current operations. Elie Arditti remembers that it was thanks to a young member of the mobile force, the GMR, who intervened with a plain-clothed police officer in favor of his sick mother, that Arditti's mother and sister were allowed to stay at their home, 13 rue d'Aubagne, although this inspector passed on the ultimate responsibility of this decision to a commissaire waiting downstairs who would settle the matter once Arditti had presented the identity cards of his relations and explained their situation. As it happened, Arditti took advantage of the absence of zeal of a GMR who allowed him to go to a toilet at the end of the stairway, where he hid their identity papers. Once arrived at the Baumettes prison, he saw a woman from another lorry complaining to a GMR that her crutches were still in the back of the police truck and that she could not walk without them. The GMR replied simply: *"Oh! Bientôt, vous n'en aurez plus besoin"* ("Oh! Soon you will not be needing them").[47] As with the question of the arrest of children, police attitude toward sick people during these arrests was most polarized in the branches of the GMR and the gendarmerie. This was doubtless a repercussion of the 1942 operations where members of these two branches had been present in the camps at the moment of the transfer of Jews and had witnessed more vividly than their colleagues from other corps the horror of these deportations, causing them to be much more definite in their reactions. Of course, even this shock did not necessarily translate into active support of the Jews in January 1943. Many were reduced to simple expressions of horror or impotence, once those they had arrested began to be transferred by the Germans on 24 January.[48]

A sense of impotence also was experienced by police officers during the second phase of the operations, that is to say, the evacuation of the population of the old *quartiers* in preparation for their destruction by the Germans. The Resistance report of police origin claimed, *"il n'est pas possible de dépeindre les scènes déchirantes auxquelles 90% des policiers assistaient impuissants"* ("it is not possible to depict the heart-rending scene at which 90 percent of the police assisted powerlessly").[49] The sense of impotence emanated from the feeling that the operations were beyond their control, and indeed, short of armed rebellion, it is difficult to see what police officers could have done to prevent the destruction of these *quartiers*. Participation in this phase was not underpinned by the same sort of choices inherent in the operations throughout the town. The involvement of the vast majority of police officers was limited to issuing instructions to people to leave their houses and offering help through words of comfort or through carrying the bags of the evacuated.[50] The Resistance report made a similar claim underlining that the police had been *"90 % avec la population"* ("90 % with the population"), although it should be noted that a certain amount of the looting from evacuated houses was subsequently attributed to the police.[51] Even previously collaborationist police officers were said to have tears in their eyes at the sight of these operations, and the police Resistance document noted, *"ils ont sans doute compris, quoique tardivement"* ("they were included without doubt, though slowly").[52]

Overall in the Vieux Port incident, the police carried out Vichy's wishes, despite strong public outcry concerning the operations. This might be taken to suggest that, ultimately, the weight of the institution counted for far more than their concern for public opinion. Many would see in police obedience an example of traditional civil servants caught in the spiral of passive acceptance of the will of their government and believing that they owed the same sort of obedience to Vichy as to the Republic. Such a view would not be entirely founded. There were certainly those who continued to believe that their function was to serve the government, but obedience had not been the dominant legacy of the 1930s. The hierarchical pressures exerted on police officers during these operations were incomparable with anything they had experienced in Third Republic France. But the emphasis on obedience would cause one to ignore any question of a community of interests between Vichy and its police. By the beginning of 1943, police officers had begun to have considerable reservations about Vichy, particularly as regards police wages and Vichy's anglophobia, but this did not exclude marriages of convenience between the two. The belief that if the operations were kept in the hands of the French they would be carried out less brutally and would offer greater possibility for selection of those to be rounded up was a common denominator between many police officers and Vichy on this issue. It was in this perspective that the police could claim to be serving the population's interests by serving Vichy. The flaw in this logic is the fact that had Vichy forces refused the operation, then the roundups would have been extremely limited indeed, as the Germans had neither the manpower nor the local knowledge to perform them on a similar scale.

NOTES

1. Paul Jankowski, *Communism & Collaboration, Simon Sabiani and Politics in Marseille, 1919–44* (New Haven & London, 1989), 93–94; A. Negis, *Marseille sous l'occupation* (Marseille, 1947), 18–19; André Sauvageot, *Marseille dans la tourmente* (Paris, 1949), 186.

2. Archives Départementales des Bouches-du-Rhône [henceforth AD BDR] 56W 71.

3. Bruno Roberty, Marseille, *Quelques notes sur Saint-Jean, son fort et ses entours* (Marseille, 1937), 28; *Le Petit Marseillais*, 24/3/36; Michael L. Kennedy, *The Jacobin Club of Marseille, 1790–1794* (Ithaca, N.Y., 1973), 3.

4. Edmond Poupe, *Lettres de Barras et de Fréron, en mission dans le midi* (Draguignan, 1910), 134–35. See also Roger Duchene, *Histoires de Marseille* (Paris, 1989), 36–37.

5. Lucien Rebatet, "Marseille la Juive," *Je Suis Partout*, 30/8/41.

6. Louis Blin, *Marseille inconnue* (Avignon, 1941), 113–19; Jacques Greber, *Ville de Marseille, plan d'aménagement et d'extension* (Paris, 1933), 44–45.

7. Blin, *Marseille inconnue*, 113–19.

8. AD BDR 5W 371, Le Préfet délégué à l'administration de Marseille à M l'Intendant de Police, n° 0/2 EMP 23/6/42; AD BDR 5W 371, Commissaire de la

Section Judiciaire à M le Commissaire Principal, chef de la section de PJ, n° 32819, 21/7/42; AD BDR 5W 368, M André P., Quai Maréchal Pétain, à M le Chef du Gouvernement, 27/7/42.

9. AD BDR 5W 368, M André P., Quai Maréchal Pétain, à M le Chef du Gouvernement, 27/7/42.

10. This project, named after the architect Eugène Baudouin, appeared in a brochure issued in May 1942.

11. AD BDR 56W 71, déclarations de Bousquet, 14/6/45; Archives Nationales [henceforth AN] 3W 92, déclarations de Bousquet, 4/10/48; Simon Kitson, "The Marseille Police in Their Context, from Popular Front to Liberation," (D.Phil thesis, Sussex University, 1995), 103–8.

12. AD BDR M6 11071, Bulletin Hebdomadaire des RG, 30/11–6/12/42.

13. AN 3W 90, Le Général von Neubronne au Secrétariat d'État près le chef de gouvt., 4/1/43; AN 3W 90, déclarations de Rolf Mühler, Commandant du SD de Marseille, 21/5/47; Christian Oppetit, *Marseille, Vichy et les Nazis* (Marseille, 1993), 42; Jacques Delarue, *Trafics et crimes sous l'occupation* (Paris, 1968), 245–47.

14. C. Oppetit, *Marseille, Vichy et les Nazis* (Marseille, 1993), 27; AN Fla 3922, CNI, 31/S/L1A/O, 28/1/43; AN Fla 3922, CNI, CE. Libe/31501, rapport n° 19, R III 9A, 11/2/43. For the Vichy circular, see AN F7 14907 [346], Ministre de l'Intérieur à MM les Préfets, n° 88, 7/5/42.

15. AD BDR 56W 71, déclarations de Bousquet, 14/6/45; AN 3W 92, déclarations de Bousquet, 4/10/48.

16. The Intendant de Police Maurice Anne-Marie de Rodellec du Porzic.

17. Oppetit, *Marseille, Vichy et les Nazis*, 28–29.

18. Ibid., 28–31.

19. AD BDR 56W 71, Le Préfet Régional à M le chef du Gouvernement, 30/1/43.

20. For the day to day unfolding of the operations see: AN Fla 3922, CNI rapport n° RIII, n° 9, Mazur 1 Ax.03. 3/14, 1/2/43; AD BDR 56W 71, résumé des rapports parvenus au Consistoire Central sur les événements survenus à Marseille du 22 au 29/1/43; Centre de Documentation Juive et Contemporaine, CCCLXIV-4, Knochen-Oberg, Pt. III, 195; AD BDR 56W 71, Le Préfet Régional à M le Chef du Gouvernement, 30/1/43.

21. AN 3W 90, the list of targets figures on an instruction issued to senior police officials on 18 January 1943 under the title *"recherches des indésirables de Marseille,"* which claimed the operation should net 8,000 people.

22. On this point see: AN Fla 3922, CNI rapport n° RIII, n° 9, Mazur 1 Ax.03. 3/14, 1/2/43; AD BDR 56W 71, déclarations de Buffet, 28/10/44; AD BDR 56W 71, rapport du Commissaire Dautun, 22/2/45; Delarue, *Trafics et crimes sous l'occupation*, 258; Oppetit, *Marseille, Vichy et les Nazis* (Marseille, 1993), 30.

23. Sauvageot, *Marseille dans la tourmente*, 208.

24. AD BDR 56W 71, Le Préfet Régional à M le Chef du Gouvernement, 30/1/43.

25. AD BDR M6 11046, L'Intendant de Police à M le Chef du Gouvernement, 29/7/43.

26. Serge Klarsfeld, *Les transferts de Juifs de la région de Marseille vers les*

camps de Drancy ou de Compiègne en vue de leur déportation, 11/8/42–24/7/44 (Paris, 1992), 39.

27. Oppetit, *Marseille, Vichy et les Nazis*, 31–32.

28. AN 2AG 82 SP10M, Aimée Cattan au Maréchal Pétain, 28/6/43.

29. The text of this law can be consulted in Serge Klarsfeld, *Le calendrier de la persécution des Juifs en France, 1940–44* (Paris, 1993), 707.

30. For the photograph see Serge Klarsfeld, *Vichy-Auschwitz* (Paris, 1983), between 160 and 161.

31. AN Fla 3922, CNI rapport n° RIII, n° 9, Mazur 1 Ax.03. 3/14, 1/2/43.

32. Foreign Office, *France Basic Handbook*, n° 2: *the Region of Marseille; part 1-people and administration* (London, 1943), 15; AD BDR 56W 101, Interrogatoire de de Rodellec du Porzic, 24/1/46 & déclarations d'Alexandre Guibbal, 31/3/45.

33. Kitson, "Marseille Police in their Context," 108–21.

34. AD BDR 56W 71, Le Préfet Régional à M le chef du Gouvernement, 30/1/43.

35. AN Fla 3922, CNI rapport n° RIII, n° 9, Mazur 1 Ax.03. 3/14, 1/2/43.

36. There were risks for police officers caught helping Jews. The Brigadier Louis Vaugier lost his job after letting a Jew escape, AD BDR 56W 15, pièce 28.

37. Oral evidence from Roxanne Algazi (née Matalon), Marseille, 18/12/92. Her evidence also features in Oppetit, *Marseille, Vichy et les Nazis*, 120.

38. Oral evidence from Ignace Doboin, Paris, 6/2/93.

39. AD BDR 55W 86, Letter from J. Ben . . . to Mme. Vinc . . . , 6/12/44.

40. Evidence from Simone Beraha in Oppetit, *Marseille, Vichy et les Nazis*, 119.

41. Oral evidence from Victor Algazi, Marseille, 18/12/92.

42. Evidence from Sarah Aboaf in Oppetit, *Marseille, Vichy et les Nazis*, 119–20.

43. AD BDR 56W71, déclarations de Bousquet, 14/6/45; AD BDR 56W 101, déclarations de Jean Magnoac, 28/5/45 & Michel Brumter, 30/4/45; AN 3W 90, déclarations de Paul Marabuto, 12/7/48; Loup Durand, *Le caïd* (Paris, 1976), 143.

44. AD BDR 56W 101, déposition de Israël Salzer, rabbin de Marseille, 5/1/45.

45. See for example the evidence from individuals in Oppetit, *Marseille, Vichy et les Nazis*, 115–37.

46. Kitson, "Marseille police in their context," 103–8.

47. Evidence from Elie Arditti in Oppetit, *Marseille, Vichy et les Nazis*, 117.

48. Jacques Delarue, who was present on the morning of the departure of the train for Compiègne, claimed that: "*Devant cette scène poignante, on se sentait saisi par la rage et la honte à la fois. Puis malgré le sentiment d'impuissance totale que l'on éprouvait, on se sentait envahi par la honte de voir des hommes se conduire ainsi, et de les laisser faire . . .*", Delarue, *Trafics et crimes sous l'occupation*, 261; AN Fla 3922, CNI rapport n° RIII, n° 9, Mazur 1 Ax.O3. 3/14, 1/2/43.

49. AN Fla 3922, CNI rapport n° RIII, n° 9, Mazur 1 Ax.03. 3/14, 1/2/43.

50. AD BDR 56W 71, déclarations de l'ancien directeur des GMR, 16/11/44.

51. André Ducasse, "Chronique du Vieux Port en Guerre, 1939–45," *Arts et Livres de Provence*, 31 (special edition) (1957): 87.

52. AN Fla 3922, CNI rapport n° RIII, n°, 9, Mazur 1 Ax.O3. 3/14, 1/2/43. For the question of pillaging see for example: AD BDR 56W 71, déclarations de Robert Auzanneau, 7/11/44; Sauvageot, *Marseille dans la tourmente*, 210.

"Trusted Servants of the Population": The Public Safety Branch and the German Police in the British Zone of Germany

David Smith

The Public Safety Branch (PSB) of the Civilian Control Commission for Element (CCG) (BE, British Element) was given the task of reforming and reorganizing the German police after World War II.[1] It is the intention of this chapter to trace the development of British policy, directed by Gerald Halland, the inspector general of PSB.[2] Halland believed that democracy in Germany could be achieved only if accompanied by a demilitarized, denazified, and disarmed police force, which would improve the prestige of the German police in the eyes of the population and encourage them to act as "trusted servants of the public"[3] with tact, courtesy, and impartiality. It was the task of the PSB to train a police force composed of new professionals guided by civilian values, with individual policemen answerable in the courts. The German police were to be freed from their numerous judicial and administrative functions in order to concentrate on combatting crime and keeping public order. Acutely conscious of the loss of civil rights in the Nazi era, the PSB wanted the German civilian population safeguarded from unlawful arrest and detention by the police.[4]

A central feature of this attempt to democratize the German police was the British insistence that national command over the police be abolished. The German police, completely centralized by the Nazis, were to adopt the decentralized administrative structure operative in Britain since the nineteenth century. Each *Stadtkreis* (large city) and each *Regierungsbezirk* (county administrative district) was to have a separate police force with self-contained speciality services controlled by a chief of police. The chief would be supervised by an independent representative police committee free from the direct control of the local political structure or the minister of the Interior. This partnership between central and local authority was one that the PSB expected to prevent the police from becoming an instrument of a political party as they had in the 1930s.

In 1945 a large number of recruits had to be found for the police as all forces were seriously understaffed. These new recruits, instructed at local and zonal training schools, and the serving policemen, free of any taint of Nazism or professional military values, were not allowed to join trade unions. The PSB felt it was important that this new police force be provided with new uniforms that reflected their changed civilian status and attitude toward authority.

The PSB, under Halland's direction, had to revise its assumptions and policies in light of the difficult circumstances faced by the German police in postwar Germany. The British realized they had to build up an efficient police force immediately, as defeated Germany was plagued with violent crime and disorder. Consequently, Public Safety Officers (PSOs) soon saw that the German police had to be armed.

As living conditions deteriorated between 1946 and 1947, Halland feared that the German police may not be reliable enough to deal with potential public opposition to the occupation. The reliability of the German police became a leading concern when large numbers of British troops, for reasons of economy, were removed from duty in Germany. This crisis of confidence and morale of the German police came at a time when it became public knowledge that the PSB had let Nazis and ex-military officers into senior posts in some police forces, while German denazification panels removed politically unreliable officers from the police.

As early as January 1947, the Foreign Office had asked the Germans to take responsibility for the development of democratic institutions themselves, and the CCG (BE) passed the direct control of the police back to the Germans. The *Länder*, however, were advised by the CCG (BE) to pass police legislation that embraced the principles the British had propagated since 1945. It will be argued that in some of the *Länder* all went smoothly, but in others ministers of the interior, opposed to a decentralized and depoliticized police force, clashed with the PSB, which supervised these legislative changes. In face of this political opposition, the PSB Inspectorate pleaded for the reassertion of greater powers over the Germans. However, the Foreign Office, sensitive to the practical need for public order, did not fully support the PSB. By the late 1940s, with the start of the Cold War, the British concept of policing was not seen to be either practical or appropriate in Germany.

In 1945, as the British army entered Germany, it followed the directives of the Supreme Headquarters Allied Expeditionary Force (SHAEF), which mandated the complete disarmament of the German police.[5] Therefore, in the summer of 1945, after the capitulation of Germany, PSOs stripped the German police of their weapons and began training local forces to operate without arms.[6] In August 1945, the PSB issued a directive that ordered the German police to reach the same degree of disarmament as the British police in peacetime. Police on the beat were never to carry arms, but a small quota of arms were to be made available at every police station to meet special circumstances. The PSB realized that the success of this policy rested on the removal of weapons from the civilian population achieved by the imposition of tough penalties for the unlawful possession of firearms. Although many civilians continued to have access to weapons in postwar Germany, the British were determined to build a civilian police force that did not carry weapons. They believed armed police lorded too much power over the public.[7] The Germans needed to be taught that police authority was to rest on respect, not to be dictated by a quasi-military force whose aggressive manner had traditionally instilled fear into the population.[8] In September 1945, the policy of an unarmed police force was reiterated in a Military Government Instruction that outlined plans for the overall reorganization of the German police. The instruction stated that policemen were never to raise their morale or personal prestige by the use of weapons. The CCG (BE) felt no action was to be taken on rearming the police at this juncture. Only in the future, when the German police reached a high standard of efficiency and discipline, would they be issued a limited number of carbines, kept securely at police stations to meet special circumstances.[9]

British officials, however, soon found that it was impractical to deprive the German police of all weapons. During the summer and autumn of 1945, many areas of the British Zone were plagued by armed and violent gangs of DPs (Displaced Persons) who terrorized the German population. The police were often victims of vengeful attacks that resulted in a number of deaths and serious injuries to unarmed officers, and local police forces were unable to protect isolated farms from attack. The PSB was concerned that if these atrocities continued unchecked, the lack of effective police protection might drive normally docile and law-abiding Germans into mob action.

As the German police were relatively ineffective, it fell upon the British army to provide some level of public order. Corps commanders desirous of support soon issued arms, on a temporary basis and under strict conditions, to German police forces. The army recognized that the German police needed some self-protection against serious criminals, especially in the vicinity of DP camps. During the autumn of 1945, corps commanders issued arms, in limited numbers, to the German police to combat DP violence. The police were forbidden automatic weapons, and carbines were issued only up to 20 percent of the authorized establishment. All these weapons were kept by British units to be used by the Germans only for specific duties.[10] The Germans welcomed the protection the guns gave them at night, although it was inconvenient to collect their weapons from distant British military barracks.[11] Despite this change of policy to meet extraordinary circumstances, Halland reminded the army that it should never lose sight of the ideal of an unarmed German police force carrying out its duties with "resoluteness." The acceptance of a small number of weapons, to be used under strict safeguards, did not mean the PSB had rejected the principle of a disarmed and civilian force. In October 1945, for example, Halland disagreed with the army commander in North Rhine–Westphalia that circumstances necessitated the limited arming of the police.[12]

British reluctance to arm the German police was in contrast to the policy of the rest of the Allies, who at quadripartite meetings wanted to move toward further rearmament. Only after a bitter debate in November 1945 did the British, after demanding stringent safeguards, agree to Directive No. 16, which sanctioned arming the police under special circumstances.[13] Halland accepted this directive with reluctance on the condition that arms were only placed in the hands of trained regular police. The British objected to French and Russian suggestions that the German police make armed patrols on the streets, as these policemen might become the basis of a new Wehrmacht.[14] While German police forces openly carried rifles and pistols in the other zones, in 1946, the British urged the use of truncheons and continued to support the restricted use of firearms.[15] The British wanted all German weapons destroyed and the police supplied with pistols made in Britain.[16] In March 1946, a Zonal Executive Instruction stressed that pistols be issued only as a last resort when military assistance was unavailable to the police.[17]

In the autumn of 1946, British authorities anticipated acts of sabotage and disorder in light of the severe food shortages in their zone. By winter, the lightly armed German police seemed barely in control, and the CCG (BE) felt insecure with the reduction of British troops. The seriousness of the situation was reflected in the winter of 1945–46, when all CCG (BE) personnel had the right to arrest any German found committing an offense. A further indication of the climate of unease was reflected in the preparation of an emergency ordinance that permitted the enrollment of British civilians in armed volunteer units.[18]

The seriousness of the situation forced Halland to suggest raising a special constabulary on British lines to support the hard-pressed police. He hoped the specials would foster a democratic and public spirit at a time when the German population was becoming bitter and disillusioned with the British occupation. This idea was soon rejected by the CCG (BE) on the grounds that such a force would siphon desperately needed funds and energy from the regular police. Some critics feared that the specials might form a military Free Corps; however, PSOs closer in touch with the hardships of daily life pointed out that Germans had no spare time for voluntary work.[19]

Although the British had opposed arming regular local police forces, conditions in the zone had necessitated the use of armed auxiliary police since the very early days of the occupation. By November 1945, some 3,000 auxiliaries had been recruited, on a temporary basis, for armed guard duty as a relief for British troops. Major General Horrocks, the commander of 30 corps in the Hannover area, had 4,850 of these auxiliary police directly under his control guarding key installations. By June 1946, the military authorities wanted to make these guards permanent with the departure of more British troops from Germany. Horrocks asked for additional auxiliaries, as Britain, unlike the United States, lacked the resources to equip a division of highly mobile and well-armed military police to suppress disorder.[20] In response to this request, Halland warned that the deployment of an armed police force under the military, rather than the local chiefs of police, was contrary to the Potsdam agreements. The PSB asserted that vulnerable strategic locations should be guarded by the military or by the regular police left free from the competition of a separate hierarchy of auxiliary police.[21]

The weak state of local police forces in the summer of 1946 led the Control Office for Germany and Austria (COGA) in London to suggest the establishment of a centrally controlled German *Gendarmerie* to repress possible food riots in the wake of British troop withdrawals. Again Halland rejected this proposal as he believed any form of *Gendarmerie*, like the auxiliary police, would draw attention away from the need to store up the morale and strength of the regular police forces. The PSB decided that the prime responsibility for quelling riots lay with the ordinary police. However, the British, clearly forced by circumstances to extend the arming of the German police, did not want the German police housed "in a barracks as a concentrated striking force of a military nature."[22] Major-General Erskine was convinced that the British army should remain the only military power in the zone and that the ordinary German police should not be trained as soldiers in a *Gendarmerie*.[23] The British had intentionally set German police forces at a high figure, able to reinforce one another during an emergency. In light of the tense situation in 1947, the PSB was forced to raise the level of arms given to the ordinary police to 50 percent of strength to deal with potential disorder effectively. Thirty percent of the weapons were kept at police stations and 20 percent remained in reserve at military HQs. Consequently, by the summer of 1947, some 20,000 revolvers and 2,643 rifles were in the hands of the German police, although the PSB remained anxious to remove the considerable number of German-made weapons and British rifles from circulation.[24] The acceptance of an armed police police force in Germany came when the CCG (BE) was deeply concerned about the reliability and adequacy of the police at a time of potential disorder. From the beginning of 1947, as economic conditions in Germany grew worse, the danger of serious civil disturbance became even more likely. PSOs lamented that direct control over the police had passed to the German local authorities on 1 January 1947.[25] They suspected that recruits, drawn from the ex-Wehrmacht and attracted to the service by extra rations, might become disloyal if a popular national movement sprang up against the British occupation. Clearly, the British felt that the German police were less reliable than in 1946 and that PSOs should observe "utmost vigilance" in the supervision of these forces.[26] However, Halland remarked that PSOs were less able to influence German senior police officers now in control of decreasingly confident forces. British influence in early 1947 was further diminished by the large reduction of PSOs.[27] In January 1947, Halland was so concerned about the reliability of the German police that he resisted the removal of his HQ to Berlin because he had to display a high profile and closely coordinate the PSOs in the field.[28]

Poor police morale and suspicions about their reliability were connected to the terrible conditions experienced by all the forces in the British Zone. In the spring of 1947, some local forces did not receive enough rations to meet their "Heavy Worker" category of 2,506 calories per day. A medical examination of 6,000 Hamburg police found 90 percent of them suffering from exhaustion because of a shortfall in rations.[29] Halland was deeply concerned about the poor condition of the police, and he argued that starving police could not be expected to perform their duties if there was a large-scale breakdown of law and order. The inspector general, ironically, was opposed to raising their occupational category to that of "Very Heavy Workers," as he believed any inequality between police rations and the general population deprived the police of their civilian status. He upheld this principle as he claimed that the police, unlike the rest of the population, lacked access to the black market and had no opportunity to search for food.[30] Fearing growing disloyalty with further cuts in rations, Halland finally compromised and raised the occupational category of the police to that of "Moderate Heavy Workers."[31]

Poor accommodation was also a serious reason for the deterioration of police morale. The lack of married quarters near police stations meant many policemen were separated from their families. Moreover, policemen forced to reside in overcrowded conditions could not sleep in the day. In addition to the lack of decent housing and food, the German police were poorly paid and inadequately clothed.[32]

By July 1947, Halland was deeply worried about the steady deterioration of the German police morale over the previous six months, "which must now cause some real concern."[33] He speculated that the defection of the police "could obviously have the most serious consequences throughout the British Zone" for CCG families and property.[34] Halland blamed the *Land* governments for their serious neglect of the needs of the police. Police chiefs had lost confidence and rapidly changed their once supportive outlook toward the British. The British regretted, because a more democratic system of local government was permitted in Germany, that senior German police officers were now forced to gain popular and political support; "they see the way the wind is blowing and are trimming their sails accordingly."[35] Many officers, appointed by the PSB in 1945, were now very apprehensive about their future, and the British feared that "when some subversion is observed all police will be inclined to take the line of least resistance and consequently subversion will grow."[36] This decline in morale was seen to be "full of danger," especially if demonstrations became violent when the British government was contemplating drastic troop reductions.

In August 1947, the Select Committee on Estimates asked Halland what measures were appropriate for training the German police in the event of further troop withdrawals. Surprisingly, he suggested that special bodies of civil police should be trained to suppress civil disturbances. Halland maintained that the Germans could develop a mobile force like the Indian police and Royal Ulster Constabulary separate from military authority.[37] After a chorus of opposition, Halland quickly rejected this idea, as he realized a special body of police might become the nucleus of a German defense force under the central government. More important, he saw that such a force would divert recruits and resources from the regular police, which would in turn further depress police efficiency and reliability. Halland still assumed that efficient local forces were the best way to cope with disorder and that military assistance should only be used in the last resort.[38] Amidst a decline in the reliability of the German police, Halland, in contrast to his position in 1946, was suspicious of German requests to enlist special constables. Dr. Menzel, the minister of Interior of North Rhine–Westphalia, supported by some PSOs, wanted Specials to protect crops from thieves in suburban areas. The Deputy Inspector General exaggerated that these innocuous units might provide the nucleus of "an undesirable formation" like the SA or the Free Corps. The Deputy Inspector stressed the use of the regular police and urged great caution against enrolling Special police that would augment the power of the minister of Interior.[39]

Despite these gloomy and anxious predictions about German police morale and reliability, Halland insisted there was still time to halt further decline if "prompt and forceful measures" were taken. The *Länder* governments were pressured to make good the deficiencies in police housing, pay, rations, clothing, and transportation before the winter set in. But if the German authorities failed to meet their obligations, Halland recommended that direct control over the police forces had to be reestablished by the PSB "for a term of years."[40]

In 1948, the majority of the German police remained ineffective in carrying out British orders, and British concern about police morale and reliability continued.[41] There was nervousness about the loyalty of police during the KPD and Trade Union–inspired strikes in the Ruhr in February 1948. Also in late 1947 and early 1948, the British authorities were concerned that they could not count on the German police to support their dismantling policy. In the most publicized case at the Holmag plant in Kiel, the workers walked out and refused to dismantle machinery. The chief of police initially disobeyed the PSOs' order to protect the plant against sabotage. The police eventually consented to occupy the factory only after the PSOs had taken over the police by executive authority.[42] The morale of the German police was further undermined by the incomplete process of denazification and demilitarization of the German police forces. In September 1945, the PSB aimed to exclude all ex-Wehrmacht officers, NCOs, and members of Nazi paramilitary organizations from the police forces. Because of the shortage of police, this policy was soon modified to accept officers recruited in wartime who had never shown any militaristic tendencies. However, the War Office insisted on a narrower category of former members of the armed services eligible for police service evaluated by German denazification panels. Therefore, some regular officers, recruited in 1945, were dismissed in 1946 and 1947 for their military backgrounds although they had been conscripted into the army and had no previous police experience.[43] Halland felt reliable men had been victimized by left-wing members on the denazification panels and suggested that "the term militarization may lend itself as an excuse for getting rid of such a type of officer on purely personal grounds."[44] The PSB urged the panels to use their discretion over officers obviously not professional soldiers and whose attitudes and connections were not militaristic.[45]

Halland complained that concern about reinvestigation produced demoralization throughout the forces as this new category of demilitarization provided no leniency for ex-Wehrmacht officers.[46] This change of policy was criticized as it "is probably based on an unrealistic appreciation of rapidly changing conditions in Germany" and because so many police would be affected by the new category. The PSB argued that the removal of these officers would have a detrimental effect on police morale and efficiency.[47]

It was assumed that many dismissed officers would leave the zone for good, while the reminder would pose problems for the British. Halland had serious concerns about the political reliability of these dismissed officers: "I feel we shall be building up a hard-core of antagonism to the British cause which may link up with undesirable political tendencies already developing amongst that section of the people who feel themselves frustrated in their efforts to rehabilitate themselves."[48]

Although worried about the political inclinations of dismissed officers, Halland continued to believe that those police officers who had joined the army during the war, and who were clearly not supportive of military values, should be able to serve in the reconstituted forces. He extended his argument to other officers who had been transferred compulsorily in 1935 from the police to the army. The PSB accepted up to 5 percent of ex–regular army officers, who were not considered dangerous, in the new police forces.[49] These men, Halland believed, had not been sympathetic to the Nazis; they just possessed the technical skills that had been needed in the expanding army of the 1930s. Halland argued that almost all suitable policemen had some military training in the 1930s, which did not always turn them automatically into men sympathetic to military values. After 1941, these officers were forced to join the SS, and Halland went as far as to consider these men suitable for public service after an investigation of their background.[50]

The relaxed policy of denazification conducted by the PSB, however, brought the German police into disrepute with sections of the German population and further lowered morale within the forces. PSOs, in their desire to rebuild the German police as quickly as possible in 1945 often turned a blind eye to officers with Nazi connections. Allegations from British Intelligence in North Rhine–Westphalia and Schleswig-Holstein purporting that the police was filled with ex-Nazis poured into the PSB in 1946.[51] The *Kriminalkommissar* at Göttingen complained that "the old gang" of arrogant Nazis was still in control. These senior police officers were themselves amazed that as party members they had not been purged after 1945.[52] In March 1946, Kurt Schumacher, the leader of the Social Democratic Party (SPD), was shocked that the police chief and several senior officers on the Hannover force were notorious Nazis.[53] The Political Branch confirmed that PSOs had blocked the appointment of confirmed anti-Nazis on denazification panels in Hannover. As a result, vetting was often left to the police themselves.[54] After the poorly conducted examinations were exposed, PSOs were told to reexamine senior police officials in Hannover. This action was not taken promptly, and dismissals only took place in late May, after further pressure from Schumacher and after questions were raised in the House of Commons.[55] Halland took responsibility for this slackness and admitted that decisive action was postponed because he did not insist that examinations were carried out promptly. Clearly, the PSB was not anxious to dismiss trained officers, even if there was suspicion about their backgrounds because of the shortage of experienced policemen in 1946 to maintain law and order. The Foreign Office, in sympathy with this view, urged the termination of the British role in denazification to provide for security in the zone in uncertain times.[56]

Halland, in defense of the PSB, argued that he never received the 800 special branch officers he requested in 1945 to carry out a thorough process of denazification. Overworked PSOs were given innumerable tasks before the winter of 1945–46 in addition to the maintenance of law and order and the formation of an efficient police force in Germany.[57] Nevertheless, senior officers, in Hannover were reexamined by special denazification panels and, after a personal examination by Regional Intelligence Officers, were dismissed.[58] A similar scandal erupted in Hamburg, where two-thirds of the senior officers were removed; the Hamburg situation led the Foreign Office to comment that if denazification was carried to extremes, there would be no capable police left in Germany.

It was amidst the climate of scandal and sagging morale that the PSB aimed to prevent the German police from becoming the basis of a new central army by transferring the primary control of the police to some form of regional or local authority.[59] Also, the establishment of a decentralized police force in Germany was seen as the first step toward bringing the police under the form of democratic control that had evolved in England. Halland was convinced that the police should never act as the executive servants of the government at any level, a practice that had been particularly dangerous under the Nazi regime, when the police helped destroy the political opposition. Hence, Halland feared the resuscitation of a centrally controlled German police force that went beyond the impartial enforcement of the penal law.[60] This Anglo-Saxon conception of policing rested on the constable, who held a civilian office and, as a representative citizen, was paid to uphold his obligations to the common law. In contrast to the police officer in Germany, the British constable was a "Crown Officer," responsible for keeping the king's peace but immune from administrative interference. Halland pointed out the great stress on local responsibility in the British system, and although a partnership had evolved with the central government, local forces had never succumbed to the direct authority of the state. Determined to impose this system on the Germans, Halland wanted to create forces modeled on Anglo-Saxon principles that maintained the correct balance between central and local authority. He opposed any federal police authority that could be attached to the defense forces and disagreed with the United States that a centralized crime detection unit like the Federal Bureau of Investigation (FBI) be introduced in the British Zone. Halland felt all crime detection was the responsibility of the *Land* police, and he feared an institution like the FBI might form "a possible nucleus for some future form of political police weapon, such as the notorious *Gestapo*."[61] The British only supported a Central Record Office in the Bizone that provided the various *Land* forces with technical and scientific support.

The Germans were expected to adopt the decentralized Anglo-Saxon system of police organization in each *Land*. In England and Wales, there was a mixture of 180 borough and county forces responsible to local authorities. Accordingly, the British proposed that every *Stadtkreis* with more than 100,000 persons establish a separate police force with its own criminal investigation and administrative departments. This arrangement meant the disappearance of the *Gendarmerie* and the *Kriminalpolizei* as separate entities under centralized control. In the rural areas, police forces were to be created in each *Regierungsbezirk* modeled on the larger county constabularies in England. These forces were formed from the old *Schutzpolzei* and *Gendarmerie* units but were unattached to any other *Land* force. Halland was convinced that a single *Land* police force opposed democratic principles and popular control: "there would be nothing easier in years to come than for a future Reich Government to combine these state police forces into one national police organization."[62] Although the United States proposed in their zone to accept separate forces in towns above 5,000, Halland felt the creation of a large number of urban forces would "result in the disintegration of the police service to a dangerous extent."[63] Halland wanted to avoid the multiplicity of very small inefficient forces that "would not have stood the test of time in the German mind."[64] Hence, by January 1947, thirty-nine separate police forces had been organized by the British composed of twenty-three *Stadtkreis* forces and sixteen *Regierungsbezirk* forces (plus five water and six railway police forces in the zone). The number of German police was determined by the same ratio of police to the population as in England and Wales, where there was one policeman for every thousand citizens in rural areas and one to five hundred in urban areas. Based on these ratios, 40,000 police were required for the twenty million Germans in the British Zone.[65]

In 1947, the CCG (BE) was anxious that the *Länder* produce legislation that affirmed this decentralized organization. This attempt, however, to transplant British ideas soon ran into considerable opposition from the Germans. In 1947 and 1948, the strongest response came from Schleswig-Holstein, which resulted in an intense struggle between the minister of Interior and the British authorities over the future democratic structure of the police in the *Land*. The British complained that the minister of Interior wanted to establish a *Land* force directly under his central authority. Subsequently the *Landtag* proposed a police bill that sanctioned setting up four police groups only answerable to the minister of Interior, not the police committees. This attempt to undermine British principles of police organization was seen by the occupation authorities "to pave the way for a police state."[66] The PSB was disappointed that these police groups mixed *Stadtkreis* and *Regierungsbezirk* forces, a fact that meant Kiel and Lübeck would not have their own separate forces. Outside of the main towns, the proposal abolished the other four *Regierungsbezirk* forces entirely.

Halland was afraid this plan permitted the police groups in Schleswig-Holstein to recombine freely into one force as they had done in 1933. He was determined to prevent the minister of Interior from gaining executive control over local forces.[67] In June and October 1947, the regional commissioner found the two police bills drafted by the *Landtag* unacceptable. Opposition to British suggestions continued in Schleswig-Holstein even after the publication of a military ordinance in March 1948, urging the Germans to frame legislation that incorporated the principles of decentralization. Halland worried that the delay in producing police legislation was detrimental to police morale, as the *Land* government had consistently disregarded British "guidance and persuasion" in matters of police organization.[68] In March 1949, a police bill for Schleswig-Holstein that conformed to the British principle of decentralization eventually was passed: Kiel, Flensburg, and Lübeck were to have separate forces, and the rural areas were divided between a Northern and a Southern force.[69]

British authorities hoped that the decentralized police forces in Germany would come under local police authorities imbued with democratic principles. In England and Wales, the police were controlled by Standing Joint Committees in the counties and Watch Committees in the boroughs. The British wanted to introduce the Germans to this tradition of local responsibility for the preservation of order shared between the police, the citizenry, and representative statutory bodies. As early as 1944, Halland saw the establishment of police committees for each *Stadtkreis* and *Regierungsbezirk* as the key to the success of decentralized and democratic policing in Germany. These committees, independent of the control of the minister of Interior, were elected separately from local government bodies.[70] It was hoped that the Germans would accept these committees that acted as "sovereign bodies" free from party politics.[71] The minister of Interior only had the right to confirm the appointment of the chiefs of police and hear disciplinary appeals lodged against them. The *Land* government had indirect control over the police, as it could, like the Home Office in England and Wales, withhold funds if levels of efficiency had not been met by the local forces.[72]

In 1946, the PSB was determined to institute the police committees, even before the *Land* governments were in operation, by reviving local councils in the *Stadtkreis* and the *Regierungsberzirke* to elect local police authorities. This reorganization was not easy, and strong opposition to police committees came from Dr. Menzel in North Rhine–Westphalia.[73] The British found Menzel "a wily creature" bent on seeking control over the local police as he wanted ministry officials to have the right to attend and control police committees. In 1947, the Provisional Police Bill for North Rhine–Westphalia produced an error in translation that allowed Menzel to slip in the right of local authorities to appoint rather than elect the members of the police committees.[74] Facing similar opposition in Schleswig-Holstein in 1947, the British rejected draft legislation that placed the *Kriminalpolizei* under the minister of Interior and under the *Bürgermeister* in each *Kreis*.[75] Throughout 1948, Menzel in North Rhine–Westphalia continued his campaign to undermine the independence of police committees by insinuating what the PSB saw as "sly provisions" into proposed legislation.[76]

Menzel argued that he needed "stricter concentration and direction of the police" because of the emergency situation that prevailed in North Rhine–Westphalia in 1948. He wanted the right to supervise local police chiefs "on special occasions affecting the people as a whole," [77] to combat serious public disturbances, and to carry out centrally directed traffic and black market checks. Menzel piquantly remarked that in England the Home Office could "wave the big stick" over police forces and could exercise emergency powers and call on the military during times of unrest.[78] However, in Germany, he noted the minister of Interior had no executive authority whatsoever. In 1948, the *Landtag* eventually produced draft legislation that restored the 1931 law that supported the democratic control of the police; however, they remained under state authority answerable to the *Land* ministry. The minister of Interior approved nominations to police committees and the police forces in the towns were controlled by the *Bürgermeister*.[79]

Unable to secure their legislative goals, the British did their best to protect police chiefs and police committees from being ridden "rough-shod over their preserves"[80] by the ministry of Interior. Conferences for police chiefs were organized so they could exchange views freely without the attendance of officials from the ministry of Interior.[81] CCG (BE) officials reflected that if a conference of police chiefs had been held in 1947 legislation supportive of British principles would have passed. Moreover, Menzel would not have dared reduce police pay without consulting local police authorities if a wider organization among chiefs had been set up.[82] The British also feared Menzel would influence other ministers against the policy of decentralization and enhance the authority of *Land* governments at Zonal Police Advisory Council meetings that excluded chiefs of police.[83]

Determined that individual German policemen be free from political pressures, the CCG (BE) wanted the police excluded from trade unions. Moreover, to prevent any political interference into the day-to-day operations of the police, and to ensure their impartiality, the German police were not allowed to canvass or openly support any political party and could only exercise their voting rights as private citizens and attend political meetings out of uniform. The police were expressly forbidden to strike, and penalties were imposed on any policeman who caused disaffection or threatened to strike.[84] All these restrictions, also imposed on all public servants (*Beamte*), were to be adopted in 1948 by each *Land* in its new police legislation. The PSB wanted the individual forces to establish police federations, based on the English legislation of 1919, to protect their rights and working conditions. Although the PSB denied they "intended to impose unsuitable British systems on the Germans merely because they are British," they could have easily revived the civil service federation that had represented the German police before 1933. The inspector general demanded that the *Land* ministries of Interior replicate the English model.[85]

The need to keep the police out of political and trade union activity was particularly acute in Berlin. In 1946, the KDP had infiltrated the Berlin police in the British sector, and the Soviets wanted the police to attend political meetings and take part in party business when off duty. The British, worried about the strong communist influence among the Berlin police, were opposed to their playing any part in politics.[86] In 1947, the situation did not improve when the Russians established police federations in their sector with the right to participate in a general strike that the PSB thought of as "the onset of a one party dictatorship."[87] Clearly the PSB saw a nonunionized force as one of the best measures to counter communism in the city.[88] In 1948, the PSB in the British sector continued to resist the Social Democratic Party pressure to unionize the police and the infiltration of the party into the force by discouraging the police from setting up Works Councils and preventing their use in the supervision of elections. The Foreign Office desired a nonpolitical police force in Berlin free from communist and left-wing sympathies and staffed with officers willing to uphold the law impartially.[89]

The PSB's policy of restricting the political rights of the police was questioned by the Zonal Secretariat of Trade Unions in a complaint to the Industrial Relations Branch of the CCG (BE). It argued that trade unions in Germany were not connected to any particular political party comparable to the association between the Trade Union Congress (TUC) and the Labour Party in Britain. Consequently, the German police should be allowed to join the independent labor movement. The Zonal Secretariat felt it was foolhardy to deprive the German police of their rights at a time when the British were attempting to transform the police to become servants of the people and when young policemen were learning to exercise their power in a democratic fashion after the experience of the Nazi period.[90] The TUC in Britain took up the cause of the German police but was reminded by the Military Government of the detrimental political role the police had played in Germany's past and of the necessity of a police federation to counteract communist influence.[91] In 1948, however, even the deputy military governor questioned the viability of police federations separate from trade unions. He noted attempts were made to impose this policy on the police when the British were encouraging the growth of trade unions and free associations in their zone.[92]

British policy was opposed by the *Länder*, which resisted the inclusion of police federations in their new police legislation. The minister of Interior for Schleswig-Holstein was convinced that the police should be members of trade unions and political parties and, in June 1949, included police federations in the legislation only after nine months of intense pressure from the Military Government. Elections for officers of the federations slowly moved forward, and in 1950 by popular demand the police in Schleswig-Holstein were allowed to affiliate with unions. The PSO wistfully remarked that the Germans had been unwilling to recognize the benefits of the British system.[93]

Dr. Menzel in North Rhine–Westphalia was adamantly opposed to police federations and supported police participation in trade union activities. The PSB was concerned because Menzel had cut police pay in the absence of a federation, which showed his willingness to make arbitrary decisions regarding the police without consulting them.[94] In March 1948, Menzel led a meeting of all *Land* ministers of Interior, which declared that police federations should be voluntary and just deal with welfare matters. The Military Government in North Rhine–Westphalia backed down and agreed to accept a welfare organization for the police, leaving pay issues to the trade unions. In January 1949, ignoring Military Government guidelines, North Rhine–Westphalia adopted a very weak police federation, which never gained the support of the police. Officers gave their loyalty to the trade union that masqueraded under the familiar name of a welfare association. In May 1949, after the Police Act was passed, restrictions on the political activity of the police were ignored, and by September the British were forced to issue a Military Government Instruction warning the police not to strike or affiliate outside of their federations.[95]

The British, to prevent a resurgence of Nazism and militarism among the German police, aimed to eliminate the many traditional nonpolice functions attached to these forces, so their duties came close to those of the British Bobby. From the seventeenth century, *Polizei* activity in Germany included a wide range of administrative activities, as the police were responsible for the prevention of danger that threatened the individual or disturbed public order and safety. As a result, a vast measure of supervisory authority became vested in the Administrative Police (*Verwaltungspolizei*) over all forms of public life. The responsibility of the *Verwaltungspolizei* included building traffic regulations, public health, roads, sale of food, and fire precautions. In 1945, the British abolished the *Verwaltungspolizei* as a separate organization when they severed the police from local government administration by setting up independent forces controlled by police committees. They wanted police activities restricted to the detection of crime and the maintenance of law and order. Consequently, considerable judicial and administrative power was removed from the police.[96] For example, the *Verwaltungspolizei* had the right to impose fines (*Zwangsgeld*) and impose short-term sentences of detention for minor offenses.[97]

British determination that the German police forces abstain from all administrative duties produced confusion and opposition among the Germans and generated "bewilderment and alarm in the minds of many German experts."[98] In response to this criticism, a special Legal Research Unit inquired into the implications of the elimination of the *Verwaltungspolizei*. In October 1945, the unit reported that restricting the German police to matters of law and order "runs counter to the entire legal basis of the German administrative apparatus, as developed throughout the centuries."[99] They concluded that the disappearance of the *Verwaltungspolizei* produced havoc and created gaps and inconsistency in German administrative law."[100] The Legal Research Unit claimed it was unfair to judge the *Verwaltungspolizei* on its operation after 1933 as administrative role of the police had been democratic and efficient under Weimar, when legislative rules received democratic approval and fines had not been imposed arbitrarily. The unit felt the administrative procedure was no worse than British police courts, and the unit concluded the activities of the *Verwaltungspolizei* saved police time. Moreover, the separation of administrative duties from the police resulted in an increase in bureaucratic expense. The abolition of the *Verwaltungspolizei* made the CCG (BE) very unpopular with the public because heavier fines were imposed for minor offenses and offenders had to pay the extra cost of their prosecution in summary courts. Moreover, without the production of new rules, local administrative authorities had no means of enforcing their authority, as it was unclear under which legal basis they operated.[101]

The PSB was willing to allow the police to retain some judicial powers as the courts became overcrowded and short-staffed resulting from the denazification of the legal profession. In 1946, the German police were given the temporary right to punish traffic offenders with fines and short prison sentences. The PSB, however, reminded the police to act impartially and to relinquish this judicial power once normal circumstances prevailed.[102] The legal department admitted to the unsettled and unsatisfactory state of the administrative law in Germany, and eventually wanted local authorities to enforce regulations with bylaws.[103] It appears there was little comprehension among Prussians why the British wanted to separate the traditional functions of the police, and reform of the *Verwaltungsgesetz* (Administrative Law) came only with great reluctance.[104]

In January 1948, the Newsome Commission, established to inquire into the progress of the democratization and centralization of the German police, presented a very pessimistic report on the state of forces in the zone. It asserted that many of the Germans interviewed only paid lip service to democratic ideals denying "that the police could be kept apart from politics."[105] It was feared that if the British left the Germans unsupervised their authority "might be used to revive ideas and practices very different from those which they purported to support."[106] With the exception of Niedersachsen, the commission thought the *Länder* had produced unsatisfactory police bills that contained "clauses inimical to a democratic police system,"[107] indicating that power had passed too prematurely into German hands. The commission lamented that in North Rhine–Westphalia the minister of Interior had direct executive control and could issue "directives" controlling the chief of police. Schleswig-Holstein wanted to set up a single *Land* force and retain the *Verwaltungspolizei*, staffed by civil servants responsible to the *Bürgermeister*. The commission was disappointed that the concept of an independent police committee was rejected in Schleswig-Holstein. It found that the chiefs of police and the clerks of the police committees in Kiel and Lübeck were appointed on political grounds, firmly under the control of the mayors of those cities. However, the report did not recommend a retreat from the principles of an independent and impartial police force. It felt a Military Government Ordinance was needed to provide specific directions for the adoption of legislation incorporating British principles "if a stable democratic government is ultimately to be firmly established in Germany."[108] The committee did not recommend full resumption of British control over the police, but asked that the deputy inspector generals in each district be given a suspensory veto to ensure British principles were carried out.

In October 1947, the Foreign Office, on instructing the Newsome Commission, officially gave support to the policy of decentralization of the German police and agreed that the political control of all forces should be kept from the *Land* governments. It recognized that if local police failed to enforce the law impartially, individual *Länder* could adopt tactics to sabotage central laws.[109] Nevertheless, in private Foreign Office officials wondered, on the eve of the Committee's visit to Germany, if "it is a mistake for us to have sought to transplant a British institution in Germany, contrary to their whole tradition."[110] J. de Saintonge, an official in the German section of the Foreign Office, after a meeting with J.R.H. Nott-Bower, deputy commissioner at New Scotland Yard, thought that the British should consider reversing their position on decentralization if the Germans opposed British policy. Nott-Bower thought it unwise to impose the British system on the Germans as "it was one which probably no other people in the world would consider to be good."[111] He reminded the Foreign Office that all continental countries had their police controlled by a political head.

In early 1948, Foreign Office defense of British institutions became even weaker. It claimed that the Newsome Committee had exaggerated the importance of establishing the British system and questioned why "independent forces should prove a more dependable bulwark for any future democratic German Government."[112] Sir Ivone Kirkpatrick, permanent under secretary of the German section of the Foreign Office, was unsure that the British model "from the point of view of creating a force on which a democratically elected German government can rely to ensure that the law is obeyed."[113] He argued that an independent police force in Germany might be a "menace" and concluded that the best way of supporting democracy was to ensure that the democratically elected government exercise firm control over the minister of Interior. Kirkpatrick realized that an independent police force could not prevent any government after an election from placing itself above the law if it wanted to change the police to suit its purpose.[114]

Foreign Office officials believed the imposition of a Military Government Ordinance would cause the Germans to "lose heart and question our good faith," and if the population were to be educated in democracy, "it is essential we should achieve our aims as far as possible by persuasion rather than direct instruction."[115] They wanted regional commissioners to explain principles to the *Land* governments as an ordinance would "inevitably result in some loss of prestige for them."[116] The Foreign Office justified the delay of the ordinance as it assumed that German opposition to English principles of police organization was "probably less due to deliberate obstruction than to genuine inability to understand properly a conception of police administration which is entirely alien to their experience."[117] PSOs were advised not to adopt a "too academic attitude" on the division of functions and only intervene when British standards "are definitely threatened" and when the German police were deprived of adequate supplies and housing.[118]

Therefore, the Foreign Office only reluctantly supported the promulgation of a Military Government Ordinance intended to give the Germans a last chance to establish a democratic system based on British organizational principles. Officials in London anticipated the lack of German receptivity to change, and if the ordinance was unsuccessful, "we should not exclude a possibility of reverting to a system of organization less alien to continental experience."[119] PSOs were cautioned against excessive interference between the police committees and the chiefs of police, and deputy inspector generals were urged not to exercise their veto power in police matters. Apparently the Foreign Office, in contrast to the officials in the PSB, felt it was too late to hope the Germans would respond to British pressure.

By 1948 it was clear that the Foreign Office realized the extent of German opposition to the efforts of the PSB to reform and reorganize the German police. The Germans were free to control their own affairs and pass police legislation without regard to British guidelines and principles. As we have seen, the Germans from the early days of the occupation, especially in North Rhine–Westphalia and Schleswig-Holstein, resisted the introduction of the British vision of a decentralized, democratic, and nonpolitical police force in Germany. The exclusion of the German police from trade unions and the abolition of the *Verwaltungspolizei* were particularly unpopular measures introduced by the British. These measures must have been felt by the Germans to be undemocratic, or at least denying the police their democratic rights.

British policy, however, did not fail only because it was alien and unwelcome to the Germans. The PSB was forced to follow contradictory policies in its attempt to impose a new concept of Anglo-Saxon policing on the Germans. Gerald Halland, as inspector general, was dedicated to the ideals of a disarmed and civilian force free from Nazism. Throughout 1945–47, the PSB assumed the responsibility for public order lay with the regular police forces, and it rejected suggestions that paramilitary forces be formed to suppress disorder. However, these ideals were often in conflict with the circumstances that confronted PSOs once they arrived in Germany in 1945. Threats to law and order from DPs, and later from the fear of a general uprising against the Occupation Forces, meant the German police had to be armed. Also in 1945, the shortage of competent police led to the induction of a number of ex–military officers and Nazis into the forces. Between 1946 and 1948, overworked and understaffed PSOs, alarmed by the reduction of British troops in Germany, tried desperately to strengthen the police in Germany, whose loyalty and reliability to the British occupation were often seriously in question. Moreover, the PSB found that the low morale and poor conditions experienced by the German police prevented these newly reconstituted forces from serving the population in the fashion conceived for them with the defeat of Germany in 1945.

NOTES

1. See The Reformation of the German Police as a Long Term Policy, Gerald Halland, Inspector General, PSB, 25 August 1944, his address on the Reorganization of the German Police to the *Oberpräsidenten* and *Ministerpräsidenten* at Detmold, 19 November 1945 and his Reorganization of the German Police System in the British Zone, 4 April 1946, PRO/FO 1050/259.

2. Military Government Instruction on the Reorganization of the German Police System in the British Zone, 25 September 1945, PRO/FO 1050/427.

3. Halland's address at Detmold, 19 November 1945, PRO/FO 1050/259.

4. PSB, Memorandum on the German Police System, November 1994, PRO/FO 1050/259.

5. Although the PSB was warned in early 1945 that violence from assassinations and guerrilla warfare perpetrated by Germans might slow the process of disarming the police down. Memo from Halland to Col. Nicoll, 2 March 1945, and the Memo by Major Foley, March 1945, PRO/FO 1050/240.

6. Memo by the PSB, North Rhine–Westphalia, 23 October 1947, PRO/FO 1050/261.

7. Memo on the Question of Arming the German Police, PSB, August 1945, PRO/FO 1050/240.

8. PSB Instruction, 29 September 1945, PRO/FO 1050/240.

9. The instruction stated, "The morale and prestige of the police, both individually and collectively, come not from a show of force by carrying weapons, but from the proper exercise of authority, a high conception of police duty and discipline, and the exercise of such qualities as courtesy, tact and strict impartiality." Military Government Instruction on the Re-organization of the German Police System in the British Zone, September 1945, PRO/FO 1050/427.

10. Control of Displaced Persons, Chief of Staff to all Corps Commanders, 17 August 1945, PRO/FO 1050/240. PSB remarked that the population in Germany was more willing to respect and obey an armed force "although this would not be possible in our country." PSB Memo, 4 July 1945, PRO/FO 1050/241.

11. PSB Officer Report, Hamburg, October 1945, PRO/FO 1050/240.

12. Assistant Inspector General, PSB Rhineland to Commander 1st Corps, 12 October 1945; Inspector General, PSB to Chief I.A.&C. Division, 24 October 1945; Inspector General, PSB to Isemonger PSB, 11 October 1945.

13. Memo of Proceedings of the PSB Committee, 4 October 1945, PRO/FO 1050/240.

14. Deputy Inspector General, PSB, to Halland, 12 October 1945, PRO/FO 1050/240.

15. Halland to HQ. BOAR, 17 April 1946, PRO/FO 1050/241. In anticipation

of riots in late 1945 the police were to keep control only with batons. See "Possible Dangers to the Occupying Power During the Coming Winter," PSB memo, October 1945, PRO/FO 1050/228.

16. HQ Military Government Directive, 3 December 1945, PRO/FO 1050/241. 28,000 pistols were to be supplied by the end of 1946 at the cost of £357,075.

17. Zonal Executive Instruction No. 21, 30 March 1946, PRO/FO 1050/228.

18. Memo from Chief of Staff, CCG, September 1946, PRO/FO 1050/226; White Paper on the work of PSB in Schleswig-Holstein, 9 September 1950, PRO/FO 1050/580.

19. Halland to the Deputy Inspector General PSB, 14 June 1946 and Simpson, I.A.&C. Division to Halland, 1 July 1946, PRO/FO 1050/267. Halland seems quite out of touch on this issue and only reluctantly gave it up. The PSB officer in Schleswig-Holstein noted how Germans were battling for survival and spent long hours working and guarding their farms. Memo to PSB, 17 October 1946, PRO/FO 1050/267.

20. CC, HQ British Army of the Rhine to HQ. CCG and I.A.&C. Division, 31 May 1946, PRO/FO 1050/266.

21. J.H.C. Simpson, HQ I.A.&C. Division to Brig. E.S.B. Gaffney, 14 June 1946, PRO/FO 1050/266. Manpower opposed a Gendarmerie of Auxiliaries because it would reduce the number of productive workers. Inspector General, PSB, to HQ. BOAR, 21 August 1946, PRO/FO 1050/125; PSB Memo, G Section, to Inspector General, PSB, 19 June 1946. In October 1947, the Kommandatura in Berlin agreed to raising 3,500 armed auxiliary police to support the regular forces. PSB only reluctantly agreed to this because they had little faith in auxiliaries and disliked the discrepancy with the rest of the zone. This force seemed less necessary as normal police in Berlin carried arms on patrol. PSB, Berlin, to Inspector General, PSB, 1 October 1947, PRO/FO 1050/105. M. S. O'Rorke, PSB HQ, to E. C. Nottingham, Deputy Inspector General, PSB, Berlin, 10 October 1947, PRO/FO 1050/205.

22. Maj. General G.W.E.J. Erskine, HQ CC, to Wilberforce, CC Office for Germany and Austria, 21 August 1946, PRO/FO 1050/266.

23. Ibid.

24. PSB, memo "Arming the German Police," 28 February 1947; Halland to O'Rouke, Deputy Inspector General, PBS, 19 March 1947, PRO/FO 1050/242. PSB, memo North Rhine–Westphalia, 23 October 1947, PRO/FO 1050/261.

25. Brig. R. W. Martin, PSB, Schleswig-Holstein, to the Inspector General, PSB, 16 January 1947, PRO/FO 1050/254.

26. E. C. Nottingham, Inspector PSB, North Rhine–Westphalia, 18 January 1947, PRO/FO 1050/254.

27. The reduction of PSOs continued throughout 1947. In November 1946 there were 915 in the zone that were reduced to 500 by July 1947. In Osnabruck, for example, twenty-one PSOs supervised local forces in autumn 1946; by July only eleven officers remained to advise 927 German police in a large area of 638,000 persons. Top Secret Report, "Morale and Reliability of the German Police," 15 July 1947, PRO/FO 1050/254.

28. Halland to the Secretariat C.C.G. Lübeck, 20 January 1947, PRO/FO 1050/254. Halland stated, "I am not prepared to say that much reliance could be placed on the German police in the event of a widespread subversive movement." Ibid.

29. Deputy Inspector General, PSB, to Inspector General, PSB, 9 May 1947; Halland to Major General Bishop, Deputy Chief of Staff, 5 May 1947, and Halland's Top Secret Report "Morale and Reliability of the German Police." In April 1947 he said, "If they [German police] are not properly fed then we must face the possibility of a serious breakdown in police morale and discipline." 15 July 1947, PRO/FO 1050/254.

30. Halland to the Secretariat at Lübeck, 24 April 1947, PRO/FO 1050/254.

31. Halland to Maj. Gen. Bishop, 12 May 1947, PRO/FO 1050/254.

32. Halland, "Morale and Reliability of the German Police," 15 July 1947, PRO/FO 1050/254.

33. Ibid.

34. Halland to the Central Secretary HQ CCG, 29 September 1947, PRO/FO 1050/427.

35. Ibid.

36. Ibid.

37. Ibid., 16 August 1947.

38. Ibid., 29 September 1947.

39. Deputy Inspector General, PSB, North Rhine–Westphalia, 7 April 1948, PRO/FO 1050/226.

40. Halland, "Morale and Reliability of the German Police," 15 July 1947, PRO/FO 1050/254.

41. See for example, Halland to the Secretariat, 11 February 1948, PRO/FO 1050/254 and the correspondence in PRO/FO 1050/230.

42. White Paper on the work of PSB in Schleswig-Holstein, 9 September 1950, PRO/FO 1050/580.

43. Halland to DAIG PSB, HQ Mil. Gov. North Rhine–Westphalia, 31 March 1947, PRO/FO 1050/352.

44. Deputy Inspector General to Inspector General PSB, 24 August 1946, PRO/FO 1050/354.

45. PSB memo on the Demilitarization of the Police and Fire Services, 2 September 1946, PRO/FO 1050/354.

46. Deputy Inspector General PSB to Inspector General PSB, 2 October 1946, PRO/FO 1050/354.

47. PSB memo on the demilitarization of the Police and Fire Services, 2 September 1946, PRO/FO 1050/354. "The light of experience has shown that the limits so far laid down are too narrow and that not only are feelings of injustice being harboured by some men who have been removed or refused employment when in reality they are not militarists, but the services of valuable and experienced officials are being lost and this is dangerously lowering the efficiency of the Police and Fire services." Ibid.

48. Ibid.

49. Halland to R. D. Harrish, Deputy Inspector PSB, HQ CCG, Berlin, 9 August 1947.

50. Inspector General of PSB, Paper on the Demilitarization of the German Police, 12 August 1946, PRO/FO 1050/350. In 1947 Halland was willing to accept forty-nine ex-officers into the railway police but stated a position closer to his instructions of 1945, that no professional Wehrmacht officers or soldiers should be

recruited or retained in the police forces. Halland to DIAG, Railway Police, 16 June 1947, PRO/FO 1050/352.

51. For example, see Halland to Deputy Chief, I.A.& C. Division, 29 May 1946, Halland to E.S.B. Gaffney, Deputy Chief, I.A.& C. Division, Bunde, 30 May 1946, PRO/FO 1050/350. Halland felt the Intelligence Division reports exaggerated the numbers of alleged Nazis in the police and gave a false impression of the situation. Halland to Albu, Office of Deputy Military Governor, 1 June 1946, PRO/FO 1050/350. A Field Officer in Schleswig-Holstein complained to the chancellor of the Duchy of Lancaster that old Nazis were firmly in place and anti-Nazis were demoted to inferior positions. He suggested, "We could do with a good purge here." Memo, April 1946, PRO/FO 945/98. For a full discussion of the failure of British denazification policy see Tom Bower, *The Pledge Betrayed: America and Britain and the Denazification of Post-War Germany* (Garden City, N.Y., 1982), 167–71.

52. *Kriminalkommissar* Schluter, Regierungsbezirk Hildesheim, Memo on the Organization of the German Police Personnel, April 1946, PRO/FO 371/5537.

53. Halland to Gaffney, Chief I.A.&C., 30 May 1946, PRO/FO 1050/350, Telegram CCG Legal Branch to the Foreign Office, 26 May 1946, PRO/FO 945/95. Adolf Schulte had joined the NSDAP in 1933 and had directed the German police at The Hague during the war and acted as the deputy chief on Himmler's staff.

54. Memo German Political Division, CCG, 22 March 1946, PRO/FO 1050/350.

55. Deputy Military Governor CCG to HQ Military Governor, Hannover, 16 May 1946, PRO/FO 1050/350.

56. Memo by A. R. Walmsley, 24 April 1946, FO/PRO 371/5537.

57. A. H. Albu to the Office of Deputy Military Governor, HQ CCG, 4 June 1946, PRO/FO 1050/350. "PSO officers have been faced with stupendous difficulties owing to lack of police officers and men of any experience who were free from the Nazi taint."

58. CCG Legal Branch to Foreign Office, 26 May 1946, PRO/FO 945/95, and Halland to Deputy Inspector PSB, Bunde, 26 May 1946, PRO/FO 1050/350. Bower argues that the policy of allowing former Nazis into the police was concealed from the Cabinet Reconstruction Committee, which was responsible for coordinating German policy. Bower, *Pledge*, 70.

59. Halland explained that what they wanted was "not so much the excessive devolution of decentralisation of powers for policy and legislation as the greatest possible measure of decentralisation on a democratic basis in the sphere of administration and supervision through strong local government machinery." Halland to HQ I.A.&C., Division 6, April 1946, PRO/FO 1050/259. Notes by Halland on the Reorganization of the German Police with Special Reference to the Problem of Centralized Forms of Control, 4 September 1947, PRO/FO 371/7590.

60. Notes by Halland on the Reorganization of the German Police with Special Reference to the Problem of Centralized Control, 4 September 1947, PRO/FO 371/7590.

61. Ibid.

62. Ibid.

63. Memo by Halland on the Reorganization of the German Police, 25 August 1944, PRO/FO 1050/260.

64. Ibid.

65. In 1945, the strength of the police in England and Wales was to be 65,000 for a population of 40 million. An additional 20 percent of police were recruited to act as an internal reserve in Germany.

66. Newsome Report, 7 January 1948, FO 371/55.

67. Halland to Lt. General Brian Robertson, Deputy Military Governor, 7 August 1947, PRO/FO 1050/261.

68. Halland to A. H. Albu, HQ CCG (BE), 9 September 1947, PRO/FO 1050/261.

69. White Paper on the Work of PSB in Schleswig-Holstein, 9 September 1950, PRO/FO 1050/580. Halland to Miss Giachardi, German Internal Affairs Department, Foreign Office, 23 June 1947, PRO/FO 371/64696.

70. See Military Government Instruction on the Reorganization of the German Police System in the British zone, 25 September 1945, PRO/FO 1050/225. It was hard to set up an identical system to the English in Germany as the later did not have justices of the peace who were represented on standing joint committees in England. After considerable discussion and the failure to find a counterpart to the JP in Germany, it was decided to do without legal representation on German police committees. The situation was also complicated in the *Regierungsbezirk*, where police committees were elected from the *Landkreis* councils. This administrative change meant depriving the *Regierungspräsident* of his police power but allowed his administration to remain functioning alongside the police committees. See Chief of the Legal Division, CCG (BE) to PSB, 27 May 1946, PRO/FO 1050/225.

71. Halland to Simpson I.A.&C. Division, 22 June 1946, PRO/FO 1050/259.

72. Halland to Simpson I.A.&C. Division, 1 November 1946, PRO/FO 1050/259.

73. Halland to O'Rorke, 30 June and 8 July 1947, PRO/FO 1050/264. There was also opposition to the transplanted British system: Because the city was also a *Land* the *Bürgerschaft* acted as both city council and local parliament. Here an advisory police committee was presided over by the Ministry of Interior. PSB was worried this organization gave too much operational control to the ministry and provided a precedent for the other *Länder* to assert their control over the police. The Foreign Office was eventually more flexible because they felt the Minister of Interior was checked by the Senate; they were willing to concede that Hamburg provided an exceptional case. Although the Foreign Office affirmed that the British wanted to prevent chiefs of police from taking orders from a political leader, acting instead as independent guardians of the law: "The Germans do not accept this conception but want to insure against independent and arbitrary police action by keeping operational control in the hands of an elected representative of the people." De Saintonge to J.R.H. Nott-Baker, 18 September 1947, PRO/FO 371/7590.

74. P. H. Miller, Deputy Inspector General, PSB to Zonal Executive Office, PSB, 8 June 1948, PRO/FO 1050/264.

75. White Paper on the work of PSB in Schleswig-Holstein, 9 September 1950, PRO/FO 1050/580.

76. Ibid.

77. Menzel's Memo, 2 October 1947, from the Landtag, PRO/FO 1050/264. Minutes of the Police Committee Chairmen, 5 May 1948, PRO/FO 1050/264.

78. See Menzel's letters in *Die Welt* on 17 February and 26 June 1948. For differences between the PSB and the *Landtag* in North Rhine–Westphalia, see F. H. Miller, Deputy Inspector General PSB to the PSB Zonal Executive Offices, 31 March 1948, PRO/FO 1050/264.

79. Minutes of the Police Committee Chairmen, 5 May 1948, PRO/FO 1050/264.

80. Halland to DIG, HQ of all *Länder*, 9 April 1948, PRO/FO 1050/265.

81. Ibid. Halland commented that the police could "put up a united front against the Minister of Interior and his police department representatives where the latter wished to take some action or issue an instruction affecting the overall sphere of the two authorities mentioned, without first consulting them."

82. Halland to S. M. Ogden, DIG Land Niedersachsen, 1 June 1948, PRO/FO 1050/265.

83. Deputy Inspector PSB, North Rhine–Westphalia, 10 May 1948, PRO/FO 1050/265. J.H.A. Emck, Chief Governmental Structure Officer to Land PSB Departments, 25 April 1948.

84. Deputy Military Governor (CCG) to Regional Commissioners, 9 August 1947, PRO/FO 1050/184; Regional Commissioner of North Rhine–Westphalia to *Ministerpräsident* for the Ministry of Interior, 17 October 1947.

85. Inspector General, PSB to HQ Military Government, Schleswig-Holstein, 12 August 1946, PRO/FO 1050/184.

86. Kit Steel, Political Division HQ CCG. Berlin to Wilberforce, 2 March 1946, PRO/FO 945/98. Allied Control Authority, Political Directorate, to Internal Affairs and Communications Branch (I.A.&C.), 21 October 1946, PRO/FO 371/55837. The NKVD were encouraging the East German CID to arrest German civilians in the Western sectors and abduct them to Soviet officials in the East.

87. PSB Zonal Executive Office to PSB, 17 July 1947, PRO/FO 1050/184.

88. I. P. Garran, Political Division, HQ CCG (BE) to P. Dean, Foreign Office, 14 January 1949, PRO/FO 371/77073. The Foreign Office felt, "So long as our relations with the Russians remain as they are, we *cannot* take the risk of giving the Germans operational control of the police."

89. The Foreign Office summed up the situation: "In other words the Germans are still far from realizing that it is invidious to root out for Arsenal one Saturday and referee Arsenal v Chelsea the next." Ibid.

90. Zonal Secretariat of Trade Unions to the Industrial Relations Branch, 10 February 1947, PRO/FO 1050/184.

91. For Lord Pakenham (written by C. M. Anderson, Private Secretary) to H. Vincent Tewson, TUC, 3 November 1947, PRO/FO 371/7590.

92. Deputy Military Governor, CCG (BE) to Regional Commissioners, 9 August 1947, PRO/FO 1050/184.

93. White Paper on the work of PSB in Schleswig-Holstein, 9 September 1950, PRO/FO 1050/580.

94. Inspector General, PSB, to Deputy Inspector General, PSB, North Rhine–Westphalia, 1 June 1948, PRO/FO 1050/265.

95. Ibid.

96. The Reorganization of the German Police and its Effects on Public Admin-

istration, Legal Division, HQ CCG, April 1948, PRO/FO 1050/233. The classification of German police functions was not clear, and there were differing opinions about the responsibilities of the *Sicherheitspolizei*, staffed by uniformed officers and detectives who mainly prevented the crime, and the *Verwaltungspolizei*. Even the duty of the police to act in the detection of a committed crime was not a basic function of the police but was imposed by special law.

97. Ibid.

98. Ibid.

99. British Special Legal Research Unit, 19 October 1948, PRO/FO 371/70831 (55).

100. Ibid.

101. Ibid.

102. Inspector General, PSB to the Legal Division, Lübeck, 27 March 1946, PRO/FO 1050/232.

103. The Reorganization of the German Police and its effects on Public Administration, PRO/FO 1050/233.

104. S. L. Howes, ATC Branch to HQ Legal Branch, 20 May 1948, PRO/FO 1050/233.

105. Newsome Report, 7 January 1948, PRO/FO 371/70831/55.

106. Ibid.

107. Ibid.

108. Ibid.

109. Foreign Office Memo in response to Halland's report on the "Adequacy of the German Police in the British Zone for the Preservation of Internal Security," 4 September 1947, PRO/FO 371/64697.

110. Memo of de Saintonge, 7 October 1947, ibid.

111. Notes on meeting between de Saintonge and Nott-Bower, 7 October 1947, PRO/FO 371/7590.

112. Foreign Office to Military Governor, HQ CCG (BE) Berlin, 6 February 1948, PRO/FO 371/55. See also Foreign Office memo, 21 January 1948, which noted that Home Office colleagues "over stress and over simplify the reputed independence of chief officers of police in Great Britain." PRO/FO 371/70831.

113. Memo by Ivone Kirkpatrick on the Newsome Report, 21 January 1948, PRO/FO 371/70831.

114. Ibid.

115. Memo by M. L. Priss, Foreign Office to the Chancellor of the Duchy of Lancaster, 13 January 1948, PRO/FO 371/70831/55. Kirkpatrick said, "bearing in mind that if after a reasonable time it [the MG Ordinance] is not working well, the alternative system is from our point of view perhaps not as bad as has been painted." Ibid.

116. Ibid.

117. Ibid.

118. Memo by Ivone Kirkpatrick on the Newsome Report, 21 January 1948, PRO/FO 371/70831.

119. Ibid.

Book Reviews

Giorgia Alessi, *Giustizia e polizia: il controllo di una capitale, Napoli* 1779–1803. Naples: Jovene, 1992. Lire 27,000

Given the paucity of police history in Italy, one can only applaud the appearance of this study of the Neapolitan police system as it evolved at the end of the eighteenth century. Firmly rooted in the juridical-political methodology that marks so much of Italian criminal justice history, Alessi's book concentrates on three different legislative attempts to reform the police during one of the most tumultuous periods in the city's history. Two major themes gradually emerge from Alessi's analysis of these reforms. First, by 1803, the very notion of policing had changed radically from an ill-defined conglomeration of judicial and municipal responsibilities to a specialized administrative institution virtually autonomous from the law courts and the communal authorities. This entailed a new specificity of function based on proactive preventive control of the "dangerous classes" and aggressive information gathering, all to be carried out by special police magistrates apparently modeled on Paris' police commissioners. Each magistrate had control over one of twelve newly created districts that were intentionally drawn so as to cut across long-standing traditional divisions of the city. Hence a new network of control was established that could compete with local patterns of privilege allocation.

The author's second them suggests that these changes reflected struggles for power among competing elites, including the nobility, the legal establishment, the monarchy, and especially the military, which she sees as both the major protagonist and benefactor of the reforms eventually enacted. Thus the original reform of 1791 directly attacked the public order functions—and hence the political clout—of the municipal corporations and the city's noble governor. Subsequent changes led to what she calls the "militarization" of the police, with the formation of a new paramilitary corps of police guards, or *Fucilieri di città* and the creation of a command structure with an army general at the top. This amounted to a total divorce of policing from the "guarantist" procedures of the powerful judges who had previously run all aspects of the criminal justice system. It also created a minirevolution in the power relations of the city as concepts of efficiency and accountability—complete with maps, censuses, street numbers, and modern registration procedures—came to dominate over the many loopholes, immunities, and overlapping jurisdictions of the past.

In laying out her narrative, Alessi offers some fascinating insights into the difficulties of policing an early modern city, checkered with privileged groups and places that carried immunity from criminal prosecution to amazing extremes. Religious houses, foreign embassies, municipal offices, and military quarters all could claim one form of legal exception or another, and the regular judicial police, or *sbirri*, constantly had to tread carefully to avoid overstepping the boundaries of such protected communities. Alessi also shows that Naples was no different from other Italian cities in the general disdain maintained by all quarters for the *sbirri*. She documents the virtual state of war existing between them and the regular army, complete with fist fights, rock battles, and occasionally, armed combat—all of which was tolerated or even encouraged by the military's high command. Of further significance, she describes the surprising sophistication of the city's various police chiefs, who consistently complained that without remedies for endemic poverty and unemployment there were limits to what they could do to combat crime, disorder, or mafia-style *camorra*.

Alessi's book, however, is not without its faults. Above all, the lack of either an introduction or conclusion makes it difficult to discern her major themes, and the reader has to work hard to piece together the overall analysis. More organizational clarity is also needed within the individual chapters, where topics and chronology are sometimes scrambled. Likewise, a series of organizational charts would be very helpful, whereas descriptions of the evolving system are strung through paragraphs often devoted to different subjects. One could quibble as well with her notion of the "militarization" of the police. Although an army general was eventually placed in charge as superintendent, the new police system remained primarily in the hands of nonmilitary bureaucrats. Likewise, it is unclear if the paramilitary police guards were ever actually a formal part of the army, as would be the case with a French-style *Gendarmerie*, and a sizable contingent of the *sbirri* remained in place to carry out those police functions thought unworthy of soldiers.

Perhaps more serious, the whole book appears to have been written in a social vacuum. The reader never really gains a sense of what was happening in Neapolitan society. Population trends, class conflicts, and general levels of crime are left unexplored. Even the enormous dislocation of the

French-induced Parthenopean Republic receives scant attention. Consequently, the author offers no clear causality behind the reforms, and one does not really know if they were the result of foreign models, absolutist pretensions, Beccaria's Enlightened precepts, social anxieties over growing public disorder, political reaction to the French Revolution, or perhaps even the individual ambitions of men at the top, such as Lord Acton or General Pignatelli, seeking primarily to expand their personal spheres of power. Alessi does bind the reforms together with a kind of Foucaultian stress on systematic control, but due to the lack of concrete, social and historical evidence from the city's streets, this tells us more about her theoretical reading than about Naples' reality.

Despite these problems, Alessi is to be commended for her work. She has opened a new chapter on police history in Italy. In particular, her book confirms what little information we have from other areas that policing was already changing prior to the arrival of Napoleon in Italy. It will certainly provide the questions that will help to guide future research.

Steven C. Hughes
Loyola University, Baltimore

Steven C. Hughes, *Crime, Disorder & the Risorgimento: The Politics of Policing in Bologna*. Cambridge: Cambridge University Press, 1994. xvi + 286 pp., index. $54.95.

In his conclusion to this important study, Steven Hughes writes of the standard approach to the history of the Risorgimento—with its preoccupation with high politics—that "it writes off the very real complaints of the day, such as crime in the streets, as just another tactic for weakening the old regime" (p. 264). The appearance of this book, together with the work of those of younger scholars like Lucy Riall and David Laven in the English-speaking world, represent a vital stage in what might justifiably be called "the normalization of nineteenth-century Italian history." Hughes' monograph on Bologna thoroughly deserves to take its place among the growing, often distinguished, corpus of recent local studies of Italy in the Restoration period.

The period 1814–48 long has been the "Cinderella" of modern European history, especially so in the context of domestic Italian history. As Hughes' industry demonstrates, this is hardly the fault of the primary sources. Those of us who have been fortunate enough to work in the Archivio di Stato di Bologna will know it as one the richest, best-organized and most "user-friendly" archives in Europe, whose riches have been relatively neglected by scholars of this period for far too long. Steven Hughes has taken great advantage of this, and we have reason to be thankful. There are few areas more ripe for archival exploration in this period than the Emilia-Romagna and the extensive range of sources Hughes brings to bear on his subject shows how assiduously he has used an archive that boasts some of the longest opening hours anywhere.

By its very nature—a local study centered on crime and policing in a neglected period—*Crime, Disorder & the Risorgimento* covers important ground. Hughes has given his readers more than an institutional history of police in the Papal States and what in fact emerges is an informed, thorough examination of the political life of a great Italian city as seen through the eyes of its police officials and the indigenous elite they sought to serve. This should broaden the usefulness and appeal of this book to all scholars of the period, even if, at times, Rome seems a little distant. It would not be an unfair criticism of so excellent a local study to draw attention to its lack of a wider perspective, both within Italy and as regards the rest of western Europe, given the richness of the modern secondary literature available, but in a time of tight money and tighter word limits, much can be forgiven in these matters. Nevertheless, in most cases, the reader with comparative perspectives in mind will have to draw his own conclusions. This can be particularly frustrating when the narrative reaches points such as the revolutions of 1831 and, especially, those of 1848–49, when the history of Bologna merges with wider European currents. There are times when the issues of popular participation in revolutionary politics cry out for an analysis that embraces the recent work of scholars of France—Agulhon and Merriman above all—while the whole issue of the nature of the struggles between radicals and liberals deserves a treatment that embraces the work on Germany done by Sperber and Sheeban. That the present reviewer should choose to criticize Hughes' book on such grounds is not intended as a slight in any way. It is rather a tribute to the importance of what Steven Hughes has to say about seminal issues in his chosen local context.

Hughes is more right than he knows in setting law and order at the heart of his preoccupations, for it was the single most important issue for contemporaries. When he writes that "it would be reductive to argue that crime and brigandage caused the ultimate dissolution of the Papal States, but the evidence indicates that these were very real issues to the elites of the legations, and not just a good publicity stick with which to beat the reactionary and absolutist government of Pius IX, what is to be regretted most is his restraint. The hard fact is that the closer to the primary sources one goes, the more dominant this issue becomes. If Braudel's dictum that history moves on three levels is still held to be true, then the history of "Level III" in modern Italy—that of generational affairs measurable in terms of direct perception, "the political level"—must belong to those historians who place crime and its consequences at the center of politics. Hughes has chronicled this admirably, for the most important single thread running through his narrative is the alienation of the propertied classes of Bologna from the Papal government simply because of its continuing failure to protect them. It is here that Hughes' book is at its best, and its approach injects a much needed dose of realism into discussions on the nature of Italian liberalism and the character of the Risorgimento. There are times when Hughes needs to press his advantage further, especially in his handling of the *Moto di Savigno* in 1843 and the subsequent attempts of Mazzinian conspirators to ally themselves with criminal elements in the years before 1848. The crucial point to emerge is that Mazzini and his followers were more out of touch with Italian realities than the Papal regime, and it needs to be driven home.

Hughes also has much to say about the character of Papal rule at the local level, and when he finally turns to the revolutions of 1831 and 1848–49, he has a clear idea of what the Risorgimento was rising against. The picture that emerges is an interesting and a complex one; Hughes' study does much to banish the already outmoded view of Papal rule as inert as well as inept, but when seen from a local perspective, many "standard" judgments deserve revision. The most important example of this is Consalvi, for when his approach to reform is judged in the context of policing, his rigid adherence to Napoleonic models of policing emerges as over-ambitious as well as "progressive." The standards he tried to set were certainly those sought by the local elite, but, equally, the evidence Hughes presents reveals Consalvi's Napoleonic methods as beyond the reach of the resources of his state. In many ways, the more reactionary Gregory XVI emerges as more realistic in his desire to involve local committees in policing; here, as Hughes points out, the ultimate failure of the reactionary government in policing stemmed from the shock of the revolution of 1831. After this "jolt," the priorities of the regime—obsessed with political subversion and disabused of decentralization—and the local elite, still in search of basic protection from common crime, progressively found more common ground. If there is a clear fool-at-large—apart from Mazzini—it is Pius IX, especially in the years after 1849. In his last major chapter, Hughes makes a telling contribution to our understanding of how the regime destroyed itself. He charts the cautious path taken to treason by the Bolognese elite with sanity and skill, in no small part because he has focused on the issue that was most important to them during the 1850s. Here, Hughes has reinforced greatly the case for the central—indeed, overriding—importance of the issue of law and order for an understanding of the period by reaching beyond the official police files. He has combed the progressive liberal journals of the 1840s, particularly *Il Felsineo*, to unearth a wealth of articles written on the subject of crime and its prevention; evidence of this kind is valuable for its very existence, to say nothing of its content.

Inevitably, perhaps, in a narrative embracing half a century, there are inconsistencies in emphasis. The earlier chapters on the 1820s raise many important issues of a social rather than a political character, particularly the apparent popularity of a return to the enforcement of traditional morality in family and sexual matters. This an important subject—it may widen our understanding of the residual popularity of reactionary rule in otherwise adverse circumstances—but it is not traced throughout the period. An overlap between town and country is unavoidable in this context, and it would have been foolish to exclude developments in the countryside from this study. Hughes has much of interest to say on rural disorder, but perhaps his work might have found more focus had a single chapter been devoted to the hinterland. The patterns of rural disorder, and of banditry in particular, Hughes discerns were already present in the vast rural revolt of 1809, and many of his observations would benefit from comparison with these previous events.

The biggest single gap in the book is undoubtedly Hughes' uneven handling of *i popolani*. "The crowd," as such, all too often appears as little more than that. Hughes points to the oscillations of their political allegiances between clerical reaction and Mazzinian republicanism. Their disorders and crimes and the specter of terror they evoked among the propertied classes are recurring themes of Hughes, yet the impression throughout is of the police shadowboxing with the faceless masses. In his conclusion, Hughes notes his attempt to make the Risorgimento appear more human, and as far as the propertied classes are concerned, he can take real pride in having done so. And, he notes, there is a dearth of studies of the Bolognese working classes for this period. By contrast, there is a superb literature on the artisan classes in the early modern period—the work of Carlo Poni above all—and it is to be hoped that the riches of the Archivio di Stato di Bologna will soon be deployed in this direction.

It would be churlish to end a review of so fine a study on a critical note, however. Steven Hughes has made a splendid contribution to the history of Restoration Italy, and he has done so exactly because of his expertise as a historian of the police and of criminality. This is a much needed, welcome contribution to a field of growing interest by a fine scholar.

Michael Broers
University of Aberdeen

Geoffrey Morley, *The Smuggling War: The Government's Fight against Smuggling in the 18th and 19th Centuries*. Alan Sutton Publishing Ltd., UK: Stroud, Gloucestershire, 1994. US: Dover, New Hampshire, 1994. £16.99

According to the publisher's blurb, *The Smuggling War* presents for the first time a factual account of the war between the smugglers and government forces during the eighteenth and nineteenth centuries. The claim is unjustified. Neville William's *Contraband Cargoes*, published in 1959, examined smuggling and the efforts made to contain it over a longer period and covered a wider territory. Morley should not be held accountable for the sins of others, and there is plenty of scope for further studies. Harvey Benham has used the Customs Outport Records to reconstruct the workings of the preventive service in the port of Harwich, and Paul Monod has opened up a new area for debate in his essay linking the growth of organized free-trading with the Jacobite networks.

Morley's work is mainly confined to the southern counties, which is not necessarily a disadvantage. The Outport Records for Hampshire, Dorset, and Devon, while far from being intact, could provide a useful basis for a detailed regional study and have yet to be exploited to any significant extent. Arnold and Forster made extensive use of the Cowes records during William Arnold's years as Collector, but it would be instructive to compare his tenure with his predecessors' terms in office. *The Smuggling War* provides some idea of what might be done in the outline of Isaac Gulliver's highly successful career as a merchant smuggler and in the extracts from Abraham Pike's journal, conveying the sheer tedium of a Riding Officer's work. Yet there is little evidence of any in-depth research, and the notes locate the Poole Outport Records at the Custom House Library when they have been at Kew for at least a decade.

An extended study would have made for more assured conclusions based on the available evidence. How did Pike's experiences around Christchurch in the early 1800s compare with that of the Riding Officers in Romney Marsh fifty years earlier? Certain errors of judgment could have been averted by paying closer attention to the historical context. Morley questions the sense of issuing commissions and letters of marque during the War of Independence: "Did the Admiralty imagine that these privateers intended to cross the Atlantic to attack the erring colonials?" Probably not; they anticipated them attacking enemy shipping in European waters. The problems the British government faced in checking clandestine importations in the early 1780s made this country a "laughing stock throughout the world." Why should it, given that protectionism and tariffs were normal practice and that other states were devoting greater resources to their own successful campaigns against smuggling?

There is useful material on the logistics of the trade, the way runs were funded, contraband purchased overseas, and the goods brought across, unloaded, and taken into the country. The problems are explained clearly, but carelessness over detail raises doubts about the writer's familiarity with the period. The prospect of making five pence a night carrying contraband off the beaches is contrasted with the farm worker's wage of one shilling a week. Life was hard, but not that bad, agricultural laborers generally making above six shillings a week and living-in. Morley also seriously understates the smugglers' rewards. According to a contemporary witness in 1749, each man was allowed "Half a Guinea a Time and his expenses for Eating and Drinking, a Horse found him and the profits of a Dollop of Tea." This could bring in another guinea at least.

Smuggling was a business conducted with considerable violence both at sea and on land. Revenue officers carried swords and pistols, and the armed services were deployed "in aid of the Revenue." The contest between government and contrabanders can be represented as a war, though some care should be exercised before making statements such as, "Both sides were squaring up for the warfare soon to break out nationwide." This implies a level of conscious, concerted rebellion on the smugglers' part, and Cal Winslow's case that the Sussex smugglers in the 1740s were defenders of the local community against the encroachments of commercial capitalism needs to be discussed.[1] The concept of social crime, central to "Sussex Smugglers" may give rise to disquiet, but it needs to be brought into any account of the contraband trade and its ramifications. Even for the searcher after interesting anecdotes, Winslow is a useful source. Morley appears unaware of the existence of "Sussex Smugglers" or the other essays in *Albion's Fatal Tree*. Once the 1746 act came into force, "capture meant automatic death at the hands of the hangman," he says. The new statute dispensed with the need to prove that an accused person was guilty of smuggling in certain circumstances, but Morley's approach simply ignores the work carried out on the functioning of the legal system and the great paradox of the Bloody Code, where the rate of hanging declined as the number of capital offenses increased. The few who were convicted and executed for smuggling alone felt themselves ill-used, the victims of a policy of exemplary punishment.

The use of proclamations as an administrative alternative to due legal process serves to illustrate the fact that eighteenth-century governments were no more encumbered by concepts of justice than are their modern counterparts. Yet Morley is quite content to accept that people in the past were given to outbreaks of irrationality when drafting new laws. So under the 1717 act, "Smugglers who refused to plead guilty" were to be transported. Far from worsening the smugglers' situation, transportation was a humane advance on the practice of pressing, when those refusing to enter a plea were slowly asphyxiated unless they changed their minds. The 1746 act did not penalize the county if a seizure of goods was made with no smugglers being arrested. There is nothing in the wording of the statute that lends itself to such an interpretation, and the bizarreness of such a measure should have occurred to the author. In any case, it was against the hundred, rape, or lathe that an aggrieved officer could seek redress in the event of an assault or a rescue if no suspects were brought in, not the county.

To unearth the complexities surrounding the case of the Ruxley gang,

Hastings pirates and smugglers active in the 1760s, would have entailed some detailed research but more accurate versions of some events or accounts more in line with contemporary evidence are more easily obtained. F. F. Nicholls makes particular mention of the fact that the Hawkhurst gang were very much in the minority in the raid on Poole warehouse and that the party probably numbered thirty men;[2] Morley insists the raid was carried out by sixty men, all members of the Hawkhurst gang. He later attributes the Galley and Chater killings to the Kentish men when it is clear the perpetrations were from West Sussex. A more careful reading of Ketcherell's letter to John Collier, quoted by Nicholls, might have eliminated the "Winham crew," an imaginary East Kent gang Morley conjures up.

The list of errors could be perpetuated; reappraisal and reform of the arm's contribution to the preventive force is dated 1748, when it was carried out in 1784. A witness before the 1745 Committee of Enquiry reckoned there were 20,000 smugglers in Britain, not just on the Sussex coast.

There are other issues perhaps more important than a lack of conformity with the existing records. A book entitled *The Smuggling War* should take as its model studies made of other forms of conflict, attempting some assessment of available resources, strategies, and tactics. Instead of filling seven pages with the instructions to coast guards issued in 1829, why not explore the question of policing the maritime counties in these years before the establishment of the new constabulary forces? Was it possible to keep the men of the Coast Guard and the Coast Blockade isolated and insulated from the communities they were supposed to be keeping in order?

Geoffrey Morley asks too few questions about the nature of smuggling both as a commercial enterprise and as a criminal activity. To grasp the extent of the problem faced by governments, the supply side needs to be brought into the analysis. Keeping Britain stocked with illicit merchandise was essential for the solvency of the various continental companies sending out ships to China to bring back cargoes of tea destined for eventual disposal on this side of the Channel and the North Sea. The Mui's essay on the Commutation Act is an excellent introduction to the realities of the smuggling trade with which Pitt had to contend.[3] The diplomatic and fiscal aspects of smuggling do need attending to, if only to escape "massive condescension" toward the people of the past. If tariff reform and free trade policies were such obvious solutions, then why were they not implemented sooner? The intellectual limitations of politicians and civil servants do not provide a satisfactory answer.

NOTES

1. Cal Winslow, "Sussex Smugglers," in *Albion's Fatal Tree* (London, 1977).
2. F. F. Nicholls, *Honest Thieves, The Violent Heyday of English Smuggling* (London, 1973).

3. H. Mui and L. Mui, "William Pitt and the Enforcement of the Commutation Act, 1784–88," *English Historical Review* 76, no. 300 (1961): 447–65.

Paul Muskett
The Open University, Milton Keynes

F. Murray Greenwood, *Legacies of Fear: Law and Politics in Quebec in the Era of the French Revolution*. Toronto: The Osgoode Society, 1993. xvi + 359 pp.

This book examines the influence exerted on Lower Canada (present day Quebec) by the French Revolution. The author demonstrates how this event created a wave of panic within the established British community in the colony. They feared that the Canadiens, the vast majority of the population, would rebel against their English masters.[1]

The first chapter of the book presents a brief outline of the legal setting within the colony during this period. After the Conquest of New France in 1759 and the judicial chaos that followed, the Quebec Act reestablished the *Coutume de Paris*. The seigneurial system, which typified the *ancien régime*, was maintained while British criminal law, somewhat modified to take into account the realities of colonial life, was also in force.

Dissatisfied with colonial institutions, petitions in favor of constitutional reform were sent to London. Those seeking reform, who were members of both the English and Canadien communities, endeavored to obtain the creation of a representative assembly that would have control over spending and would be independent of the judiciary. They also advocated adopting British commercial law. Opponents to these changes were concerned that they would lead to the establishment of a system of taxation as well as signal the end of the *Coutume de Paris*. Neither of these groups was defined along ethnic lines, as would subsequently be the case. Adherence was instead based upon the social class of a person. British authorities accepted constitutional reform using British institutions as a model.

As the historian Evelyn Kolish has demonstrated, the anticommercial character of French law and the superiority of English law were not the subject of any elaborate demonstration during this period. The devotion of the business community to the British system was based upon cultural considerations.[2]

The creation, by London, of a House of Assembly has been described, at the time as well as subsequently by historians, as a stratagem aimed at stopping the spread of ideas from the French Revolution. Greenwood gives little credence to this theory. The author proposes that, through its actions, Great Britain hoped to reduce its financial backing of the colony, to calm the English minority, and to stifle the propogation of American republicanism.

When it began, the French Revolution had been welcomed in Great Britain as well as in Canada. Sympathy, however, was rapidly replaced with disgrace. Support began to evaporate with the imprisonment of Louis XVI and disappeared following his execution. After 1793, paranoia gripped the English colonial elite, who feared invasion of Lower Canada by French Republicans. The presence of French agents in the United States, activism within the colony, and the refusal of the Canadiens to enlist in the defense of the country in case of conflict with the Americans produced an atmosphere of terror. Canadien opposition to the Road Act (1796), which relegated to each citizen the task of maintaining the roads, only added to the sense of distrust. The authorities sought to subdue the inhabitants of the colony. Even though they were met with stiff resistance, outbreaks of unrest were quickly put down in Montreal.

Despite the agitated atmosphere, the Canadien population remained loyal to the new Sovereign and showed no signs of rebellion. The British colonial elite remained distrustful and developed a garrison mentality. Greenwood provides the reader with a description and a detailed analysis of this mentality in Lower Canada.

Far from being imaginary, this fear was real. Apprehending coming revolt by the Canadien population, the British found signs foreshadowing imminent upheaval in diverse political events. Furthermore, demographic disparities clearly favored the Canadiens. The memory of the American Revolution, clearly lodged in the minds of many in the colonial elite, offered little reassurance.

In order to secure the colony, the governor manipulated legislative and judicial power. The comings and goings of strangers, principally from France, were controlled. Seditious acts were quashed. Although criminal proceedings were brought against rioters, the court, at the governor's behest, was lenient in order to avoid public outrage to what could have been perceived as provocation. Those guilty of political crimes received light sentences.

For David McLane, however, the mercy of the court was not available. Recruited in the United States to be a French agent, he was sent on a spy mission to Canada in 1796. McLane sought the support of the colonial population in order to provoke a rebellion. Denounced, he was arrested and charged with high treason.

In minute detail, Greenwood follows the trial and demonstrates where fear can lead during troubled times. The accused suffered from the partiality of the judge, the inexperience of his lawyers, and the makeup of the jury. After declaring him guilty, Judge William Osgoode condemned McLane to be hung, eviscerated alive, and dismembered. McLane was the unfortunate victim of mistrust, if not paranoia, among the colonial elites, who feared the danger that came with the spread of revolutionary ideas.

The British, frought with a garrison mentality, believed that the acknowledgement of Canadien cultural values by the Quebec Act was no longer appropriate at the end of the century. A strategy that included the creation of an English public school system, the abolition of the seigneurial system, and strict controls upon the religious hierarchy was devised to anglicize the colony. Greenwood proposes that these policies were aimed at assimilating the Canadiens in order to make them loyal subjects of the British Empire. Far from achieving these results, the measures intensified tensions between the two ethnic groups.

The distrust that gripped the colonial elite during the French Revolution persisted long afterwards. Fostered by the state of war between Great Britain and France, the fear of invasion and revolt never disappeared. In these circumstances, it is not surprising that the authorities tried to maintain efficient control over the colony. To this end, the House of Assembly approved the Alien Act, which gave the governor wide powers to facilitate the identification of spies, as well as their arrest or expulsion. In this setting, the rights of habeus corpus were set aside easily for a person suspected of high treason.

Acts of repression, originally aimed at outsiders, eventually focused upon the Canadien population. Maneuvers by the *parti canadien* in the House of Assembly, as well as articles published in the newspaper, *Le Canadien*, provoked an angry reaction from Governor James Craig, who arrested and imprisoned the Canadien political leaders.

In his conclusion, Greenwood emphasizes the effect of the events punctuating this period. Were it not for the development of a garrison mentality, the bourgeois alliance could have been maintained. Had this alliance survived, it probably would have permitted the coexistence of new and old British subjects. In the following decades, historians and politicians offered these acts of repression as fundamental to the development of nationalist thinking in Quebec. The author also views this period as a defining moment in the relationship between French and English in the colony.

Leading historians, including Claude Galarneau and Jean-Pierre Wallot, have already contributed important studies regarding the advent of the nineteenth century. Greenwood's book brings an original perspective to this period. The strength of this book lies in the author's analysis of the use of the law and the judicial apparatus by the colony's legal and political elite to cement their power and authority during this turbulant period of Canadian history.

NOTES

1. During this period, the word *Canadien* was used to describe French speaking members of the new British colony. The word English described British subjects who had come to the conquered colony.

2. Evelyn Kolish, *Nationalismes et conflits de droit: le débat du droit privé au Québec, 1760–1840* (Montreal, 1994), 165–76.

Sylvio Normand
Laval University, Quebec

Hereward Senior, *Constabulary: The Rise of Police Institutions in Britain, the Commonwealth and the United States*. Toronto and Oxford: Dundurn Press, 1997. 192 pp., index.

Studies of police institutions have been a growth industry in this decade as scholars explore the ever-increasing boundaries in societies ancient and modern. The author, a Canadian historian at McGill University, seeks to survey the history of policing from the amateur of the middle ages to the professional of modern times across the globe, striving to present a comparative study within a common-law tradition. The results, unfortunately, are not very credible.

In Medieval England, Norman institutions are read into the Anglo-Saxon era, and by the thirteenth century rural society and the forests are seen as closely controlled. This control increased in the sixteenth and seventeenth centuries, until a crime wave emerged after the evil Cromwell's Commonwealth. (The crime wave was actually over by then, and in decline to the late eighteenth century.) There is more on Henry Fielding and the London Metropolitan Police than on policing in England in the era of the industrial revolution.

Turning to New York and the United States, the colonial era is largely bypassed, as well as the early national period. Policing is seen as rather benign. But the story picks up in coverage and credibility for the 1830s through 1850s. Montreal, and Canada at large, fall into the same scene. There is nothing on the early period until the 1830s, and no discussion of what the police did on the ground, in the streets, and how that was regarded by the people who were there. The chapter on Australia 1788–1911 is slightly better in both organization and content.

Finally, for the western United States, which is one of the largest chapters, there is more on the Southeast and Texas than there is on the West. There is a brief history of vigilantes, with the chapter ending on the Pinkertons. How the West was policed, when, and to what effect, escapes the author. Western Canada falls into a similar scene as well: little on policing itself, no meeting of the problem of conflicting jurisdiction between federal, provincial, and city forces, and virtually no discussion of the policing of towns or cities.

There is an abbreviated conclusion. However, it is largely a collection of one-paragraph summaries of the chapters. One of the author's major interpretive problems is that he sees the rule of law and due process (from Anglo-Saxon times and Magna Carta) as creating an environment that precludes, a few exceptions aside, absolutist practices. Therefore, he fails to see state power in the common-law world, how it grew, and how it was exercised. Contrasts with the "absolutism" of continental European countries simply do not pass muster in our contemporary world of scholarship.

An overriding problem is that the author's historiography is approximately thirty years old. For England, he considers the best sources to be F. W. Maitland, John Coatman, George Howard, and Charles Reith. For the United States, Joel Tyler Headley, James Richardson, and Walter Prescott Webb. His literature is not much better for Australia, Canada, and India. What is perhaps most surprising is that none of the studies of Clive Emsley, David Philips, or Robert Storch are mentioned, let alone modern American scholars such as Eric Monkkonen, Wilbur Miller, Samuel Walker, or Eugene Watts. Nor is the magisterial history of justices of the peace (JPs) in the common-law world mentioned: Sir Thomas Skyrmes' three-volume *History of the Justice of the Peace* (London 1991). Without JPs, there would have been no law enforcement. The work of this judge and scholar, a Bencher of the Inner Temple and founder of the Commonwealth Magistrates' and Judges' Association who was Secretary of Commissions for England and Wales 1944–77, could have been used for both structure and interpretation.

Louis A. Knafla
University of Calgary

Thomas H. Holloway, *Policing Rio de Janeiro: Repression and Resistance in a 19th-Century City*. Stanford: Stanford University Press, 1993. xvii + 369 pp. £35.

The historiography of Latin America has always emphasized subjects of contemporary concern. It is, therefore, quite surprising that studies of police and crime had been so scarce when the role of violence in the building of social order appears to be so essential. This scarcity can be ascribed in part to the difficulties of obtaining the proper sources for such studies, which are still real, in spite of the wave of democratic reform in the area. But it must be acknowledged also that there existed a repugnance from academics to deal with matters of daily violence, reinforced by a strong conviction that members of the criminal justice system, and particularly the police, were only instruments exercising the instructions of a ruling elite. One strong indication of this is the fact that even if the use of criminal sources has increased in the 1980s, they have been employed to study various elements of daily life, never having crime and the criminal justice system as their main subjects.

Holloway's new book must, therefore, be welcomed as shedding some light on a much deserving subject, and we can only hope that it can be followed by other studies. He has amassed a vast quantity of new archival material from police sources to try to demonstrate his thesis that policing in Rio de Janeiro was part of the concerted efforts of the ruling elites to control a rebellious population through the exercise of sheer force. He considers the independence process as being only the transferring to the state of the monopoly of force that was formerly diffused among the seigniorial groups during colonial times, providing "a glaze of modernity over traditional attitudes and relationships, protecting and strengthening them." In the process of building the new police forces, the ruling elites attempted to replicate the European models that were also emerging but ultimately found that a militarized police was the best option in their circumstances, where the issue of policing was not to be part of the building of any sort of consensus, but purely a repressive instrument. If the purpose of the elites was solely to repress, the population was left with the only alternative of resisting, either through acts of rebellion or through crime or passivity.

In a sense, Holloway further elaborates the original approach to the role of the police in Brazilian history without really changing it. The police force was indeed an instrument of oppression and its own history of reforms and changes attends more to the ruling elite's whimsical wishes for a modern outlook than to difficulties experienced in exercising control or any need of building a more consensual model of authority. From the official files he draws a picture of an overpoliced city, where "force [was met] with superior force and insult with subjugation. To maintain hierarchy it was not enough to fight for a draw. Every battle in the social war, large or small, had to be won" (p. 143). The evidence shows the calls of the higher authorities for a tough police approach, especially from Feijó in the 1830s, and can present many cases where the use of violence was the norm. Relying on evidence from the higher official ranks of the police, Holloway presents a case for what seems to have been a very successful experiment on repressive police.

This is where some points must be raised: Did the police system really work as effectively as he indicates? Two issues need to be addressed. First, Holloway has difficulties in explaining how the police achieved the necessary cohesion to repress, and second, were the police really able to keep the city under such tight control? It is conceivable that while the whole population was resisting, the police acted as a docile instrument of the elites, rewarded by the "intangible psychological rewards" (p. 280) of military esprit de corps, keeping distant of the people they policed? More concrete rewards, such as the earnings of a policeman or the policy on promotion, are passed over briefly. If the salary in the police was small compared with other occupations, and the requirements of the job exhausting, it is still necessary to try to have a closer evaluation of the impact of rewards for arrests on the income of policemen. The policy of promoting from the ranks in the military police is a theme that altogether escaped Holloway's attention.

The effectiveness of such a model is very doubtful, since it was inevitable that policemen had their own social networks and spent most of their lives on the streets in close contact with those they policed. The high turnover in the forces that Holloway points to suggests that the policemen also resisted and found ways of reconciling the exigencies of the job with their own personal motivations, which most of the time are absent from the official reports.

The problem of how well policed Rio was remains difficult to answer. From the official files Holloway is able to present both stories of successful repression and cases where the excess of violence got out of control, but in general, he gives the impression of a very efficient, if unpleasant, police system. Yet, is not this, in fact, contradicted by the observation of their failure in keeping daily order in a city rife with *capoeiras*, the characteristic street fighters of Rio, and considered as a typical hideout for runaway slaves? Property crimes, which occupied an important place in the criminal statistics presented by Holloway, are an unknown quantity, in the sums involved as well as in the results obtained by the police in prosecuting. The police ability to cope with major disorder was not threatened during most of the nineteenth century, but from the Vintem riots of 1880, and especially in the early republican period, it became clear that the police were unable to deal with such cases.

Holloway provides a vivid account of urban conflicts and a useful framework on how the political elites conceived the police role during the nineteenth century. But the policeman on the job remains throughout the book the most noticeable absence, allowing the repressive model of Brazilian history to go on unchallenged. This can be a result of a total lack of sources or of the disorder of police archives, where much is still to be found. In any case, Holloway's book presents many challenges for future research.

Marcos Luiz Bretas
Federal University of Rio de Janiero

Elizabeth Cancelli, *O Mundo da Violêcia: A Polícia da era Vargas*. Editora Universidade de Brasília, 1993, 227 pp.

Curiously, studies of dictatorial regimes have commonly ignored the role of their police forces as a subject for study. The long period of Vargas' rule in Brazil from 1930 to 1945 is no exception. Elizabeth Cancelli's book intends to bridge this gap, offering a view of the importance of the police in the maintenance of power. It originates from a doctoral dissertation, in which the title referred to the police state in the Vargas period. The substitution of the "police" for "police-state" in the book is misleading and may bring some disappointment to readers. The book is concerned with the establishment of what Cancelli considers a totalitarian regime in the 1930s, which, in common with its European counterparts, relied heavily on repressive and secret policing. Even if we accept the general argument about a totalitarian regime in Brazil, which is not altogether a widely accepted definition, the role of the police in achieving and maintaining such a goal is not satisfactorily proved.

Cancelli relies on a definition of policing that emphasizes its political role, with only scarce reference to its role in dealing with crime or its other routine activities. According to her, Vargas took over the police of Rio de Janeiro in 1930 and transformed it into the police of a centralized state, exerting influence over the other state police forces and occupying a vital place in the propaganda apparatus of the state. She bases her conclusions on the police reforms implemented by the new rulers, which involved both a modernizing and reorganizing of the police and a complete replacement of the officials in the higher ranks. Here she misses the fact that the same type of reforms, substitution of personnel, and claims for modernization characterized the police administrators throughout the so-called old Republic (between 1889 and 1930); second, the impressive volume of law that reorganized the police in July 1934 was strongly reminiscent of the last great reorganization of 1907; third, the subordination of the police to the Minister of Justice, overlapped by a de facto control by the president, was already perceived in 1917 by the chief of police, Aurelino Leal, who called for the elimination of this bureaucratic control by the minister. In sum, much of what the Vargas regime did to the police was very similar to what had happened before.

This is not to deny that new features appeared with the new regime. Certainly, the fact that Felinto Muller remained as chief of police for about ten years was unprecedented; this indicates his closeness to the dictator and probably a degree of efficiency in performing the tasks he was given. The role of the police in censorship—which had begun in the mid-1920s—and propaganda for the regime represented a new development that certainly was important, although much has to be investigated about the relationship between the police and the Departamento de Imprensa e Propaganda (DIP).

The political disorder of the 1930s certainly underlined the police role in the surveillance of political opposition, especially on the left. But what I found particularly noticeable about the extensive evidence of political policing presented by Cancelli is that most of the names on the reports are those of military officers rather than policemen. This seems to suggest that political policing was a business too important to be left in the hands of the policemen, who were replaced in this task by army officers in a pattern established already in the 1920s.

The lack of information about policing before the Vargas period is again noticeable when Cancelli discusses the targets of police action. The attention focused on vagrants, foreigners, and domestic servants can hardly be considered a new feature, since these were the object of police interest since the nineteenth century. The extensive information that the police were supposed to collect about every corner of the country and the cases of denunciation presented by Cancelli have to be taken with care, and questions about its effectiveness are essential. Certainly bureaucracies in dictatorial regimes demand extensive amounts of information, but it is not certain whether they really obtain the required cooperation and whether the information is put to any concrete use. The detailed questionnaire sent to all municipal authorities asking questions ranging from the history of the place to the number and nationality of the prostitutes can be a very interesting source for historians, but of what value was it to the police? Knowledge, rather than power, can offer a justification for growing bureaucracies. Denunciations of "criminals" or government enemies are also a common feature of police work, and certainly grew everywhere during the Second World War. This is another problem presented by the evidence that is not dealt with properly: how much of the concern about "government enemies," spies, and German and Japanese colonies was part of a spirit common to all countries involved in the war? More comparative information, together with a look into the past practices of Rio's police, would certainly enrich Cancelli's undoubtedly thorough use of the sources. But even with all these problems, the book still offers some valuable new information on a subject frequently set aside by most of the historiography of the Vargas period. Particularly interesting is the last chapter dealing with prisons, which offers new data and illustrates the structuring of the prison system and the treatment of political prisoners. Once again the question might be posed: How different was this from the old Republic? But knowledge about the subject is very scarce.

Finally, it must be welcome that the press of the Universidade de Brasília has again started to publish academic books. Nevertheless, more care with the treatment of the books is necessary, because printing errors frequently distort the author's argument and make reading much more difficult.

Marcos Luiz Bretas
Federal University of Rio de Janiero

Stefan Petrow, *Policing Morals*. New York: Clarendon Press, 1994, xiii + 343 pp. £35.

Dr. Petrow's book is an important contribution to the history of the London Metropolitan Police between 1870 and 1914, when it became a "recognisably modern, professional police force" with a greatly increased range of powers and responsibilities. Petrow's concern is the Metropolitan Police's role in the enforcement of a legally enshrined code of public morality. This moral policing was directed principally at four areas of concern—habitual criminality, prostitution, drunkenness, and betting. According to Petrow this necessitated the growth and transformation of the Metropolitan Police under the direction of the Home Office. Policing methods changed dramatically and demanded the creation of a new strata of police bureaucracy. The institutional growth of the Metropolitan Police in this period became vitally important for the inauguration of modern mechanisms of control and the future of English "liberty."

Petrow studies a number of important issues: first, why and how the Metropolitan Police were directed to enforce a legally defined morality; second, the nature of the legislation used to tackle habitual criminality, prostitution, drunkenness, and betting; third, the activities of moralists who sought new powers for the Metropolitan Police; fourth, whether the police desired these powers for moral or institutional reasons, or resisted them because of impracticalities; finally, how effectively were the new powers enforced and how did policing methods change in the process. In doing so, he examines some themes in the history of policing and the policed raised by Robert Storch in his seminal work of the 1970s. Two points are crucial to Petrow's analysis of policing. He emphasizes that a new era of policing began around 1870. Hitherto, policing in London—and elsewhere in England—had been a matter of patrolling the streets, observing people and property. Henceforth, there was a steadily increasing bureaucratization of police procedures with the creation of specialist departments staffed by administrators. Also from about 1870 the image of the police began to change. From its inception, the Metropolitan Police had been able to argue—rightly or wrongly—that it was independent and impartial, an instrument of the people, not the state, enforcing laws untainted by class bias. However, after 1870 the powers conferred on the Metropolitan Police as a result of moral legislation forced policemen to repress activities that they, and others, did not regard personally as "immoral," socially undermining, or hazardous.

The advocates and supporters of moral reform came mainly from the professional middle class (particularly doctors and criminologists) and lower middle class, but a significant amount of support came from elements of the working class and not just from the labor aristocracy. In London, a commercial and renter city where manufacturing industry was less important than the service sector, the influence of the professional middle class was considerable, and within this group the moralists were especially influential. Opponents of the moral reformers were more diverse, comprised of the "pleasure-seeking" aristocracy and working class, middle-class interests in the drink and entertainment industries, and middle-class socialists. Intellectually, they were led by a group of libertarian thinkers who opposed, in principle, attempts to increase police powers at the expense of the individual. Of the two groups, the moral reformers were more powerful politically, and the police were forced to respond to their demands for action against habitual criminals, drunkards, gamblers, prostitutes, and their clients. Although opinions on this subject varied markedly inside the Metropolitan Police according to rank, policing experience, upbringing, and religious observance, the force generally regarded violent crime and the militant activities of political extremists as more threatening to the fabric of society than any "immoral" behavior. Most Metropolitan policeman did not sympathize with moral reformers, and even the minority that did tended to believe regulation of immorality was preferable to its legal suppression. As far as the police were concerned, their primary objective was fighting crime and maintaining order; it was not their job to enforce a code of morality.

The enforcement of moral laws accelerated the growth of the Metropolitan Police and the Home Office and aggrandized police power over all citizens. But it also undermined public confidence in the police, whose impartiality was increasingly questioned. The powers of the Metropolitan Police were augmented in three related ways. First, the campaigns of moral reformers in well-organized pressure groups claimed that public morality and, hence, national efficiency and survival were being undermined by certain kinds of "immoral" behavior. Despite being unable to marshal any hard evidence to support their arguments, the moral reformers, with the help of sympathizers in Parliament, managed to secure the passage of draconian legislation to punish immoral behavior. Their opponents defeated or diluted some of the more extreme measures, but generally the moralists achieved most of their aims. Second, in the short term, public opinion was alarmed by moral panics, in part driven by moral reformers' manipulation of the press. These panics were directed at various groups between the 1860s and 1914: ticket-of-leave men, prostitutes, and habitual criminals. They resulted in increased powers being given to the police to combat the perceived threat. Third, the responses of the law enforcement authorities themselves—the Home Office bureaucrats and senior police officers who came together to formulate official policy and discuss new police procedures—who identified with some of the moral reformers' concerns but opposed their more extreme proposals, preferring licensing and regulation (e.g., liquor licensing) to prohibition on the grounds that the latter would force immoralities underground, making them harder to control. The implementation of new procedures encouraged the bureaucratization of the police, which also multiplied under its own impetus and became more specialized.

However, this crusade of moral authoritarianism was far from being effective. It is here that Petrow pursues some of Storch's themes. Although the moral legislation, and its enforcement by the police, reduced the range of behavior that was acceptable and submitted the remainder to a higher degree of supervision and control, the police had to bargain with those that they policed, because the latter exhibited a high degree of independence and resistance. Moreover, often the ordinary policemen sympathized more with those who broke the law than with those who urged its enforcement. Also, it should not be forgotten that despite the tremendous growth of the Metropolitan Police between 1870 and 1914, it still did not have the manpower or the financial resources to comprehensively enforce the moral legislation. This was a minor problem compared to others encountered. Bribery among the lower ranks of the Metropolitan Police—inspectors, sergeants, and constables—although not endemic, was not scarce either. This could range from substantial sums given by professional criminals to inspectors, to a few shillings received by a beat constable from a street bookmaker for "looking the other way." Many constables and sergeants did not view street betting, drunkenness, and prostitution as serious offenses and, in parts of London, took no action against them unless they became a transparent public nuisance, partly as a way of avenging themselves against senior officers who ignored demands for improvements in pay and working conditions. Ultimately, the moral legislation had very little effect on individual behavior and the practices that were targeted for coercive treatment. People of all classes who wanted to drink, gamble, and become involved with prostitutes continued to do so, and many providers of these wants continued to evade the law with or without the connivance of policemen. The enforcement of moral laws may have affected the time and place at which some of these wants were satisfied, but they achieved little more.

Petrow's book is a commendable example of scholarship in the tradition of liberal history. It is empirically based, detailed, and generally thorough, but in places the facility of the style is interrupted by too many short quotations and the sheer amount of detail tends to blunt the sharpness of the argument. Furthermore, its failure to provide even the most basic theoretical framework is disappointing. For example, Petrow's analyses of the bureaucratization and institutional development of the Metropolitan Police, the classifying (or "labeling") of certain behavior as immoral and the implementation of control mechanisms to regulate that behavior are well argued but could have been improved by a discussion of the different theoretical perspectives relevant to each area. Important though his work is, Petrow overestimates the part played by moral policing in the growth and development of the Metropolitan Police. Concerns about "conventional" crime (especially robbery and burglary), public order in general, and specifically the violent activities of Fenians and militant trade unionists, socialists, anarchists, and suffragettes were far more important as reasons for the tremendous increase of police powers and numbers than any fears about "immoral" behavior. Regrettably, Petrow does not juxtapose the two as a way of putting the moral policing in its proper context. Nevertheless, none of this should detract from what is a fine and important book and one that will be of great interest to police historians. This period in the Metropolitan Police's history has been relatively neglected, and *Policing Morals* should act as a stimulus to new research.

D. R. Welsh
University of Hull

Barbara Weinberger, *The Best Police in the World: An Oral History of English Policing from the 1930s to the 1960s*. Aldershot: Scolar Press; and Brookfield, VT: Ashgate, 1995, 224 pp., illus.

The reality of some low-crime "golden age" of policing in England between the 1930s and the 1960s has become a largely unchallenged part of public debates about law and order. It has remained unchallenged because there has been little research done into the administration of criminal justice in this period. Instead, the public image of the police has come to be defined by the normative and often complacent descriptions of practice contained in official reports and memoirs of the time.

Barbara Weinberger has set out to test the thesis of the "golden age." At the same time, by filling this gap in the historiography, she has succeeded in providing a major contribution toward the history of twentieth-century policing. Although she has utilized a wide range of source material, what distinguishes her work is the attempt to counter the bias of the records by checking the official version against the recollections of a representative selection of police officers from borough, country, and metropolitan forces who served between the 1930s and 1960s. This is a necessary corrective, particularly since, as an official admitted in 1920, "At the Home Office one does not get much in touch with individual policemen."[1]

At times her methodology has enabled her to be spectacularly successful in eliciting confirmation of conclusions that otherwise could be drawn only tentatively from more conventional sources. For example, Sergeant Minch of Birmingham was more informative than a string of *Parliamentary Papers* discussing the criminal statistics when he said:"We wanted to say at the end of the year that crime's gone up ten percent because we haven't got enough policemen. And the CID, because their gaffers kept saying 'we're having too much crime', they tried to write it off" (p. 87). However, the danger with an oral history approach is that the psychological insights revealed can give the impression, as has been given by some sociological field work in later periods, that police practice was largely determined by a form of apolitical "cop culture" that emerged as a result of the "authoritarian" personality type attracted to the service. Fortunately, Weinberger's wide contextualization does not allow this to happen. Throughout, the reader is kept aware that the manpower problem, economic stringency, and the formidable discipline exerted by senior officers were major forces controlling the constable.

The book's excellent discussion of training reveals how the authoritarian attitude was instilled into the young constable. For example, some were drilled that "Law, as defined by Blackstone, is a rule of action prescribed by a superior which an inferior is bound to obey" (p. 28). With such a grounding in the law, it is no surprise that the unemployed in Jarrow who had been lying on the pavement were taught to rise "like zombies" when a constable appeared. Meanwhile, in London, barrow boys were expected to lift "the handles of their barrows to make a show" when a policeman passed by (pp. 31–33).

A wide spectrum of policing issues is covered, all of which, to some extent, impinge on the central issue of the book—police/public relations. Until the car intruded, the principal contact that the police had with the public was on the beat. Fundamentally, Weinberger argues, it was the exercise of authority in the maintenance of public order and the "tributes in the form of respect and obedience" that gave the uniformed policeman on the beat his purpose and "main job satisfaction" (p. 183). The policing of prostitutes, bookies, and demonstrations and marches are all presented as variants on the same theme of public order. The chapter on policewomen and police wives delves into a much-neglected area of policing. The discussion and oral descriptions of "the representative function of police families" provides the reader with considerable insight into the preventive function of the police as moral educators for the rest of society (p. 104).

As regards police/public relations, while there is much disquieting evidence in the book of police violence, brutality, and corruption, ultimately Weinberger argues that the police "may not have been 'the best in the world' but they were certainly exceedingly well adapted . . . to the policing demands made of them" (p. 208). The evidence for this assertion is somewhat thin, and the author assumes that there was a much greater moral consensus and cultural homogeneity in the past. This is very hard to prove one way or the other. But surely, no discussion of the police image can be complete without taking into account its politics. Why was it important to the imperial government that the British police be seen as the "best in the world"? How close were the links between Whitehall, senior police officers, and such media organizations as the Fleet Street Proprietors' Association, the BBC and the British Film industry, and how reliable is the information we obtain from such sources? Since these questions are really beyond the scope of the book, the conclusion must be that the thesis of the "golden age" remains unproved.

Although the book deservedly should become the first source to consult to discover what real policeman did on the beat, in the CID, on traffic duty, during the war, or at demonstrations, and how these specialisms developed, the overall analysis of the policing function is not as penetrating as might have been hoped for. Why is this? Possibly because the age limitations of the interviewees determined that the history should start in 1930 rather than ten years earlier, at the end of the First World War. There, as the statistics show, significant discontinuities, particularly as regards crime and the composition of the police forces, abruptly marked postwar police practice from the Victorian and Edwardian period.

By 1930, the car had come to occupy a great deal of police time, and the Home Office had begun to take the policing of crime more seriously than it had done before. Neither of these developments was inevitable in 1918. Unfortunately, the analysis does not reach back those few extra years that are necessary to understand the politics. Consequently, there is at times a whiff of Whiggism to the book's argument, because the official justifications for policies already in place are accepted without enough discussion of the original structural changes in policing that created those policies. For example, Weinberger accepts the official line in the 1930s, that the Home Office wanted police amalgamations for straightforward reasons of efficiency and economy, and dismisses their opponents as basing their arguments "more on sentiment than on logic" (p. 38). This greatly oversimplifies a long and complex debate without advancing our understanding.

In conclusion, this is a major addition to our knowledge of the police, and it illuminates many aspects of police work that previously have been explored little. It will remain, for many years, the standard work on police and organization. Hopefully, this pioneer work will stimulate much future research into this period of policing.

NOTE

1. Evidence of H. B. Simpson, Assistant Secretary, Home Office, "Committee on the Police Service of England and Wales (Desborough)," *Parliamentary Papers* 22 (1920), 6.

Howard Taylor
Gonville and Caius College, Cambridge

Charles Townshend, *Making the Peace—Public Order and Public Security in Modern Britain*. Oxford: Oxford University Press, 1993, 264 pp.

Charles Townshend's study comes after a succession of investigations by British academics, mostly historians or sociologists, into the historical roots and the evolution of what we could call the "public order system" in Britain. These investigations have developed mainly during the last two decades. One can situate Professor Townshend's contribution among those who try to describe and characterize what he himself identifies as a specific "British way" of dealing with public disorder. Townshend, like most of the others, is seeking to understand why "somewhere between Brixton and Bogside, Grunwick and Gibraltar, sometime in the last decade, the British way seems to have petered out. It looks as if we must now do it somebody else's way" (p. 201).

Although the exact and scientific definition of the concept is not absolutely clear, one can conclude from reading a great part of the British literature that the "British way" of maintaining public order is characterized by the existence of a decision-making process concerned with the search for political and social consensus, the exercise of tolerance, and the respect for individual and public liberties. Charles Townshend's perspective does not seem to depart from this general trend of analysis. The weight of this "definition" in English academic circles (and various other circles, notably political ones) has been enhanced greatly by the invocation of foreign models as alien countermodels, especially the French, German, and Russian "ways" as they are understood in the Great British mythology of public order; Charles Townshend can take rightly as a starting point of his book the "English image of order."

The author's contribution to the discussion takes the form of a historical analysis of the various concepts on which the "law and order debate" has been founded since the middle of the nineteenth century. Participating in the very British belief in the primary importance of the law in governing the machinery of public order, as well as in expressing the deep spirit and motivations of the political regime, Townshend mainly focuses, on the legal aspects and their management. His analysis, as well as the examples chosen, show very clearly how much the belief in the efficiency of the law as an instrument of the maintenance of order (as opposed to a general reflection on the organizational and technical aspects of that task) has dominated British public order "policy" until recently. Indeed, one may reflect that if there has been an alteration of the "British way" in the last two decades, as the author suggests, it could be precisely because of a rather new preoccupation of the public authorities, both central and local, as well as of the police themselves, for the organizational and technical aspects of public order maintenance (hence the process of "professionalization" of the police), rather than a distinctive shift in the nature of the legislation.

Townshend's book touches upon many of the subjects involved in the study of the peace-making process in the British society, but the main theme of his analysis has been developed already in some of his previous books, like *Britain's Civil Wars* and *Political Violence in Ireland*, primarily his perception of the vagueness and ambiguity of definition as characteristics of the British governmental response to public order problems and challenges. For Townshend, this ambiguity is particularly obvious at the legal constitutional level, and manifests itself in particular through an implicit refusal by the authorities to "look at the whole of the law of public order from a coherent principled standpoint" (p. 61). It originates partly from the unwritten character of the British constitution and, correspondingly, from the dominant place of the common law and, therefore, the crucial importance of judicial interpretation in that domain in this particularly sensitive field (e.g., pp. 125–31 on emergency powers). Consequently, Townshend observes a recurrent intractability of the problem of the definition of a conception of "order" and correspondingly of "disorder" that could form the base of public order policy, but we could say that this situation is similar to that of most liberal-democratic political regimes. Beyond that, the "British way" in public order management historically distinguishes itself by several features expressing those ambiguities and lack of definition mentioned above. Townshend insists on the difficulty of identification of the relevant law applicable according to the circumstances; he develops his case convincingly, notably through the analysis of the extraordinary problems and contradictions caused by the imposition of Martial Law in Ireland in 1921 (pp. 77–79) and the elaboration of, and vote on, the first Public Order Act (pp. 104–11). He pursues this fundamental idea into the contemporary period, in linking directly, for example, the second Public Order Act to the first one and to the "British way": Both in its preparatory stages and its definite form, the 1985 Public Order Bill seems to have been no more than, in the words of the author quoting Chris Smith, "an attempt by the Government to be seen to be doing something" (p. 164).

Another crucial dimension of the same general problem can be mentioned, even though it does not constitute the main part of the author's reflection: It is the problematic identification of the competent authorities and services supposed to intervene *in the concrete field of public order*, as well as the limits of their competence. A particularly topical example is that of the place and the role of the Armed Forces (alluded to on p. 75), a historically recurrent problem ranging from the question of the status and constitutional definition of the powers of those services (cf. pp. 77–78 for instance) to the very concrete issue of their operational control. The modernity of this question is particularly familiar to any student of the Northern Irish conflict.

Another particularly interesting example is that of the place and the use of bodies of citizens in public order. Townshend briefly evokes the cases of the Defence Force and the Civil Constabulary Reserve in the 1920s, and one must of course add to them, even more significantly, the constant problem of the status of the "Specials" and of the citizens' associations, which notably have caused troubles in Ulster in the contemporary period.

One can draw many conclusions from the reading of this interesting, although not extremely original, book. Some of them are brought about by a question left only partly answered by Townshend at the end of this book: Have "the stresses of modern political violence . . . exhausted the flexibility which has always been the chief virtue of the unwritten constitution"? The problem is that "the common law tradition could deal with traditional war, but is stranded on the reefs of *low intensity* rebellion and terrorism, just as the policing tradition has been disintegrated by *slow rioting*" (p. 201). His presentation of the most recent developments in the field of public order as fostering a real shift in British political culture, notably its "militarization" and the redefinition of the "traditional" space alloted to the public in the discussion of those fundamental matters, can be seen as pessimistic, at least if one follows the logic of the specifity of the "British way."

Finally, the theory and the description of the decision-making process in the public order sphere in Britain are yet to be built. Professor Townshend's sometimes rather brief accounts of the genesis of some of the most crucial decisions and pieces of legislation in the history of public order make us regret our lack of not only complete descriptions, both historical and sociological, of that political reality in Britain, but also a theoretical framework of analysis for the study of this political process. Townshend does not really approach this, even though it is clearly a fundamental problem for social scientists. We are sent back to the larger question of what a public order policy is, as much as what "national" characteristics are or can be. Indeed, all of these remarks can be applied to the study of the public order decision-making process in general. The problem of ill-definition is partly related to the essentially imprecise nature of the public order "sphere" in any society, but also to the attitude of political scientists. Interest in public order and internal security problems *as parts of the study of the political system* has taken a considerable time to emerge, and is still not very well established.

Anne Mandeville
Centre d'Études et de Recherche sur l'Armé
Université de Toulouse I

Michel Bergès, *Le Syndicalisme policier en France (1880–1940)*. Paris: L'Harmattan, 1995.

Until relatively recently the study of the police in France was at a primitive stage, but within the last five years a number of texts have appeared to fill this scholarly vacuum. In particular, the period of Third Republic France (1870–1940) has begun to become a focus of specialist attention, owing partly to the ready availability of source material but also to the insights this period offers regarding the development of policing in modern societies. Bergès' book comes after two excellent studies of Third Republic policing by Jean-Marc Berlière and Marie Vogel.[1]

In his text, Bergès reproduces, with a few very minor alterations, the thesis he wrote under the supervision of one of France's leading police specialists, Jean-Louis Loubet del Bayle.[2] He charts the evolution of police trade unionism from the nineteenth century through to the 1930s. The title of the book is a little misleading in this respect, because the analysis rarely goes beyond 1932, Bergès concluding, incorrectly, that there is little source material beyond this date. Also not evident is that the book focuses largely on trade unionism in two cities—Marseille and Bordeaux—and that the associations studied are for the most part limited to those of the Gardiens de la Paix (equivalent of constables or patrolmen) and Commissaires (superintendents or captains) with the movements of the Inspecteurs and Secrétaires de Police being pretty much ignored. Such limitations are almost inevitable in a study of this kind given the complex nature of the questions tackled and allow a closer analysis of the aspects chosen.

The author traces back police associationism to origins in the mid-late nineteenth century, giving examples of activity in this embryonic stage. He stresses the importance of the widespread diffusion of a newspaper for Commissaires de Police, which from 1855 offered debates on the question of whether the police should be controlled nationally or locally and drew attention to manpower shortages, denouncing budgetary restrictions. Developing corporate identity and demonstrating the desire of members of the institution to participate in the construction of their administration, Bergès argues convincingly that such a newspaper helped sow the seeds of the later associations. Similarly, a mutual aid society established in December 1882 acted as a precursor to later activity. More formal associations began to take root shortly after the turn of the century, their development being influenced by the growth and politicization of the civil service as well as evolutions in society at large such as the sharpening of working-class consciousness and a shift toward greater suffrage. The establishment of a police-friendly society in Bordeaux in June 1904 is the first example of a more formal mechanism for self-protection within the institution and this type of grouping began to be coordinated nationally with the founding in Lorient in 1906 of a national federation of police associations, which continued to grow up until the First World War. Bergès traces two main phases in the interwar development of police trade unionism. In a first period, running from 1919 to 1924, the associations engaged in a form of aggressive trade unionism including the use of strikes and revolutionary rhetoric. Between 1924 and the 1930s, they adopted a more corporatist stance striving for co-management of their institution.

Evolving from associations for mutual aid and protection into more assertive and demanding organizations, police trade unions followed a similar course to that pursued by the professional associations of other public service. Their relationship with these associations varied considerably during these different periods. Police attempts to form closer relationships with nonpolice federations were not always viewed positively, with the suspicion that police trade unionists might be acting as spies for the administration. Although there were moments of rapprochement with other unions, such as the Marseille police strike of 1919, the police usually wallowed in their specificity. Indeed, it was difficult enough to establish trade union unity within the police itself without searching to establish it beyond the corporation. Too often police unions were divided by jealousy between different branches and categories of personnel, not to mention the disputes arising from personal or political hostility between the leaders of these associations. The administration encouraged these divisions working on the age-old theory of divide and rule and when the senior hierarchy of the institution felt the associations were becoming too aggressive or a danger to discipline severe repression would ensue. The repression of these organizations encouraged their politicization. Faced with incomprehension from their own hierarchy, police trade unionists contacted local politicians, who took up their cause for their own political ends, some politicians using this as a means of reinforcing their local power base and thereby bypassing an increasing centralization of police services. It is when dealing with the relationship between police and politics that Bergès is on the firmest ground, and he comes up with a number of interesting and important insights.

However, despite its strengths, it is probable that this text will be considered somewhat unsatisfactory by all types of readership. The general reader undoubtedly will find the cumbersome writing style a little stodgy and indigestible. Those interested in the study of the localities of Marseille and Bordeaux will be surprised that little attempt is made to understand the particular sociopolitical climate of these two towns. For the specialist reader the level of scholarship is often found wanting. The author falls into anachronisms and cannot resist the temptation of seeing the 1930s as Vichy before Vichy. There is no index, and the footnotes are entirely unsatisfactory—inconsistent and impossible to follow. Quotation marks are thrown into the text without any indication of where the quotation originated. Too often the text is careless and slapdash. Many of the names of police trade unionists are misspelt. Little imagination has been used in the search for archival material and some documents are misread. On p. 306, Bergès claims that Paul Allard's book *Anarchie de la Police* was directly inspired by the Commissaires' trade union (of radical and Masonic inspiration) when, in fact, Allard, of right-wing persuasion, denounces this union as an occult movement working for the Free Masons. While Bergès can be forgiven easily for not consulting the rich CGT archives (which at the time he researched this book were available but still in the process of reclassification), it is somewhat surprising that he apparently has made no attempt to consult trade union newspapers such as *l'Étatiste*, which was readily available in the Bibliothèque Nationale.

It is to be hoped that Bergès will draw on the strengths of this text, continuing to make use of clearly displayed qualities of intelligence and natural perception, and will reissue it in a form that is both more readable and more careful.

NOTES

1. Jean-Marc Berlière, "L'Institution policière en France sous la Troisième République, 1875–1914" (Thèse, Université de Lille, 1991); Marie-Thérèse Vogel, "La Police des villes entre local et national: *l'administration des Polices urbaines sous la IIIe République*" (Thèse, Université de Grenoble II, 1993).
2. Michel Bergès, *"Corporatisme et construction de l'État: le champ policier (1852–1940)"* (Thèse d'État de Science Politique, Toulouse, 1994).

Simon Kitson
University of Birmingham

Maria de Conceição Ribeiro, *Policia Politica no Estado Nova 1926–1945*. Lisbon: Editorial Estampa, 1995, 314 pp.

Twenty-one years have passed since the so-called "carnation revolution" in Portugal, but only now has the first piece of serious academic research specifically focusing on the political power of Salazar's authoritarian regime been published. This is, however, not a situation limited to the history of political police. Studies of the history of police in general, of crime, and social control with a nonjuridical perspective are also almost nonexistent and do not appear to interest academics in Portugal, though there is a constant fascination among the media.

Given the scarce bibliography, but perhaps more seriously the practical difficulties of approaching and researching the former Portuguese political police archives, Ribeiro manages to collect an impressive amount of information and also to provide a perceptive and lucid analysis of the subject. As the title indicates, the book, which is based on a thesis undertaken at the *Universidade Nova de Lisboa*, explores the Portuguese political police within the period 1926–45. It centers especially, however, on the *Policia de Vigilância e Defesa do Estado* (PVDE), created in 1933 after the legitimation of Salazar's regime—the *Estado Novo*—by the constitutional plebiscite and the new constitution of the same year.

As a starting point, Ribeiro focuses on "the [novelty] of the political police forces created within the frame of the authoritarian regimes which emerged in the period between wars in countries such as Italy, Germany, Portugal or Spain, in a complex and historically diversified reaction to the crisis of the liberal State model." A brief comparative analysis of these authoritarian regimes and their political police forces points out a number of aspects common to them all, within the context of "a redefinition of the institutional role of political violence" and a movement that both centralized and restructured the repressive apparatus. The "novelty" of Salazar's political police requires an analysis in national terms of the multiple police organizations with political functions during the preceding period—the first Republic, 1910–26. The complex transition from the military dictatorship installed in 1926 to the *Estado Novo* in 1993 is also analyzed with the same purpose. Ribeiro's work here is important, as it delineates lines of continuity and points of rupture in relation to the political police of Salazar's regime.

The core of the book is a detailed analysis of the *Policia de Vigilância e Defesa do Estado* from 1945 until 1993. Ribeiro chronicles its genesis, structure, functions, legal framework, powers, constitutional elements, training, its formal and informal connections with and influences from other contemporary political police forces, and its relationship with the government, especially the head of the government. There is also a brief discussion of the representation of the police among the political opposition and their response to this repression. The text is supported by an appendix containing statistical data on political imprisonment, prisoners, and penalties in charts and graphics, as well as some contemporary underground illustrations of the PVDE's torture methods.

The result is a comprehensive and solid study displaying the real dimension of the PVDE's organization and behavior that is usefully juxtaposed with the substantially different common "image" of this very political police. The *Policia de Vigilância e Defesa do Estado* almost controlled an entire justice system without any external judiciary restraint whatsoever and with devastating consequences. The imperfections, vagaries, and roughness of both its structure and its members are exhibited clearly here and set alongside the common, almost mythical image of an immense, rigorous, and all-powerful organization.

Lenor Sá
Museu Nacional de Criminalistica de Policia Judiciária,
Instituto Nacional de Policia e Ciências Criminais
Lisbon, Portugal

Index

About the Editor and Contributors

MARCOS LUIZ BRETAS is Professor of History at the Federal University of Rio de Janiero. He is the recent author of *A Guerra das Ruas: Povo e Policia Na Cidade do Rio de Janiero* (1995) and *Ordem Na Cidade: O Exercicio Contidiano da Autoridade Policial No Rio de Janiero, 1907–1930* (1997). He is currently working on theatre and censorship in the 1920s.

MICHAEL BROERS is Reader in Modern European History in the Department of History, King's College, at the University of Aberdeen. He has authored major books on *Europe Under Napoleon* (1996), *Europe After Napoleon* (1996), *Napoleonic Imperialism and the Savoyard Monarchy, 1773–1821: State Building in Piedmont* (1997), and *The Politics of Religion in Napoleonic Italy: The War against God, 1801–1814* (2001). He has also published recent articles on culture and politics in *The English Historical Review* 114 (1999), *War in History* 8 (2001), *Historical Journal* 44 (2001), and *Past & Present* (2001). Currently he is engaged in a study of culture imperialism in Napoleonic Italy and a history of Europe from 1715 to 1815.

MARK CLAPSON is Senior Lecturer in History at the University of Luton, where he also directs the degree program in contemporary history. The author of *"A Bit of a Flutter": Popular Gambling and English Society c. 1823–1961* (1992), he is currently studying new towns and cities and researching a comparative study of "suburbanization" in Britain.

CLIVE EMSLEY is Professor of History and co-director of the European Centre for the Study of Policing at The Open University. He has published second, revised editions of the popular *The English Police: A Political and*

Social History (1996), and *Crime and Society in England 1750–1900* (1996), a major study of *Gendarmes and the State in Nineteenth-Century Europe* (1999), and has co-edited with Richard Bessel, *Patterns of Provocation: Police and Public Disorder* (2000). He is currently working on several aspects of policing the state in modern Europe.

BARRY GODFREY is Lecturer in the Criminology Department at Keele University. He has published essays on the factory, workplace theft, and white-collar crime in the *British Journal of Criminology* 39:1 (1999), *Crime, History and Society* 3:2 (1999), and *Northern History* (2001). He has a book chapter in press on " 'Rough' Girls" in *Criminal Girls*, ed. C. Adler and A. Worrall (2002). Current research interests focus on violence and its prosecution in the lower courts, and he is using oral histories in England and Australia to examine the meaning of violence and popular attitudes toward crime at the turn of the twentieth century.

STEVEN C. HUGHES is Professor of History at Loyola University, Baltimore. The author of *Crime, Disorder and the Risorgimento: The Politics of Policing in Bologna* (1994), he has published several articles on crime and disorder in Italy in *Manzoni: Societa, storia, medicina* (2000) and *Le Carte e la storia* 6:2 (2000). He is currently completing a study of the history of duelling in nineteenth- and twentieth-century Italy.

RICHARD W. IRELAND is Senior Lecturer in Law at the University of Wales, Aberystwyth. He is the co-author of *Imprisonment in England and Wales: A Concise History* (1985) and *Punishment: Rhetoric, Rule and Practice* (1989); and is a contributing author to *English Legal History: A Bibliography and Guide to the Literature* (1990). He has published articles on the pictorial representation of the penal system in *Art Antiquity and the Law* (1997 and 1999), and the impact of the railway on the history of crime in *Continuity and Change* (1997). Currently he is engaged in a study of the inmates, staff, and administration of Carmarthen jail in the nineteenth century.

SIMON KITSON is Lecturer at the Department of French Studies, University of Birmingham. His publications include "The Police in the Liberation of Paris," in H. R. Kedward and Nancy Wood's *The Liberation of France: Image and Event* (1995); "La reconstitution de la police a Marseille (aout 1944–fevrier 1945)," in *Provence Historique* 178 (1994); and "Les policiers marseillais et le Front Populaire," *XXe Siècle* (January 2000). Recent essays have expanded his research on Marseilles in Bessel and Emsley's *Patterns of Provocation* (2000), Guillon and Mencherini's *La Resistance et les Europeens du Sud* (2000), and Berlière and Peschanski's *La police francaise* (2000).

LOUIS A. KNAFLA is Professor of History at the University of Calgary. He is the author of *Kent at Law 1602: The County Jurisdiction* (1995) and has co-edited with Susan Binnie, *Law, Society, and the State: Essays in Modern Legal History* (1995), and with Clive Emsley, *Crime Histories and Histories of Crime* (1996). He currently has the second volume of his Kent at Law project in press, as well as an edited book of essays on the history of the law in the Canadian plains and northwest territories, 1670–1940, entitled *The Middle Kingdom* (2002). He is currently working on the courts of Star Chamber and Chancery in the late sixteenth and early seventeenth centuries.

LENOR SÁ is Director and Curator of the Museum of the Portuguese Police Service, Lisbon, Portugal.

ANNE MANDEVILLE is a Political Scientist at the University of Toulouse I. She has published several articles on public order in the United Kingdom with particular reference to Northern Ireland.

PAUL MUSKETT is Associate Lecturer for The Open University. He has published several articles on smuggling in England during the eighteenth century.

SYLVIO NORMAND is Professor of History of Law and Civil Law at the Faculty of Law, Laval University, Quebec. He has published several articles on Quebec legal history.

ELAINE A. REYNOLDS is Associate Professor of History at William Jewell College. She has recently published a study of the pre-1829 night watch system in London, entitled *Before the Bobbies: The Night Watch and Police Reform in Metropolitan London, 1720–1830* (1998). Her current work is a joint project with Ruth Paley on the comprehensive history of early-modern policing in London.

DAVID SMITH is Professor of History at the University of Puget Sound. The author of a challenging article on "Juvenile Delinquency in the British Zone of Germany, 1945–1951," *German History* 12 (1994), he has published recently "The Formation of the British State: 1525–1945," in *A Visitor's Britain: Exploring Culture Past and Present*, ed. Martin Upham and Patricia Tatspaugh (2001), and has forthcoming " 'No Work No Feed' Policy Towards Displaced Persons in the British Zone of Germany, 1946–1949," in *German History* (2002). He is presently working on a history of the Save the Children Fund and Anglo-German relations at the end of both world wars.

HOWARD TAYLOR is Fellow of Gonville and Caius College, Cambridge. His principal research interest is the history of the construction and use of criminal statistics. His essay on "The Politics of the Rising Crime Statistics of England and Wales, 1914–1960," won the annual Herman Diederiks Prize for Crime, *Histoire et Sociétés* (1998).

D.R. WELSH is a Graduate Teaching Assistant in the Department of Criminology, Buckingham Chilterns University College, in High Wycombe, Buckinghamshire, and is doing research on early nineteenth-century policing in England at the University of Hull.